RADICAL DOCUMENTARY
AND GLOBAL CRISES

RADICAL DOCUMENTARY AND GLOBAL CRISES

Militant Evidence in
the Digital Age

RYAN WATSON

INDIANA UNIVERSITY PRESS

This book is a publication of

Indiana University Press
Office of Scholarly Publishing
Herman B Wells Library 350
1320 East 10th Street
Bloomington, Indiana 47405 USA

iupress.org

© 2021 by Ryan Watson

All rights reserved
No part of this book may be reproduced or utilized in any form or by any means, electronic or mechanical, including photocopying and recording, or by any information storage and retrieval system, without permission in writing from the publisher. The paper used in this publication meets the minimum requirements of the American National Standard for Information Sciences—Permanence of Paper for Printed Library Materials, ANSI Z39.48-1992.

Manufactured in the United States of America

First printing 2021

Library of Congress Cataloging-in-Publication Data

Names: Watson, Ryan, author.
Title: Radical documentary and global crises : militant evidence in the digital age / Ryan Watson.
Description: Bloomington : Indiana University Press, [2021] | Includes bibliographical references and index.
Identifiers: LCCN 2021013734 (print) | LCCN 2021013735 (ebook) | ISBN 9780253057990 (hardback) | ISBN 9780253058003 (paperback) | ISBN 9780253058010 (ebook)
Subjects: LCSH: Documentary films—History and criticism. | Documentary mass media.
Classification: LCC PN1995.9.D6 W375 2021 (print) | LCC PN1995.9.D6 (ebook) | DDC 070.1/8—dc23
LC record available at https://lccn.loc.gov/2021013734
LC ebook record available at https://lccn.loc.gov/2021013735

For Philipp, Ruby, and my parents

Contents

ix
Acknowledgments

1
Introduction: Radical Documentary, Global Crises, and Militant Evidence

31
1. Digital Active Witnesses and the Limits of Visible Evidence

85
2. Prisons, Palestine, and Interactive Documentary

131
3. Amateur Counterarchives in Iraq

167
4. Syria and Abounaddara

207
Conclusion: Militant Evidence and the Future of Radical Documentary

215
Bibliography

229
Index

Acknowledgments

THIS BOOK BEGAN as some vague thoughts more than fifteen years ago, after I had seen James Longley's film *Iraq in Fragments* (2006) and had watched the amateur documentaries from the Independent Film and Television College (IFTC) in Baghdad attached to the bonus disc in the two-DVD set. These films sparked my thinking about the importance and possibility of documentary media made by people on the ground who suffer the profound effects of wars, occupations, and human rights abuses. *Radical Documentary and Global Crises* has been influenced by many friends, colleagues, and mentors who have helped me along the journey to its realization. First and foremost, I thank Indiana University Press and editors Janice Frisch and Allison Chaplin. I first met Janice at the Society for Cinema and Media Studies (SCMS) conference in Atlanta in 2016, and she was an enthusiastic champion of the project, guiding me through my first book-publishing experience with grace, compassion, and a keen editorial eye. Allison Chaplin took over for Janice after she left IU Press and made a seamless transition. I could not have asked for better editors. Both Janice and Allison have shaped this book in so many helpful ways. The peer reviewers selected by Janice and Allison were careful, enthusiastic, critical, and generous, and their very thorough feedback propelled generative revisions of the book. In the later stages of the production process, David Miller and Rachel Rosolina have both been exceedingly helpful. I thank Janice, Allison, David, Rachel, and everyone at IU Press from the bottom of my heart for their support of this project—it would not be in your hands without them.

Many of the groups and artists I write about were quite generous with their time and quick to respond to requests for permissions as well as other requests. I thank them for their support and for all of their urgent and necessary work. At WITNESS, Sam Gregory, Ambika Samarthya-Howard, Palika Makam, and Jackie Zamuto have all graciously offered assistance. At B'Tselem, I thank Amit Giltutz and Roy Yellin for their help. Zohar Kfir and Sharon Daniel have both been kind enough to provide images from their projects, and I thank them for their support of the book. I'm so grateful to the Rousl Group for permission to use the cover image which a still from the documentary *Still Recording* (dir. Saeed al-Batal and Ghiath Ayoub, 2018). I thank Saeed al-Batal as well as Ali Atassi and Rola Kobeissi at Bidayyat for Audiovisual Arts for their assistance. I also thank Charif Kiwan at Abounaddara for his help. In addition, I thank Misericordia University for summer research grants and course releases that gave me the time to complete the book. Many parts of the book were given as papers at a number of SCMS, American Comparative Literature Association (ACLA), and Visible Evidence conferences throughout the world. I thank the audiences and the many friends and colleagues there that I have engaged with about ideas in this book over the years.

From my days as an undergraduate student to my current job, a number of people have had an influence on this book in myriad ways, large and small: Rick Altman, Paula Amad, Allan Austin, Phil Barash, Jaimie Baron, Jennifer Black, James Cahill, Amanda Caleb, Kara Carmack, Dana Chalupa, Grace Chen, Bernie Cook, Nilo Couret, Corey Creekmur, Stephen Crompton, Joe Curran, Jeffrey Okla Elliott, Erika Fritz, Kristen Fuhs, Christina Gehrhardt, Daniel Grinberg, Tom Gunning, Sarah Hamblin, Patrick Hamilton, Dale Hudson, Chuck Kleinhans, David Oscar Harvey, Tim Havens, Elisa Korb, Colin Leslie, Heidi Manning, Josh Malitsky, Karen vanMeenen, Kathleen Newman, Rebecca Padot, Gregg Perkins, Michele Pierson, Brook Rosini, George Shea, Patrick Smith, Rebecca Steinberger, Steve Ungar, Rachel Urbanowicz, Tom Waugh, Ryan Weber, Margot Wielgus, Glenn Willis, Brian Winston, Steve Wurtzler, Nadia Yaqub, Yanqiu Zheng, and Patty Zimmermann. In addition, my parents, Gary and Ellen, have provided immense support and love, and I deeply appreciate them. Finally, I thank my husband and best friend, Philipp. He has seen this project (and me) through many ups and downs. I could not have done this without him.

Parts of chapter 2 appeared in "Affective Radicality: Prisons, Palestine, and Interactive Documentary," *Feminist Media Studies* 17, no. 4 (2017): 600–615, and parts of chapter 3 are from "Art under Occupation: Documentary, Archive, and the Radically Banal," *Afterimage* 36, no. 5 (March/April 2009): 7–12. I thank Taylor & Francis, Ltd. (http://www.tandfonline.com) and the University of California Press for allowing permission to reprint portions of the articles here.

RADICAL DOCUMENTARY
AND GLOBAL CRISES

Introduction
Radical Documentary, Global Crises, and Militant Evidence

THE SHORT DOCUMENTARY *REC* (2012) begins silently with a black screen and words, in white: *Hama 1982*. All of a sudden, the sounds of bombs and rapid gunfire invade the silence as the screen remains black and the words turn to red.[1] A dissolve reveals another black screen followed by the words *Hama 2012* and the sounds of men chanting in Arabic. Then, for the first time, moving images appear. Low-quality cell phone video provides glimpses of the chanting men and the ensuing protest in Hama. Red boxes and a blinking red "REC" in the left corner frame the video, evoking an old VHS camcorder viewfinder. The anonymous Syrian filmmaking collective Abounaddara made the video and posted it to the video-sharing site Vimeo amid the current war and inchoate revolution. In 1982, Hama, Syria, was the site of a massive civilian slaughter by current president Bashar al-Assad's father, former president Hafez al-Assad, who was cracking down on protests by members of the Muslim Brotherhood, an opposition group who defiantly demonstrated against his authoritarian Baathist regime. But there were no cameras present to capture the event. Today, the Syrian war is "the most socially mediated civil conflict in history."[2] This hypermediation is the direct result of ubiquitous cell phones and digital cameras in Syria, like in many countries across the globe. Image-making technology is now in easy reach for billions of people. Never before has the means of producing documentary images been more widely distributed. In addition, in the networked digital age, these images can be shared instantaneously, displayed publicly, and stored indefinitely. The most urgent, radical documentary media is produced by amateurs,

Figure i.1 Still from *REC*.

Figure i.2 Still from *REC*.

Figure i.3 Still from *Media Kill*.

artists, and activists with cell phones and digital cameras documenting the horrors they face in places of global crises. To understand their militant uses of documentary media or work in solidarity with them to fight against these crises, it is imperative to center their perspectives and rigorously engage with their media, films, demands, and the generative partnerships they form.

REC also underscores the importance of capturing visible evidence within the specific global crises of war, occupation, mass incarceration, and human rights abuses. The traditional conception of this practice is that with increased documentation within these circumstances, people will be moved to "do something," and as a result, perpetrators of violence and violators of rights are exposed and then brought to justice. Yet this often does not occur. For example, in another of Abounaddara's films, *Media Kill* (2012), a closely shot, silhouetted (to protect his anonymity) man speaks directly to the camera and says, "The documented human rights violations are enough to bring down at least three regimes. Isn't that enough?"[3] While there is wide access to documenting, capturing, and presenting visible evidence, the sheer ubiquity of images and their corresponding affective and effective appeals demanding attention at a given moment within a variety of media and other ecologies often dull their importance, force, and activist potential.

This overwhelming image-making and image-receiving environment fosters a number of fundamental questions: Can documentary media actually do anything to change the material conditions of ordinary people, engender justice, or catalyze radical movements and revolutions? And, despite the futility referenced in *Media Kill*, why do people across the globe keep making documentary images and capturing visible evidence? What are they trying to accomplish? In her book *Precarious Life: The Powers of Mourning and Violence*, written in the wake of 9/11 and at the beginning of the ruthless global war on terror, Judith Butler asserts that "the question that preoccupies . . . in the light of recent global violence is, who counts as human?"[4] Within the discourses of terrorism and national security deployed after 9/11, dehumanizing language and categories were used to justify wars, torture, and occupations. Faced with this pervasive violence, Butler's question is crucial; it also begs two larger ones: How can we act as humans to intervene in and abolish the regimes of violence that surround us and how can everyday people assert their values, voices, and political agencies amid global crises?

Radical Documentary and Global Crises considers these questions through an examination of the status and use of documentary image making in a post-9/11 world, which is defined by the interminable "Global War on Terror," wide use of cell phones and social media, rapid economic globalization, and the massive spread of digitally networked images. Through individual smart screens connected to networks 24/7 and equipped with cameras, much of the world's population is armed and ready to capture and share documentary images. Because of these technological developments, recent and ongoing global crises, such as the Iraq War, the occupation of Palestine, the war in Syria, and the routine killing of Black and brown people by police in the United States, have become sites of overmediation. Yet there are also many spaces and places the world is barred from seeing or representing, such as life inside prisons under mass incarceration in many US states, the workings of Central Intelligence Agency's (CIA) global "black sites," and state repression in Western Sahara and North Korea to name just a few. The representation of reality has never been easier, more fraught, or more important.

As global crises continue to emerge and strengthen unabated, there has been a widespread and urgent interest in deploying documentary moving images to intervene within them by Abounaddara as well as a plethora of other media collectives, human rights and activist groups, artists, and ordinary citizens. For all of them, documentary images are tools in the struggle for rights, representation, and in some places, emerging revolution. It is in these instances of extremity and desperation, the places and interstices where complex issues boil up into violence and repression, that the will to document, witness, and testify—to confidently assert one's voice and human agency—manifests with ferocity. This is the new international avant-garde, less concerned with theory and aesthetics and more concerned with deploying documentary evidence militantly in the service of recognition, survival, and radical change.

In *Radical Documentary and Global Crises*, the analyses of both overmediated global crises—such as the Iraq War, the occupation of Palestine, and the recent war in Syria—and undermediated ones—such as mass incarceration in the United States and child-soldier conscription in the Democratic Republic of Congo—are approached from a microhistorical perspective, privileging the images and testimonies produced by on-the-ground amateurs, artists, activists, and ordinary citizens who bear the brunt of the many detrimental effects of these crises. Further, *Radical Documentary and Global Crises* ties together a number of strands emergent in previous historical models of radical documentary film to connect their militancy to contemporary projects, theorize what a radical documentary practice encompasses today by drawing on lessons and conceptions from previous iterations, and think through how current radical documentary practices can be most effective when employing digital technologies within vast, globalized networks.

From Dziga Vertov's wish for a "factory of facts" in the 1920s to the term "visible evidence" coined after the wide dissemination of the Rodney King tape in the 1990s, radical documentarians have had, as a fundamental basis of their work, a concern with the illumination of the usually "unseen" and the strategic uses of witnesses and archives. They also put great emphasis on the concepts of testimony and evidence (both effective and affective) as a means of persuasion. There is also a concomitant desire for greater ease of filming and mobility: the wish for a plethora of cameras and observers who are activated, informed, and attuned to the vagaries of their worlds. This is coupled with the will to give access to representation for marginalized groups in the cause of global collectivity and exchange. Finally, there is a wish to capture, accumulate, and deploy documentary evidence as counterinformation against mainstream narratives and, as such evidence accumulates, to produce counterarchives that can be further mined and weaponized. These desires are underscored by an avant-garde approach to form and/or content as well as an openness to experimentation with technologies, collective and bottom-up filmmaking practices, and, importantly, a militant political and/or ideological stance. These are works that seek to activate their spectators and catalyze radical change. The historical global development of radical documentary relies on the visible evidence produced by the camera and the ecologies and networks such images circulate within as they become forceful, nonviolent weapons in political struggles that are deployed in the tasks of activism, advocacy, revolution, and intervention against regimes of state violence and repression.

Further, the radical documentary tradition grew out of and continued drawing inspiration from the early modernist avant-garde movement seen in the work of Vertov, Jean Vigo, and Joris Ivens as well as later experimental practices exemplified in the work of filmmakers associated with Third Cinema in Argentina and throughout Latin America, post-Revolution Cuban cinema, filmmakers and film collectives in France in 1960s and 1970s and the Newsreel collective in the United States, the AIDS activist collective AIDS Coalition to Unleash Power (ACT UP) and their video arm Damned Interfering Video Activist Television (DIVA TV), as well as feminist media artist Martha Rosler in the broader 1980s "new documentary" art movement, and the discourses surrounding the Rodney King tape and bystander video in the 1990s.[5] These varied approaches, artists, and collectives root the deployment of "militant evidence" in contemporary articulations of radical documentary practices. These particular examples mentioned above, while a very partial genealogy of global radical documentary practices, are explored in the book because each have shaped conceptions of radical documentary history and theory, have received sustained critical attention, and the artists and groups involved often collaborated with and/or influenced one another. By rereading and reevaluating some of their key manifestoes, texts, and films, a set of common parameters is woven throughout the four chapters of *Radical Documentary and Global Crises* for how the radical documentary was defined and codified regarding form, content, distribution, access, and spectatorship since the early 1920s.

These radical or "committed" documentary film practices have been integral to political movements, revolutions, and demands for social change around the world since the early twentieth century.[6] The word *radical* derives from the Latin word *radicalis*, which translates to "having roots." By the mid-1600s, the word expanded to contain the meaning of "going to the origin" and again by the 1800s to include an upward, political tone: namely change "from the roots." *Radical Documentary and Global Crises* engages "the roots" of radical documentary by analyzing the aforementioned strains of interconnected transnational filmmaking practices as oppositional forces for political and social intervention. These documentary practices encompass a diverse range of filmmakers, formal techniques, and groups. Yet, despite this heterogeneity, a set of recurring impulses, wishes, and inclinations emerge as their ambitions often outpaced available technologies. Now that these technologies have exceeded their wildest expectations, it is time to return to this set of films, filmmakers, and writings to historicize the development of today's practices and root an analysis of how they operate in the digital age.

Despite this seemingly coherent historical genealogy, the development of radical documentary history is not linear or technologically determined, and this is particularly true among the filmmakers and practices delineated above—and the many others not mentioned. Emerging from spaces and situations of global crises, today's radical documentary practices draw on the legacies, ambitions, and groundworks laid by previous generations while they are also at the forefront of emerging conceptions of radicality, activism, and the militant uses of documentary images. Radical documentary practices in the digital age are a set of mutable practices where "militant evidence" is instrumentalized and/or deployed within and from spaces of conflict, emergency, and protracted struggle. They operate not simply as representations of reality but as interventions, catalysts, and shaping forces. These urgent practices necessitate an expansion and rethinking of how a documentary is defined, how and why they are made, what they can do in the world, and how and where they function.

Chapter 1 examines the work of two human rights organizations that successfully deploy militant evidence within larger advocacy strategies. The first, WITNESS, a Brooklyn-based nonprofit, partners with groups globally in a range of human rights situations to create and use militant evidence in settings determined by the most effective means of ending abuses in a given context. The second, B'Tselem (Hebrew for "in the image of"), is an Israeli group working in partnership with Palestinians in the occupied territories. Their camera distribution project, once dubbed "Shooting Back," arms individual Palestinians with video cameras to capture images of routine abuses that are then deployed by B'Tselem as forms of evidence in a range of legal, government, policy, and media settings. Both WITNESS' and B'Tselem's transmedia documentary practices bring about an "effective radicality." Chapter 2 considers interactive documentary projects by new media artists Zohar Kfir and Sharon Daniel. Kfir's project, *Points of View* (2015), investigates the Israeli occupation of Palestine through a strategic deployment of selections from B'Tselem's vast video archive. Daniel's *Public Secrets* (2006) explores the human toll of the prison industrial complex in California via six hundred audio statements recorded by Daniel with female inmates and algorithmically displayed. In these projects, the interactive form allows viewers/users a multifaceted affective encounter with a range of subjects and militant evidence, engendering an "affective radicality," which moves viewers/users into larger networks of political discourse, activism, and practices of resistance.

Chapter 3 analyzes three short, student documentaries made in conjunction with the short-lived Independent Film and Television College (IFTC) in Baghdad, Iraq, during the most recent war and subsequent US occupation. These films, as forms of militant evidence, constitute counterarchival practices and the creation of public domains of communication outside of the mainstream. They also employ a representation of the everyday as a radically banal act of resistance in the wake of the spectacle of Operation Shock and Awe. The IFTC films create a space for humanity and empathy to emerge outside of dominant media narratives and sets the stage for a renewed independent film and media culture in Iraq. Finally, chapter 4 investigates the mass of short, anonymous videos, an "emergency cinema," produced weekly and posted on Vimeo by the Abounaddara collective since 2011. These films and the documentary practices of the collective comprise what Abounaddara calls "emergency cinema," an anonymous and forceful deployment of militant evidence to advocate for a universal "right to the image" for Syrians amid the current war as they work to provoke and sustain revolutionary fervor despite massive devastation. Their creative work, like that of the IFTC, also serves as a catalyst for a renewed amateur media and independent film culture that continues to challenge existing structures of entrenched power in Syria.

The documentary practices and projects analyzed in *Radical Documentary and Global Crises* emerge directly from the people (often amateurs) who live in places and situations of crises. They are also part of larger partnerships and advocacy and political efforts (on multiple levels) where documentary images and stories are enmeshed within networks for meaningful representation, counterinformation, counterarchives, and/or adjudication. Each example is particularly attuned to the ethical concerns inherent in representations while they also rely heavily on witnesses, testimonies, and appeals to a common humanity. Further, the collectives, groups, and artists leverage new and emerging media technologies in their documentary practices as a way to heighten impact. And each projects' form and aesthetics are used in service of instrumentalizing the images and stories in various contexts. The aforementioned contemporary groups and artists create and/or use what I call "digital active witnesses," who produce militant evidence that, when strategically targeted, can intervene within specific social and political situations. Because the ubiquity of cameras has led to a mass of witnesses and countless hours of filmic evidence, stored in impossibly vast quantities in various digital archives, to succeed in advocating for a particular cause, radical documentarians around the world must present this plethora of evidence tactically and strategically while employing the logic of amassing as a militant intervention. In their own ways and for very different reasons, each of these groups, artists, organizations, and individuals examined in this book accumulates, shapes, and targets militant evidence within various media, legal, artistic, and activist ecologies and networks of distribution for a variety of audiences.

Militant Evidence

The documentary image is highly spreadable, but a single image is no longer enough to catalyze change, bring forth justice, or even sustain one's attention—there is simply too much to be aware of in the modern media environment. In addition, the instantaneous nature of the digital age shapes expected timescales for results, occluding the deliberate pace and work required for lasting political and social change. The concept of militant evidence refers to both what is produced and how it is used. Its production and use draw their power from two main elements. The first is the accumulation and corroboration of images, events, witnesses, and testimonials. The second is that each piece of evidence builds on the force of others when accumulated to a great degree. This collection of affective and effective forces rendered by militant evidence helps to reveal the long-standing and systemic effects of wars, occupations, and human rights abuses. In terms of the name of the concept, the "militant" aspect refers to unyielding, nonviolent struggles on the part of digital active witnesses, who purposefully or through circumstance capture documentary images to intervene in their world. Further, it is a reference to the long-standing, global and militant documentary practices that root the analysis throughout *Radical Documentary and Global Crises*. Moreover, it is an unyielding assertion of fact and reality in a pervasive climate of "fake news" and a digital environment where individual images and deep-fake videos can be produced, appropriated, altered, and recontextualized ad infinitum—subject to skepticism and doubt and easily dismissed. The "evidence" component of the term refers to both its effective and affective uses in order to theorize *how* militant evidence is deployed in a radical or activist way across varied global contexts.

The effective form of militant evidence attests to the fact something has occurred and can be used in the policy, legal, governmental, or other official domains governed by strict rules regarding the forms and veracity of the evidence presented. When used for radical or activist purposes within official domains, militant evidence can generate effective radicality. Affective radicality, on the other hand, relies on the accumulation and targeting of affective evidence to foster identification and solidarity for a variety of audiences, moving them into radical practices of resistance. Here, of course, concrete impact and results are more difficult to quantify yet that does not render the affective component any less important. Finally, militant evidence is an extension and update of the term "visible evidence," coined at the dawn of the digital age in the 1990s in the wake of the Rodney King tape and verdict. As militant evidence, videos, and other documentary media are considered beyond simple visibility, deployed within various ecologies and framed as affective and effective forces by individuals, activist groups, artists, and amateurs who demand justice by countering official narratives and generating solidarity and incitement toward collective action and practices of resistance.

What types of images and other forms of documentary media are deployed as militant evidence? Most often, it is poor images. Hito Steyerl argues for the vast potentiality of the circulation, in various ecologies, of poor images, or images of lower quality.[7] They are the detritus of the digital age and their meaning is always emergent and shifting, depending on context and mode of deployment. For Steyerl, the poor image testifies "to the violent dislocation, transferals, and displacement of images—their acceleration and circulation within the vicious cycles of audiovisual capitalism."[8] Such images, she argues, "refuse mainstream elitist means of production," creating a "more realistic 'people's cinema'"[9] Poor images, when paired with a militant political stance or radicality, are also a part of a longer historical lineage that encompasses the uses of what Kodwo Eshun and Ros Gray have called the "militant image," which they define as "any form of image or sound . . . produced in and through film-making practices dedicated to liberation struggles and revolutions of the late twentieth century."[10] The techniques and approaches that Eshun and Gray reference are certainly heterogeneous, but they are bonded together as oppositional documentary practices with forceful commitments to the ideology and goals of revolutionary political and social change across the world.

Steyerl locates poor images as functioning in a similar way, importantly emphasizing both the "circuits" of art and activism that define their distribution and the rich genealogy they provide as a lens on current practices in the digital age. She contends that "[from] Vertov's 'visual bonds,' [to] the internationalist workers' pedagogies . . . [and] the circuits of Third Cinema and Tricontinental . . . the poor image—ambivalent as its status may be—thus takes its place in the genealogy of carbon-copied pamphlets [and] cine-train agit-prop films."[11] Further, Steyerl argues that the use of poor images "re-actualizes many of the historical ideas associated with these circuits, among others Vertov's idea of the visual bond."[12] The visual bonds she refers to in relation to Vertov are the affective and effective glue that binds dispersed subjects to one another around common thoughts, feelings, ideologies, or understandings. Whether connected with revolutionary fervor or the documenting of war, occupation, mass incarceration, and human rights abuses, these visual bonds are routinely appealed to as a catalyst for empathy or action and to create an alternative economy of poor images. The massive circulation, degradation, and recontextualization of the poor image within a global network of communication, sharing, and remixing "creates a circuit, which fulfills the original ambitions of militant and (some) essayistic and experimental cinema—to create an alternative economy of images, an imperfect cinema existing inside as well as beyond and under commercial media streams."[13] The poor image "reconnects dispersed worldwide audiences," and it "constructs anonymous global networks just as it creates a shared history. It builds alliances as it travels, provokes translation or mistranslation, and creates new publics and debates."[14]

The power to participate and create within these networks relies on the accumulation and deployment of poor images, and they are produced by ordinary people in great number. These images are the materials in the construction of alternative networks, alliances, and connections anonymously functioning against the status quo while forging deep, mutual partnerships and creating counterpublics. When they are documentary images and testimonies that emerge from spaces of war, occupation, mass incarceration, and human rights abuses, part of their authority and power derives from their location and the amateur status of those who make them. Furthering this notion, in a lecture titled "On Documenting," Steyerl argues that these types of images "are active agents in warfare" that can catalyze resistance if we think of them as a form of evidence or fact that emerges from a space of war or other extreme condition because then they gain in stature.[15] Moreover, as Andre Bazin reminds us, "during a war, facts have an exceptional amplitude and importance."[16] *Radical Documentary and Global Crises* extends this amplification and importance of fact and evidence amid wars and similar perilous situations, arguing that the accumulation and deployment of militant evidence in a targeted fashion is a vitally important radical intervention and a force for affective and effective radicalities in the networked digital age.

Conceptualizing the Radical Documentary

As a concept within documentary history and theory, radicality emerges in specific ways, depending on the unique confluences of historical and political forces, available technology, mode of persuasion, and intended audience—in other words, it is always contextual. A radical film in one country or political situation often will not function in the same fashion outside of its immediate sphere of influence, though like-minded filmmakers and ideologies may influence it. The term "radical" is used throughout the book rather than the other popular term "committed," which has also been used to define this particular strain of documentary. Commitment, while an accurate term for much of the development of this subgenre, invokes a tethering to a particular type of ideological stance and encompasses communist and socialist politics as they manifested in various iterations and countries between 1917 and 1989. The dynamic nature of the iterations often renders the term "commitment" both too broad and too specific. While radical, on the other hand, evokes a stance of opposition that is not dependent on a particular ideology and can be more easily and universally applied.

This is especially true after 1989, in the aftermath of the fall of the Berlin Wall, when the traditional approach of Cold War–era state communism perished. The wake of this collapse, coupled with rapid developments in communication and representational technologies, as well as the shift from analog to digital, relocated sites of power to the digital world, where documentary images in particular spread virally and could shape reality in an instant. But this same digital world is tightly regulated by private corporations and powerful governments. Computer codes, algorithms, and networks that are largely hidden track, surveil, and advertise to consumers and social media users while influencing the news and other content that they see. Theoretically, there is access to a vast quantity of information, but nearly everyone is enmeshed within highly curated news systems, particularly via social media, which reinforces pre-existing views, altering perceptions of reality in a subjective, atomized way that makes it nearly impossible to build larger notions of community, shared values, or communal practices that benefit the greater good.

As mentioned in the discussion above regarding tactical media, if power and control have migrated, so too must oppositional practices. As Patricia Zimmermann argues regarding radical documentary practices, they must "abandon thinking in modes left over from the political and social struggles of the 1970s and 1980s in order to reinvent itself for the next century's formidable challenges."[17] Zimmermann was writing more than two decades ago, in the wake of twenty years of public arts defunding, about a state of emergency in the production and exhibition of independent, politically left, radical, and militant works. That state of emergency and the seemingly endless states of emergency and exception in the post-9/11 world have elevated the formidable challenges on the horizon at the beginning of the new millennium into a state of war. This a war fought on many fronts: ceaseless conflicts, repression, and occupations in the Middle East and parts of Africa, mass incarceration and racial injustice in the United States, rising right wing nationalist movements in Europe, Asia, and North and South America, mass surveillance and data collection, climate change, pandemics, and a sclerotic, increasingly fragile global neoliberal economic order of vast, unsustainable inequality, to name just a few. In this milieu, moving images have been unleashed from a status of representation from above where early ethnographic and other forms of documentary "captured" images of indigenous peoples to study and thus "salvage" their traditional culture and old models of participatory documentary that reproduced power and knowledge hierarchies to models based on self-representation, documentation, community, and partnerships. These new documentary practices are a vital currency in the production of and intervention in reality, as evidence of abuse or criminal conduct and as a conduit to action on a variety of fronts.

While the projects and practices examined throughout *Radical Documentary and Global Crises* are defined as radical, the word is used in the oppositional, strident, ground-up sense, as they do not necessarily exist within easily defined political ideologies, other than the fact they are all on the left, broadly construed. Rather, despite their diversity of contexts, struggles, and reasons for filming, there is a broad and uncompromising stance toward improving the material reality of people's lives within spaces of war, occupation, incarceration, and human rights abuses. These projects all in their own way make an appeal to common humanity—a "radical humanism," which reimagines the idea of humanism from the Enlightenment notion to one of more radical potential.[18] As Edward Said argued late in his career, "Humanism is the only . . . resistance we have against the inhuman practices and injustices that disfigure human history."[19] Thus, the appeal to a universal idea of the human, free from categorization or caveat, as the fundamental basis for recognition, where dehumanization is challenged with a militant assertion of humanity.[20] As part of an emerging international avant-garde, these projects and partnerships are at the forefront of global crises. They wage a confrontation on the terrain of politics and images by wielding militant evidence to improve the material conditions of life for those in situations of great struggle and peril.

Today's practices are also situated within what has recently been heralded the "documentary turn" in contemporary art, as well as among other contemporary "turns" toward the archive as a site of power, contestation, and inquiry and the digital turn, which revolutionized technologies of communication, storage, production, and dissemination.²¹ Within these larger critical turns are of course historical ruptures and technological developments that have both acted as conduit for and shaped our understanding of various global documentary practices. The first two trajectories that undergird the argument in the book concern the development of radical documentary practices as a distinct branch within the history of documentary and the parallel emergence of new media technologies that emphasized interaction, immersion, participation, searchability, and the ability to reckon with copious data, images, and other forms of mediated information. Finally, the third trajectory, and unique to documentary, is changing conceptions of evidence, indexicality, and the "real," as manifested in the use of visible evidence as a weapon in the struggle against genocide, oppression, and abuse. The turns and trajectories referenced here are not major "breaks" in approach. Rather, they shape a long, global history of radical documentary practices and use of media technologies within a larger internationalist avant-garde movement.

Broadly, the first trajectory concerns the development of the modernist avant-garde in the interwar period in Europe and Russia and the emergence of a global radical documentary tradition in its wake. In Russia, Vertov and Esfir Shub experimented with form to create new realities and ways of seeing the world with non-fiction images edited into revolutionary montages in service of the communist project. While artists within the interwar period in Europe moved from a concern with form to a stress on nonfiction and political engagement that led to the notion of "social cinema," first put forth by filmmaker Jean Vigo in France, which dominated until World War II. The postwar period was marked by the development of lighter weight cameras and synch-sound recording; the emergence of militant cinema around the global events of 1968; collaboration between filmmakers in the West and militant revolutionaries and filmmakers across the Third World; and the development of first person or subjective documentary in the 1980s and 1990s, a melding of the personal and political.

The second trajectory encompasses the decades of development in new media, or the convergences between computing and art, that eventually led to video games, interactive documentary, and virtual reality, single-viewer immersive experiences. Lev Manovich posits the current form of new media as a convergence of two separate histories: that of computing and media technology.²² The convergence of these two histories form Manovich's definition of new media: the translation of all existing media into numerical data that is searchable and accessible through computers and other devices. This process, in which graphics, text, sound, and moving images are digitized, is also known as "remediation," or the transcoding of older forms of media into a digital language.²³ The transformation of form through numerical representation enables modularity, variability, automatism, and also, importantly, a high degree of interactivity. In addition mass digitization has led the world to "accumulate an unprecedented amount of media materials: photo archives, film libraries, audio archives" that beget "the need for new technologies to store, organize and efficiently access these media materials," leading to our current age, which is "now concerned as much with accessing and re-using existing media as with creating new one."²⁴ Equally important to add in the digital age is the idea of "networked architecture," where various media and devices are accessed and used by connecting to a network within a decentralized system.²⁵ These transformations—especially the concept of interactivity—are both what is "new" about new media and what provides novel ways of thinking about documentary activism and engagement. The latter point is particularly relevant as the development of documentary converges with parallel developments in the uses of new media technologies as a means for intervention in the networked digital age.

Lastly, the third trajectory concerns the status of film and video as evidence. And it is also where the convergence between militance, evidence, and the uses of film is pushed to a new level. Paul Rotha notes an important shift that occurs in 1942, with the United States on the brink of entry into World War II, in the conceptions of how various forms and archives of documentary media were affectively weaponized by the US government to foment fervor among young men to wholeheartedly commit them to fight in the war. He writes,

> The problem in 1942 was how to turn the youth of a nation, so recently and so predominantly isolationist, into a fighting force not only effectively trained and equipped but armed, too, with the conviction that his country's entry into a world war was not only just but the inevitable answer to serious wrongs. A series of films seemed to offer the best means of so indoctrinating him. It was clearly realized that by the minds behind production that no drama or replica of the historical facts and events under consideration would serve the purpose, but that only first-hand, factual, actual, ocular evidence would be convincing. The whole series was therefore compiled from existing documentary and news-reel film, drawn from every conceivable source including the enemy, put together after considerable study and with considerable thought, and furnished with a narrative commentary which sometimes described and complemented the visuals but at other times went beyond their subject-matter to add supplementary information or comment.²⁶

The group of films that Rotha is referring to were part of the US government's propaganda series *Why We Fight*. The films are, unsurprisingly, hyperbolic, jingoistic, and unabashedly nationalist. Viewing the "first-hand, factual, ocular evidence," which must have seemed quite new and exciting at the time, coupled with material "drawn from every conceivable source" and a didactic narrative to guide you if the visual propaganda was not enough is certainly laughable today. But it signals the beginning of a larger trend toward the instrumentalization and weaponization of evidence ("documentation") that is concretized by two important watershed moments in documentary history.

The first was the film footage at the Nuremburg trials between 1945 and 1946 used to convict, for international war crimes, a slew of Nazi commanders and second was the constant broadcast in 1991 of the Rodney King tape, which depicted a Black man being horrifically beaten by a group of Los Angeles police officers during an arrest.[27] The King video succeeded in fomenting broad public outrage, but it was not sufficient enough to convict the officers charged with using excessive force in his beating. In its time, the video was quite rare—a momentary glimpse into the routine abuses of Black people at the hands of police broadcast for months on the nightly news. The much discussed, widely seen tape helped to reconceptualize the scope of documentary practices and focus of scholars, with a renewed interest in witnesses armed with portable cameras, the increased possibility of documenting and capturing visible evidence, and an acknowledgment of its interpretive instability.

There is now a third turn to evidence. In 2021, a lack of evidence or visibility of this type is not the problem. There has never been a greater ability on the part of the everyday person to document the world around them. For example, the United States is overcome with a vast accumulation of images of police violence on social media, streaming, and video-sharing sites. Writing in 2016, Benjamin Balthaser argued that "videos displaying police violence—some infamous, others obscure—play almost constantly... repeat on major and independent news channels as both evidence and incitement. They have become one of the dominant means by which racial violence is measured, known, and consumed."[28] The debate about the purpose and impact of these deadly encounters with police moves between a resistance to such images as dehumanizing, macabre, and trafficking in the spectacle of violence against Black people, which harkens back to the long history of lynching photographs in the United States, to a militant desire to keep such images at the forefront of public consciousness through activism by the groups that make up the Black Lives Matter movement (BLM), which catalyzed nationwide protests by situating images of police violence within direct actions and protests as well as discourses about racism, state violence, and demands for systemic change. BLM was highly active and visible again in 2020, when cell phone footage of the murder of George Floyd at the hands of a Minneapolis police officer spread quickly on social media and sparked truly massive multiweek protests across the United States and many countries around the world. Yet, while this pervasive image environment allows for the capture of state violence, it can also be used against activists. Part of this fraught nature emerges from a paradox of visibility. In regard to this paradox, activists are, more than ever, targeted with sophisticated surveillance, monitoring, and harassment engendered by the same sorts of technologies they use to intervene in the world. Social media sites such as Facebook, Instagram, and Twitter were the medium of choice for activists in the BLM movement to organize large-scale protests and connect with allies and comrades throughout the nation and the world. But, just as those platforms provided a space for organizing, they also tracked their activities and locations for the police during protests in Baltimore, Maryland (2015), and Ferguson, Missouri (2014).[29] There is a similar concern when dealing with video of human rights or other abuses, where victims testify about their experiences on camera and expose their identities, which often leads to revictimization and raises fundamental questions about the ethics and politics of the image. "It is the sheer versatility and multiplicity of global media," argues T. J. Demos, "the circulatory flux of images, their expanding distribution networks—that render the task of documentary filmmaking today more fraught than ever."[30]

Radical Documentary History: Tool, Weapon, Witness, Evidence

In documentary history, there are five major pivot points that reorient the concerns of radical documentary practices. Explicating this historical genealogy allows access to fundamental questions of impact, audience, tactics and strategy, dynamism and adaptability, and global circulation. It also serves as a prehistory for today's explosion of documentary media, which seeks to represent and intervene in global crises. The first pivot begins with the emergence of the interwar modernist avant-garde in Europe and Russia mentioned above. This encompasses a diverse range of filmmakers, theorists, and groups, including Jean Vigo, Vertov, Shub, Joris Ivens, and the US-based Film and Photo League and develops in fits and starts through ciné club screenings and personal exchanges between filmmakers throughout Europe, the United States, Russia, and other parts of the world up until the beginning of World War II.

The second pivot, after the war, was the emergence of the Third World as a politically viable actor in global consciousness. Third, in the same period, was the emergence of the New Left in Europe and North America in the late 1950s through the late 1960s. The New Left signaled a move away from earlier, more doctrinal Marxist and socialist movements, which were premised on class struggle and militant labor unionization, turning instead to concern with broader global issues, particularly the Third World, as well as radical cultural reforms focused on race, gender, free speech, and antiwar sentiment.[31] All of these movements trace a line of development culminating in the large-scale, global protest events of 1968. It is within context of the aforementioned political shifts where militant cinema develops in the work of Santiago Álvarez in Cuba, the broader Third Cinema movement in Latin America, Chris Marker and the Left Bank group in France, and the US-collective Newsreel. These groups and artists draw heavily on the legacy, styles, manifestoes, and frequent collaborations with the previous generation.

Fourth was the explosion of *cinéma-vérité* and direct cinema styles spurred by advances in documentary technology coupled with the rise of television, which set off sixty years of dizzying technological developments that democratized access to the means of film production. Since 1967, when the advent of the Sony Video Rover combined portability, synch-sound, and consumer affordability, the personal video camera steadily became a common possession. The trend continued with Sony's introduction of the first VHS camcorder in 1983 followed by similar models by RCA, Panasonic, and Hitachi. The ability to record and edit footage cheaply gave rise to activist collectives in the United States, such as Paper Tiger Television, founded in 1981 in New York City by Dee Dee Halleck to subvert corporate media and increase media literacy, and DIVA TV (Damned Interfering Video Activist Television), a group aligned with the AIDS direct action collective ACT UP (AIDS Coalition to Unleash Power). In England, the influential Black Audio Film Collective was founded in East London in 1982 and brought a Black diasporic perspective to overwhelmingly white British television, film, and museum audiences.

As Deidre Boyle noted in 1992, in the "years since the video Porta Pak launched an independent television movement in the United States, a new generation of video activists has taken up the video camcorder as a tool, a weapon, and a witness."[32] A plethora of groups, including DIVA TV, broadcast amateur video projects that fit their activist agendas on public access television stations throughout New York City. Such a strategy allowed for radical media projects to be shown alongside traditional television channels within the space of the home, reorientating traditional models of spectatorship that relied on the projection of film in defined spaces of exhibition. Founded in 1968, the Public Broadcasting System (PBS) emerged as an additional avenue for dissident points of view not seen in corporate media. At the same time, public organizations like National Education Television (NET), which launched the influential television program *Black Journal*, also brought educational and diverse content into US homes. In England in the early 1980s, Channel Four broadcast work by the Black Audio Film Collective and other diasporic British voices. In 1987, PBS premiered the series *P.O.V. (Point of View)*. The series broadcast the work of independent documentary filmmakers that often expressed leftist political and social ideas. Between 1988 and 1991, PBS also worked to establish the Independent Television Service (ITS), a coalition of independent film producers and documentary filmmakers who worked to underwrite and fund progressive documentary projects on PBS airwaves. Many of the films broadcast in this period included a range of voices, including members of underrepresented groups and first-time and amateur filmmakers empowered by cheaper access to video-making equipment.

This leads to the fifth pivot: as these films tended to focus on the more personal aspects and effects of political and social policy, they fostered a subgenre of documentary that Patricia Aufderheide calls "first-person filmmaking." Aufderheide defines this approach as "somewhere in between the essay, general reportage and the well-told tale. It is marked not only by the first-person voice in testimonial, but also by the bringing of the viewer into the world of the storyteller's experience. Often socially engaged, it is rarely polemical. Indeed, it typically does not make a direct argument, but an implicit request for the viewer to recognize the reality of the speaker, and to incorporate that reality into his or her view of the world."[33] This personalization of political and social issues recasts previous notions of witness and testimony by calling on the spectator to engage and empathize with the personal story of the subject through their own self-representation. In this way, political and social struggles are moved from the realm of the claims and ideologies of large-scale political movements and personalized through a heterogeneous and subjective lens. Macroissues are distilled into microexperiences; a call for recognition and empathy becomes a means for further engagement with larger issues for viewers.

Throughout the 1990s and early 2000s, a number of other issues came into play with the advent of affordable personal video-recording devices with built-in synch-sound technology; further globalization and transnational consolidation of media production; and the emergence of digital and new media technology in the realm of communication and representation. Increased access to video cameras has been furthered by the advent of consumer-grade digital video (DV) cameras, first released by Sony, Panasonic, and JVC in

1995; consumer-grade high-definition (HD) cameras first made available in 2003; and the current near ubiquity of camera and video functions on personal cell phones. These developments, coupled with the integration of the internet as a vital part of everyday life, have meant that filmmakers and activists have never had more power to capture and edit images digitally and share them widely by uploading such work to video-sharing sites. In the digital age, a piece of video shot in one corner of the world can be made available via upload to networked sites nearly instantaneously.

While filmic evidence has a long history within legal cases, especially in the United States, its relationship to documentary film is concretized by two major events mentioned above, seemingly shaped by incontrovertible evidence: the Nuremburg trials, where graphic evidence was paired with a complex legal argument about the rules of war and the Rodney King tape, which was inadequate visible evidence to convict four LAPD officers.[34] The concept of visible evidence, a phrase coined after the King tape, relies heavily on theoretical formulations of the real and indexicality. Questions of the real and indexicality have dominated past debates in documentary studies because unlike other cinematic genres, documentary makes unique truth claims. In terms of the radical, Gaines argues that "indexical privilege contributes something to one of the forks of the radical cause—the *evidence* of material conditions."[35] The evidence presented therefore seeks allies, collaborators, and potential militants. Thus, the realism of documentary relies on the capture of a certain kind of fact—a "pathos of fact."[36] This sort of fact is often effective and relies on the generation and reception of affect for its impact. The emphasis on the affective and bodily dimensions of documentary spectatorship have also been examined by Gaines in regard to the concept of "political mimesis." Political mimesis, she argues, "begins with the body and is about a relationship between bodies in two locations—on the screen and in the audience—and it is the starting point for the consideration of what one body makes the other do"—specifically what the "committed documentary wants us to do."[37]

Mimesis and affect, for Gaines, revolve chiefly around "images of sensuous struggle," often of large demonstrations, riots, and clashes with authorities. Documentarians use these images because they represent real historical struggles but also "because they want audiences to carry on that same struggle" to "make that struggle visceral." Mimesis, however, is not mere mimicry, which "carries connotations of naïve realism" and "even animality."[38] Instead, mimesis focuses both a potential "change in consciousness" and "making activists more active—of making them more *like* the moving bodies on the screen."[39] In other words, it is a provocation to move one's body in the service of and solidarity with the struggle presented.

In addition, the use of documentary as a form of evidence must take place, argues Nichols, "within a discursive or interpretive frame," where evidence is thus part of a larger discourse. "Facts become evidence when they are taken up in a discourse, and that discourse gains the force to compel belief through its capacity to refer evidence to a domain outside itself."[40] Meaning and impact also emerge from the questions we ask of images, events, objects, or sounds where evidentiary status emerges from the questions we pose and the work we ask of them.[41] Within the domain of radical political concerns and a saturated media environment, the questions we pose to documentary practices involve how to present militant evidence in such a way as to effectively intervene within the context of wars, occupations, and human rights abuses.

One productive way of thinking about this that undergirds the approach in *Radical Documentary and Global Crises* is offered by Helen de Michiel and Zimmermann, who argue that "documentary . . . is undergoing a profound change in its direction of travel . . . [where] the rhetoric surrounding the use of moving images as a tool of social action [is] acquiring a fresh lease of life."[42] They advocate for considering documentary as an open space. It is a place, they argue, "where producers and subjects and audiences work together through dialogue in grounded production, deploying a wide variety of tools and moving across many versions and iterations of a work that are endlessly adapting."[43] De Michel and Zimmermann's theorization is cognizant of the dynamic nature of networked documentary images, which move across platforms, spaces, contexts, and devices simultaneously. It also evinces a collective project where producers, subjects, and audiences interact and collaborate by employing documentary images as tools for social action. In these ways, the concept of the open-space documentary places media makers and artists in a position where they are "context providers rather than content providers, creating scenarios that facilitate dialogue, participation, collaboration, shared experience and interconnections across boundaries," which works to collapse the boundaries between artists, amateurs, and activists who wield images as forms of militant evidence.[44] There is one truth that is emerging that binds these individuals, collectives, groups, and artists documenting these spaces in the globalized digital age: visibility is no longer enough. Militant evidence must be accumulated and deployed tactically within broader partnerships and larger strategies of activist intervention, counterarchives, interruptions of dominant logics, and/or radical practices of resistance.

Efficacy, Impact, and Tactics

When discussing radical documentary projects, notions of their relative success involve the larger question of political efficacy and concerns about how impact is measured. Brian Winston argues that "films exist in too complex a socio-political space for demonstrable outcomes to be expected."[45] Similarly, Bill Nichols asserts that when filmmakers, particularly those with militant or radical political motivations, have "someone's idea of social impact measurement tools thrust upon them," it does them a "gross disservice" by "narrowing options, diminishing priorities, and side-stepping radical visions."[46] While these assertions are generally true, and the question of impact can be a loaded term, there have been recent developments where documentary and video evidence are placed within larger transnational advocacy networks and ecologies that are used in the service of changing state and legal policy, a development examined in greater detail in chapter 1. For as Bhaskar Sarkar and Janet Walker argue, "Documentary studies scholarship . . . has neglected the policy considerations and wider networks through which individual documentary films make meaning," and this neglect has occluded one potential avenue for profound change, despite its seemingly nonradical, reformist approach.[47] Further, the power of documentary images lies not in and of themselves as singular objects of art or evidence but in the discourses they engender and within the discourses and contexts in which they are placed. In the networked digital age, the study and practice of radical documentary demands a multifaceted approach and an openness to expanding definitional boundaries of what a documentary is, how it functions, how it circulates, how it accumulates evidence, and how its impact is measured.

The questions of impact and efficacy are also directly linked to matters of tactics and strategy, or *how* documentary images are deployed. Some uses of militant evidence in the digital age are forms of "tactical media," a conception that is articulated by Rita Raley, who updates its use from Critical Art Ensemble (CAE). Because capitalism, political ideology, and social power increasingly function as part of a globalized, immaterial, and digital realm, activism, in CAE's view, must shift to "take material life struggles into hyper reality."[48] Raley's use of the word *tactical* is meant to convey a form of activism, through a multitude of artistic practices, that encompasses a brief intervention or "disturbance." In Raley's estimation "tactical media is a mutable category that is not meant to be either fixed or exclusive. If there were one function or critical rationale that would produce a sense of categorical unity, it would be disturbance . . . tactical media operates in the field of the symbolic, the site of power in a post-industrial society."[49]

Her use of the word *disturbance* is particularly apt because tactical media, a fluid category of many possible approaches, makes its interventions within an immaterial, symbolic realm premised on speed, security, and adaptability.

Ultimately, Raley's arguments lead to an emerging line of thinking about the function of art, media, and political activism within a world dominated by digital technology and seemingly immaterial forces of power. She positions these emerging forms of media activism, and the concept of tactical media, as opposing outmoded notions of protest and resistance that rely on overthrowing institutional power blocs through revolutionary, epoch changing methods—"storming the barricades," so to speak.

Power, in Raley's estimation (following Gilles Deleuze), is no longer centralized; rather it is nomadic and network based. In this sense, she argues that "activism and dissent, in turn, must, and do, enter the network . . . these projects are not orientated toward the grand, sweeping revolutionary event; rather they engage in a micro politics of disruption, intervention, and education."[50] This reorientation of activism from the streets to the digital network shifts both the idea of what a revolution is or can be; it does not, she argues, "need to be a singular or spatial event . . . it does not need to be a moment of spectacle."[51] In this way "tactical media activities provide models of opposition rather than revolution . . . we need not, and indeed should not, think of political engagement strictly in terms of concrete action, organizational movement, or overt commentary."[52] That is, tactical media is about the development of counterpractices, disruptions, and interventions that think beyond traditional conceptions of radicality.

More recently, Raley has theorized the conflation of everydayness, location, and the radical—and this informs the analysis of the uses of militant evidence in *Radical Documentary and Global Crises* as well. She argues that for both spectators and media makers, locally focused, collective, and often amateur projects have an affirmative force. They work daily to provide alternative frameworks, networks, and practices of resistance. The collective and communitarian aspect here is particularly important in that, Raley asserts, "community is enacted rather than captured or exploited in the process of collective action" and "resituate[s] social activity as a form of life."[53] It is not a revolutionary moment where everything changes but a long, deliberate process where the practices of documenting and media making as well as wielding militant evidence are affirmative, collective building aspects within larger projects of resistance for local communities. Additionally, that process of change is one that is often forgotten in a digital age of the instantaneous.

Using Militant Evidence in the Digital Age

How and why do digital active witnesses capture, construct, and deploy militant evidence? Amateurs, artists, activists, and everyday people around the globe are an on-the-ground force engaging in collective, collaborative, often transnational documentary practices that are largely instrumentalized—acts of survival rather than entertainment. The urgency of the situation—capturing images or giving testimony as an act of intervention—takes precedence over aesthetic considerations, though they are still important. These works move fluidly between video-upload sites viewed on cell phones to the spaces of the gallery, the film festival, the courtroom, the remote village, and the classroom. At once evidentiary and aesthetic, affective and effective, local and global, personal and political, anonymous and visible, they reflect the radical use of documentary in the digital age as they shape its future.

Chapter 1 explores the work of two human rights organizations that use video advocacy as their primary means of activism: Brooklyn-based WITNESS and B'Tselem, the Israeli Information Center for Human Rights in the Occupied Territories, located in Jerusalem, which advocates for Palestinian rights in direct partnership with Palestinians. Both groups focus on the quantifiable and/or material impacts of their transmedia advocacy work as it manifests in court cases and legal or policy changes. They also rely heavily on the capture and amassing of firsthand witness testimonies as sites of empathy and markers of evidentiary truth within their videos, which are made in partnership with various on-the-ground groups and are strategically targeted for maximum impact within specific contexts. The chapter argues for practices of transmedia advocacy that can enable "effective radicality." In these practices, militant evidence is obtained by locals to be contextualized, narrativized, and disseminated by partner organizations. It is then aimed at various government, legal, media, and policy apparatuses that are in a position to adjudicate or stop human rights abuses and make material changes in a given situation.

Chapter 2 analyzes two interactive documentary projects: Sharon Daniel's *Public Secrets* (2006), an exploration of the prison industrial complex through the testimonies of female inmates in California, and Zohar Kfir's *Points of View* (2014), which maps Palestinian video advocacy projects made for and/or disseminated by B'Tselem. The interactive documentary form, as deployed by Daniel and Kfir, draws on the legacies of radical documentary practice but offers new possibilities for engagement and intervention. The interactive documentary form also functions as a structuring device for a wealth of affectively powerful witnesses, testimonies, and varied forms of evidence. The chapter explores how interactive documentaries allow viewers/users a multifaceted affective encounter with a range of subjects and evidence. This form, in concert with a radical political stance is a locus for the representation of viewer/user critical engagement with broad systemic problems. Daniel and Kfir deploy militant evidence to render visible hidden structures of violence and power enable "affective radicality," which moves viewers/users into larger networks of political discourse, militant activism, and practices of resistance.

In chapter 3, IFTC films are analyzed as militant evidence in four ways, which have intertwined affective and effective functions: First, they form a contemporary version of what Paula Amad has called "counterarchives," which, in this context, create a record of a microperspectival view of history and memory that both account for Iraq's past, document its present, and help to shape its emerging future.[54] In the wake of war and amid occupation, artists and filmmakers look to reorient the history that was derailed during Saddam Hussein's reign between 1979 and 2003 and during the initial phases of the war when massive official document, art, film, government, and media archives were destroyed. These counterarchives are also a challenge to the reconstruction of the official state archive, which is detailed in the first part of the chapter. Second, they helped to foster new "public domains," spaces of recognition, empathy, and communication both globally and in Iraq through transmedia efforts of promotion, distribution, exhibition, and education.[55] Third, these practices served a radical function in the specific time and context of their making and circulation, a notion called the "radically banal," an assertion of humanity amid the ruins of war. And finally, these radically banal images and emerging documentary practices laid the groundwork for future and continued media development, and protests and the emergence of an independent Iraqi film culture.

Chapter 4 analyzes the mass of short, militant political documentaries (an "emergency cinema") produced clandestinely by Abounaddara, an anonymous Syrian film collective founded in Damascus in 2010. The group attempts to intervene in the conflict in Syria by deploying militant evidence on a number of levels: first, to reinscribe humanity, personhood, and human suffering into the images of war-ravished landscapes strewn with ruins; second, to assert a "right to the image" within a holistic interpretation of international human rights law; and third, to actively resist the brutal oppression and media censorship under the regime of Bashar al-Assad by strategically deploying their films as "sniper shots" in an ongoing revolution. Through a mass of short films, Abounaddara presents an affectively radical version of Syria to challenge both mainstream representations and the power of Assad regime. The films, which range from witness accounts, photomontages, newsreel/film-tracts, mock advertisements, and recontextualized historical images, are shared widely on social media and video-sharing sites, such as Vimeo and YouTube, forming a living archive of Syria in war and revolution.

To explore how militant evidence operates across this range of countries, crises, and ecologies, the analysis in *Radical Documentary and Global Crises* is not only deeply rooted in documentary theory and the history of radical documentary, but also draws heavily on work in human rights theory and practice, law, media studies, political theory, philosophy, critical theory, and from journalists. This interdisciplinary approach not only fosters fresh thinking and perspectives about documentary media and its use, it also attempts to draw academics and researchers, artists, coders and technologists, journalists, community groups, lawyers, collectives, activists, and amateurs together across disciplines, industries, and borders to fight the myriad global crises that increasingly intersect and affect everybody. This book opens the purview of documentary studies away from feature-length, auteur-driven filmmaking and toward a focus on documentary media produced by those directly affected by the brunt of global crises specifically in places of war, occupation and incarceration, or where human rights abuses occur. The works analyzed in *Radical Documentary and Global Crises*, which instrumentalize images and stories, must be examined not only for their form and content but also in and through the ecologies in which they make meaning, through the vectors of targeted spectatorship, access, and distribution that they flow within and between. The alternative economy of poor images produced by digital active witnesses and distributed in partnership with other groups are the connective tissue that binds alternative networks, counterpublics, counterarchives, and powerful alliances. These images function as militant evidence in a new mode of radical documentary practice, as a force and tactical intervention for resistance, abolition, revolution, counterrepresentations, counterarchives, and justice.

Notes

1. See https://vimeo.com/36130185.
2. Mark Lynch, Deen Freelon, and Sean Aday, "Syria's Socially Mediated Civil War," *United States Institute of Peace*, January 13, 2014, http://www.usip.org/publications/syria-s-socially-mediated-civil-war.
3. See https://vimeo.com/47100634.
4. Judith Butler, *Precarious Life: The Powers of Mourning and Violence* (New York: Verso, 2004), 20.
5. See Bill Nichols, "Documentary Film and the Modernist Avant-Garde," *Critical Inquiry* 27 (Summer 2001): 581–610. Nichols argues that dominant histories of documentary too easily divorced the influences of the concomitant 1920s modernist avant-garde due to an overreliance on John Grierson. The theories of Grierson, he contends, repress the role of the avant-garde within the development of documentary and too easily separate the avant-garde and documentary based on genre conventions and artistic groupings. Nichols posits that such a

repression is not simply about frustrating an aesthetic affinity but also hinders a radical potentiality that includes the exploration of new subjectivities and new modes of consciousness. It also encompasses the contestation of state power engendered by an experimental cinema practice, rooted in the nonfiction image, that questions dominant aesthetic forms and ways of seeing the world. For the relationship between militant evidence, state violence, and the King tape, see Ryan Watson, "In the Wakes of Rodney King: Militant Evidence and Media Activism in the Age of Viral Black Death," *The Velvet Light Trap* 84 (Fall 2019): 34–49.

6. See Thomas Waugh, "Introduction," in *Show Us Life: Toward a History and Aesthetics of the Committed Documentary*, ed. Thomas Waugh (Metuchen, NJ: Scarecrow, 1984), xiv. The idea of commitment, as Waugh alludes to, emerges within the context of a specific political positioning in service of a larger allegiance. For much of the development of the committed or radical documentary, this positioning involved a larger commitment to various factions of the socialist and communist parties and then splintered into a plethora of loosely allied movements after 1968 as the pace and reach of technological changes in mass communication rapidly accelerated.

7. Hito Steyerl, "In Defense of Poor Images," *e-flux* 10, November 2009, http://www.e-flux.com/journal/10/61362/in-defense-of-the-poor-image/.

8. Ibid.

9. Ibid.

10. Kodwo Eshun and Ros Gray, "The Militant Image: A Ciné-Geography," *Third Text* 25, no. 1 (2011): 1. This is the introduction to an excellent issue of the journal on the development of the militant image.

11. Hito Steyerl, "In Defense of Poor Images."

12. Ibid.

13. Ibid.

14. Ibid.

15. Hito Steyerl, "On Documenting [Lecture]," filmed Utrecht, the Netherlands, December 12, 2005, https://vimeo.com/63638712.

16. Andre Bazin, "On Why We Fight: History, Documentation, and the Newsreel (1946)," in *Bazin at Work: Major Essays & Reviews from the Forties & Fifties*, ed. Bert Cardullo (New York: Routledge, 1997), 187.

17. Patricia Zimmermann, *States of Emergency: Documentaries, Wars, Democracies* (Minneapolis: University of Minnesota Press, 2000), xxiii.

18. Kieran Durkin, *The Radical Humanism of Erich Fromm* (New York: Palgrave Macmillan, 2014).

19. Edward Said, "Orientalism," *Counterpunch*, August 5, 2003, http://www.counterpunch.org/2003/08/05/orientalism/.

20. This line of thinking in regard to documentary has been developed by Michael Renov in his writings on documentary ethics and engagement with Emmanuel Levinas's work on humanism. See Michael Renov, *The Subject of Documentary* (Minneapolis: University of Minnesota Press, 2004).

21. Erika Balsom and Hila Peleg, ed., *Documentary Across Disciplines* (Cambridge, MA: MIT Press, 2016).

22. Lev Manovich, *The Language of New Media* (Cambridge, MA: MIT Press, 2001).

23. Remediation is a term used by J. David Bolter and Richard Grusin. See J. David Bolter and Richard Grusin, *Remediation: Understanding New Media* (Cambridge, MA: MIT Press, 2000).

24. Manovich, *The Language of New Media*, 35–36

25. Leah Lievrouw, *Alternative and Activist New Media* (Cambridge, UK: Polity, 2011), 11–12.

26. Paul Rotha, *Documentary Film* (London: Faber and Faber, 1963), 349–350.

27. Both events are discussed at greater length in chapter 1.

28. Benjamin Balthaser, "Racial Violence in Black and White," *Boston Review*, July 13, 2016, https://bostonreview.net/us/benjamin-balthaser-racial-violence-black-and-white.

29. Craig Timberg and Elizabeth Dwoskin, "Facebook, Twitter and Instagram Sent Feeds That Helped Police Track Minorities in Ferguson and Baltimore, Report Says," *Washington Post*, October 11, 2016, https://www.washingtonpost.com/news/the-switch/wp/2016/10/11/facebook-twitter-and-instagram-sent-feeds-that-helped-police-track-minorities-in-ferguson-and-baltimore-aclu-says.

30. T. J. Demos, *The Migrant Image: The Art and Politics of Documentary During Global Crisis* (Durham, NC: Duke University Press, 2013), 74.

31. The term "New Left" derives from French editor Claude Bourdet, who in the pages of the weekly newsmagazine *France Observateur* proffered the tenets of what would become the *Nouvelle Gauche* movement, which, as Stuart Hall argues, opened a "third way in European politics" in the post war period "independent of the two dominant left positions of Stalinism and social democracy." See Stuart Hall, "Life and Times of the New Left," *New Left Review* 61 (Jan/Feb 2010): 178.

32. Deidre Boyle, "From Portapak to Camcorder: A Brief History of Guerilla Television," *Journal of Film and Video* 44 (1992): 1–2.

33. Patricia Aufderheide, "Public Intimacy: The Development of First-person Documentary," *Afterimage* 25, no. 1 (July–August 1997): 16.

34. For an excellent account of the use of motion picture evidence in US courts, see Louis-Georges Schwartz, *Mechanical Witness: A History of Motion Picture Evidence in US Courts* (New York: Oxford University Press, 2009).

35. Ibid., 13.

36. Jane Gaines, "Political Mimesis," in *Collecting Visible Evidence*, ed. Jane Gaines and Michael Renov (Minneapolis: University of Minnesota Press, 1999), 84–102.

37. Ibid., 90.

38. Ibid., 93.

39. Ibid.

40. Bill Nichols, *Speaking Truth with Film: Evidence, Ethics, Politics in Documentary* (Berkeley: University of California Press, 2016), 99.

41. Ibid., 109–110.

42. Helen de Michiel and Patricia R. Zimmermann, "Documentary as Open Space," in *The Documentary Film Book*, ed. Brian Winston (London: British Film Institute/Palgrave Macmillan, 2013), 355.

43. Ibid., 358.

44. Ibid., 258.

45. Nichols, *Speaking Truth with Film*, 258.

46. Ibid., 227.

47. Bhaskar Sarkar and Janet Walker, "Introduction," in *Documentary Testimonies: Global Archives of Suffering*, ed. Bhaskar Sarkar and Janet Walker (New York: Routledge, 2010), 2.

48. Ibid., 93.

49. Rita Raley, *Tactical Media* (Minneapolis: University of Minnesota Press, 2009), 6.

50. Ibid., 1.

51. Ibid., 46.

52. Ibid., 151.

53. Rita Raley, "The Ordinary Arts of Political Activism," in *Global Activism: Art and Conflict in the 21st Century*, ed. Peter Weibel (Cambridge, MA: MIT Press, 2015), 295.

54. See Paula Amad, *Counter-Archive: Film, the Everyday, and Albert Kahn's Archives de la Planète* (New York: Columbia University Press, 2010).

55. A term used by Patricia Zimmermann. See Patricia R. Zimmermann, "Public Domains: Engaging Iraq Through Experimental Digitalities," *Framework* 48, no. 2 (Fall 2007): 66–83.

1. Digital Active Witnesses and the Limits of Visible Evidence

Radical documentary practices have two essential, intertwined functions: to prove and to move. These practices must produce and prove facts to viewers for a range of purposes, from creating the state and new ideologies in the aftermath of revolutions to representing an injustice that is worthy of attention. They also have to spark new ways of seeing and experiencing the world in order to move the spectator toward political action. Historically, provoking the viewer in this way involved matters of aesthetics and the affective functions of content and form and was often accomplished with appeals to empathy, shame, anger, and other strong emotions while exciting the eyes, mind, and body with montages and interactive multimedia screening events. But there is also a more instrumental tendency in the radical use of documentary images and sounds where such practices are used to accumulate and deploy visible evidence to persuade targeted audiences and/or official bodies to act based on effective law and policy appeals.

This chapter focuses on the latter function, primarily examining the interventions of human rights–based visible evidence within legal, policy, and governmental realms. While these areas are not normally considered radical and appeals to them could be considered mere reformism, they have both immediate and potentially long-term transformative impacts both inside and beyond official arenas but only when visible evidence operates within the proper frames of reference and networks and ecologies of circulation for targeted audiences. When made and/or used in a targeted way, properly contextualized and accumulated visible evidence can be successfully deployed for radical and activist purposes. Utilized in this way, the images become "militant evidence," a concept that expands on a long global legacy of radical documentary and possesses the force to catalyze revolutionary changes and movements in the networked digital age.

To explore and explicate one aspect of this concept, how militant evidence is used to generate "effective radicality," the projects of two organizations working at the intersection of media activism and human rights are analyzed: Brooklyn-based WITNESS, which collaborates with groups across the globe on a range of projects and B'Tselem: The Israeli Information Center for Human Rights in the Occupied Territories, which partners with Palestinians working to end the occupation on a variety of fronts. In a globalized digital world, both groups have pioneered bringing forth effective radicality by establishing lasting frameworks for the militant evidence produced by digital active witnesses and providing models for justice and accountability inside and outside official venues. Due to the widespread use of cellphones with cameras and other digital recording devices, documentary media can conceivably be produced by anyone. This circumstance fundamentally alters the potential of the witness while blurring the lines between the roles of the amateur, the activist, and the artist. The term *digital active witness* represents the capacity and vitality of the everyday person, wielding common consumer technologies, to intervene in a radical or activist way. This position of self-representation is not a mode victimhood or appeal to suffering but rather one part of many agentive interventions and contributions to larger collaborative activist efforts.

The digital active witness is any person who purposefully or through circumstance produces militant evidence and then personally or through partnerships shares it to engender accountability in some form in an effort to transform the world around them. The concept of the digital active witness draws on and updates John Durham Peters's definition of the "active witness," who is "a privileged possessor and producer of knowledge."[1] The notion of a producer of knowledge gives voice and force to the witness who captured the media and/or gave personal recorded testimony based on first-hand knowledge. Further, the idea of privilege puts the witness in a position of momentary power, particularly when such evidence comes from witnesses and survivors of war, violent crime, rights abuse, or other situations of extremity. This chapter explores the role of the digital active witness as it emerges from a rich legacy of transnational documentary practices and works in effectively radical ways. Digital active witnesses, in partnership with larger organizations, engender forms of accountability that range from urgent local information sharing and digital archiving in affected communities, to prosecutions in trials for international war crimes.

The digital world of "cameras everywhere" has transformed the standards and expectations for legal persuasion and argument, particularly in human rights cases.[2] Because these venues for accountability demand verifiable visible evidence, digital active witnesses possess and produce privileged forms of proof. However, as Jay Aronson notes, the recent massive proliferation of documentary-based "visual data" in the human rights world has led to concerns about preservation, archiving, and the ethics of use.[3] In addition, digital active witnesses are often in dangerous situations and take a number of risks that must be accounted for, including securing immediate safety while recording and/or avoiding retaliation for having done so. On the one hand, Aronson advocates for a humanistic approach that foregrounds the needs of witnesses and survivors over the demands of laws and archives. On the other, he is mindful of the critical importance of preserving and using relevant visible evidence and other forms of data. Beyond the many risks, access to these avenues for adjudication is precarious and limited, even in the face of clear evidence and especially for minority groups and/or those living amid wars, occupations, mass incarcerations, and human rights abuses. Digital active witnesses thus often depend on partnerships and collaborations to realize the full impact of the militant evidence they have captured or provided.

This balancing act, between the need to adjudicate, archive, and preserve but also partner with and protect witnesses and other survivors is clearly demonstrated in the efforts of WITNESS and B'Tselem. Both groups, in direct collaboration with digital active witnesses, deploy militant evidence through expanded video advocacy, or "transmedia advocacy," accumulating and circulating documentary media for specific audiences across a host of platforms and ecologies within the context of larger advocacy projects with quantifiable goals. The idea of transmedia advocacy builds on Sasha Costanza-Chock's notion of transmedia organizing, which is defined as "on the ground, social movement media-making" that is "cross-platform, participatory, and linked to action . . . (within a) broader media ecology" that provides specific frames of legibility and meaning for the accumulated media to circulate within.[4] Transmedia advocacy encompasses the multiplatform media, legal, and governmental ecologies that WITNESS and B'Tselem operate within as well as the broader ripples of impact beyond wholly quantifiable measures. In addition, the emphasis is not on professional media makers but rather "grassroots, everyday social movement media practices"[5] or, in this context, digital active witnesses. In transmedia advocacy regarding the realm of human rights, a multifaceted, loosely affiliated but collaborative group of activists, journalists, lawyers, technologists, artists, media makers, and everyday people, intervene in perilous situations across the globe while wielding militant evidence in an instrumental way.

Further, through their practices of transmedia advocacy WITNESS and B'Tselem, in partnership with local digital active witnesses, bring forth effective radicality through their deployment of militant evidence. The concept of effective radicality as an outcome is a potent force, and this power derives from two components. The first is the idea that lasting, meaningful changes with beneficial material effects on everyday people can occur through the targeted use of documentary media within official channels of accountability. These changes would include new laws and policies, legal adjudication, and/or forms of restorative justice and compensation. The second component involves the wider, unofficial generative effects on populations, activist movements, and social, cultural, and legal norms. This chapter, which examines two human rights organizations working at the nexus of law and policy, draws on what Seyla Benhabib calls the "jurisgenerative" effect of human rights claims. This effect defines some of the less immediate or quantifiable effects of transmedia advocacy and the effective radicality generated. In her formulation, the more rights claims made in the public sphere, the more new social actors, particularly those traditionally excluded from public discourse, will be enabled to "develop new vocabularies of public claim-making and to anticipate new forms of justice." Social actors exercising their right to expression and association, guaranteed by the Universal Declaration of Human Rights (UDHR), is crucial for "the recognition of individuals as beings who live in a political order."[6] Importantly, Benhabib emphasizes a bottom up, citizen-generated approach to rights spurred by the use of communicative technology as a way to assert oneself as a member of the political order with a fundamental right to be heard and become a digital active witness.

In these ways, even when rights claims and other forms of public witnessing and testimony do not lead directly to official forms of justice, they can positively affect future cases by laying the groundwork for the legibility, via digital media, of the claims of previously marginalized voices. Building on Benhabib's formulation beyond the context of rights and legal justice, the impacts of transmedia advocacy campaigns also have sociogenerative effects, including the efficient dissemination of vital information, the creation of local archives and accountability structures outside of the government and courts, and the benefits of engendering collective forms of resistance for catalyzing future activism and assertions of rights. The jurisgenerative and sociogenerative effects of transmedia advocacy are crucial aspects of the idea and power of effective radicality because they work slowly but persistently to change the norms of law, culture, and society.

For WITNESS and B'Tselem, documentary media is instrumental for transmedia advocacy and engendering effective radicality, as forms of militant evidence are used across legal, governmental, and community settings.[7] As Leshu Torchin argues, groups like these can go beyond mere "exposure of abuse" by using "strategies to place video within a promotional movement that takes into account multiple factors in order to best direct attention and to produce action."[8] Without harnessing the militant evidence and providing the proper frameworks and networks for action and legibility, a single traumatic or graphic moving image can devolve into what Louis Georges-Schwartz calls "image events," which are defined as "images that must be shown but cannot be properly responded to."[9] WITNESS and B'Tselem provide the proper frames of reference so the images captured can be properly responded to. They also help catalyze movements and direct resources into the hands of local groups while building a culture of official rights claims, which produce jurisgenerative and sociogenerative effects beyond their specific quantifiable goals and outcomes. Even when documentation of a human rights crime does not lead to official adjudication, other forms of emerging activism and practices of resistance can generate and galvanize.

To contextualize the analysis of the deployment of militant evidence by WITNESS and B'Tselem, in this chapter, two important turns to evidence within the history of documentary film are assessed. First, the use of film evidence of the Holocaust at the Nuremburg trial in the aftermath of World War II. And second, the wide, constant television exhibition of grainy video of Rodney King being beaten by a group of Los Angeles Police Department (LAPD) officers in 1991. The tape was also a key piece of evidence in the trial of the officers the following year. Today, the widespread availability and circulation of similar images, particularly graphic ones, has not radically altered the landscape of human rights abuses, genocides, or police brutality, as all still frequently occur. The Nuremburg trial and the King tape demonstrate that the affective impact of visible evidence, no matter how powerful, does not guarantee successful outcomes in official settings. Rather, often more mundane, yet accumulated, targeted, and deployed images, effectively engender material impacts for survivors and communities.

Beyond these evidentiary flashpoints, the concept of the digital active witness is rooted within a global genealogy of practices, tendencies, and wishes that sought to create engaged and ideologically informed witnesses from the ranks of artists, activists, and amateurs all armed with cameras to "capture facts" to be used in the service of revolutions and demands for social change. These practices, both within the history of the radical or committed documentary and political cinema more generally, are often engaged through questions of aesthetics as a way to trace opposition, in both form and ideology, to dominant structures and modes. Yet, there is an important and often overlooked tendency among radical documentarians of accumulating and instrumentalizing images for specific purposes, relying on the fact of the event as the main currency for manifesting and spreading radical politics and revolutionary ideas within larger, emerging transmedia efforts. This chapter employs an analysis of highlights from this genealogy through an examination of the work and writings of Dziga Vertov in the wake of the Russian Revolution and the emergence of factography after Vertov's dizzying aesthetic approach fell out of favor; the growth of the Film and Photo League in the United States, whose members adopted some of the Soviet approaches in the 1930s; the work of Octavio Getino and Fernando Solanas and the development of Third Cinema in Argentina in the late 1960s and early 1970s; and the multimedia and direct activist efforts of the AIDS Coalition to Unleash Power (ACT UP) and their video advocacy arm, Damned Interfering Video Activist Television (DIVA TV) in the 1980s and 1990s.

These groups and artists are considered in this chapter not for their aesthetic acumen or innovations, which are vast and well documented, but for their commitment to capturing and deploying militant evidence for instrumental ends within broader media activist efforts. These groups and artists are also part of a larger, loosely integrated transnational legacy of opposition and counterinformation that relied on circulatory networks of technologies, films, people, and causes. This chapter highlights the instrumental tendencies of the aforementioned groups to historicize one important way that images come to have radical power in the digital age. These intertwined histories and evidentiary turns are foundational for understanding the wider media and activist ecologies that militant evidence circulates within. Harnessing the power of militant evidence, and informed by the legacies set by the high-profile successes and failures of visible evidence at Nuremburg and the Rodney King trial, WITNESS and B'Tselem cultivate and expand the seeds planted by earlier generations of radical media pioneers through the effective radicality of their transmedia advocacy.

Transmedia advocacy as deployed by WITNESS, B'Tselem, and similar groups challenges and expands the concerns of documentary studies while realizing some of the impact envisioned for documentary images by the early pioneers of the radical documentary. In transmedia advocacy projects, form and content follow the most effective means of documenting the specific situation at hand to have the greatest material impact on populations suffering mass human rights abuses. For both groups, transmedia advocacy is collaborative and involves participation and training of local groups and people in peril. Thus, transmedia advocacy creates the space and modes of legibility for everyday people to work in service of generating effective radicality and a politics of resistance to human rights abuses by using documentary media as a forceful tool of witnessing, testifying, and illuminating underrepresented struggles.

In both historic radical documentary practices and modern transmedia advocacy projects, impact is intimately tied to the question of spectatorship, particularly through witnessing and testimony. Witnessing and testimony are important foundations for the work of both groups, as their advocacy strategies rely on a combination of media shot by local citizen-witnesses, video from human rights workers, and films actively constructed using a collage of militant evidence from various sources. The WITNESS and B'Tselem advocacy projects are thus created and contextualized for specific audiences and consciously encompass both affective and evidentiary appeals. But unlike previous conceptions of the documentary spectator, these projects are made chiefly for an audience of law and policy makers, international criminal courts, humanitarian relief groups, and local citizens directly affected by the problems being exposed. These transmedia advocacy efforts are not simply made to "raise awareness" of a generalized audience; they are made in the hopes of ameliorating concrete issues in specific locations and contexts, a concept WITNESS program manager Sam Gregory calls "smart narrowcasting."[10] Evidence demands context and narrative, as well as accumulation, to be effective, and it also needs a targeted, empowered viewer who is moved to act in a specific way. With the idea of smart narrowcasting, the viewer is left with a concrete space for action, a path forward toward justice and accountability spurred by the militant evidence presented.

Finally, the idea of militancy often evokes a sense of violence, but here, the unyielding but nonviolent and generative nature of the term is emphasized rather than its potential savagery. As WITNESS founder Peter Gabriel argues, "Sometimes, documenting a human rights crime doesn't directly lead to justice. But it can galvanize a movement. It can be proof regardless of what a jury decides. Most importantly, it can transform public opinion as well as national and international policies. We may not see the outcome we want when we want it, but there is power in arming truth with evidence."[11] The idea of "arming truth with evidence" moves beyond the radicality of previous generations and updates it for the digital era. Here, the camera is not conceived of as a gun but rather a productive weapon, a tool of intervention, justice, and community building. Evaluations of the efficacy of radical documentary media must be reorientated to what Liz Miller has called "slow resilience," which she defines as a "gradual and rooted strengthening, enacted through processes that involve creativity . . . and new collaborative frameworks . . . people working together, taking actions over time, often in quiet but resourceful ways."[12] Groups like WITNESS and B'Tselem, in collaborative frameworks with digital active witnesses, engage in the slow work of justice and accountability. And they do this work within larger ecologies of media activism and human rights projects where impact involves conceiving a more militant notion of evidence whose efficacy relies on targeted circulations and framings for specific spectators in ideal venues for adjudication. The idea of targeting specific visible evidence within formal legal proceedings in this way emerges from lessons of the first two turns to evidence in documentary history—the Nuremburg and Rodney King trials—and reveals the limits of the affective power of visible evidence.

The Limits of Visible Evidence

While assessing the horrors of the recently liberated concentration camps, the Allied soldiers shot hundreds of hours of film that revealed, in graphic detail, a glimpse of the immense scale and brutality of the events of the Holocaust. Despite the overwhelming nature of the evidence, the question of legal culpability exceeded the bounds of traditional criminal law in scope and jurisdiction. In order to prosecute the Nazi high command, members of the Allied nations, including the United States, France, the United Kingdom, and the Soviet Union, collaborated to form the International Military Tribunal. This tribunal held the Trial of the Major War Criminals from November 20, 1945, to October 1, 1946, at the Palace of Justice in Nuremberg, Germany. The four-count indictment included charges of conspiracy, crimes against the peace, war crimes, and crimes against humanity. The last charge is particularly important as it established a legal precedent for circumscribing acts of such magnitude they exceeded the boundaries of simple war crimes. The formal charge, as elucidated in the London Charter of the International Military Tribunal, defined crimes against humanity as "murder, extermination, enslavement, deportation, and other inhumane acts committed against any civilian population, before or during the war; or persecutions on political, racial or religious grounds in execution of or in connection with any crime within the jurisdiction of the Tribunal, whether or not in violation of the domestic law of the country where perpetrated."[13]

To prove the guilt of the twenty-three Nazi commanders on trial, especially in regard to the newly defined charge of crimes against humanity, the tribunal took the unprecedented step of granting themselves wide latitude when it came to evidentiary rules. Article 19 of the aforementioned charter states that "the Tribunal shall not be bound by technical rules of evidence. It shall adopt and apply to the greatest possible extent expeditious and nontechnical procedure and shall admit any evidence which it deems to be of probative value."[14]

This confluence of newly created crimes and lax rules of evidence is important to understand as context for the role of filmic evidence in the trial. Nearly eighty thousand feet of film shot by Allied soldiers after liberation in 1944 and 1945 was compiled and edited by the US Department of Defense into an hour-long documentary, *The Nazi Concentration Camps* (1945).[15] Hollywood director George Stevens directed the film, which was shown at the Nuremberg war crimes trial on November 29, 1945. Legal scholar Lawrence Douglas observes that "the use of film was necessitated, so the prosecution argued, by the nature of the crimes the Allies had assumed the burden of proving . . . The filmic witness could offer pictures where speech failed; it could produce visual knowledge of atrocities that resisted summary in the words of eyewitness testimonials."[16] The film consists of twelve different sections, each focusing on specific concentrations camps, such as Buchenwald, Dachau, and Bergen-Belsen, as well as associated institutions, such Hadamar, a makeshift asylum and medical-testing unit. Each section is accompanied by the common expository documentary trope of dry, matter-of-fact "voice of god" narration and includes horrific iterations of emaciated prisoners, descriptions of atrocities, indirect and direct testimony of prisoners and allied soldiers, as well as reenactments of brutality. As the film progresses, the images of corpses become increasingly graphic, including the ghastly depiction of bodies being bulldozed into common graves in the final images of section 12 at Bergen-Belsen. Beyond these monstrous images, the film stands out in two ways. First, it routinely employs the use of "witnessing witnesses," depicting German townspeople and Nazi officials forced to view the gruesome aftermath of the camps. Second, the film consciously attests to its own veracity as a witness and as evidence through affidavits that buttress the images at both the beginning and the end of the film. The use of affidavits and other legal tools regarding witnesses, testimonies, and evidence in the film do not work to establish the existence of a genocide per se, despite the horrific imagery, but rather they work to prove more legally applicable crimes that involve conduct within the logic of military operations. The film thus works, as Torchin argues, to "promote both rational and affective cases" simultaneously.[17] And it is the rational or effective case that seals the fate of the Nazi commanders because the visible evidence is properly contextualized within the pertinent legal discourses. If the affective case can be said to rely on the power of the images presented to overwhelm the spectator, the rational or effective case lies in the attempt to properly insert the film into a legal discourse of both authentication and culpability. For the former, the film relies on affidavits that attest to the its veracity.[18] Such attestations seek to assuage the possibilities of photographic manipulation while girding against the viewer dismissing the excessive imagery as simply not real or possible. While seemingly focused on the veracity of the images presented, the affidavits also validate the lesser noticed, but perhaps more important, information. Douglas notes that beyond the shocking imagery of the film, there lies a less affective, but likely more effective, accretion of seemingly mundane statistical details that greet the viewer during each section of the film. The evidence makes its case here. The narrator inserts details such as facts about the exact number of political prisoners who died during various periods at specific camps and the nationalities of those held captive. The details presented are of a clinical nature and do little to enhance the power of the images. Yet their effectiveness comes from the prominence they hold within the legal argument presented.

Thus, Douglas argues that despite the striking imagery, the film itself, within the context of its use as evidence, is not really about genocide. Rather, the "film is about political terror and the excesses of war," and it "understands extermination in terms of the perverted logic of political control and military conquest" where the crimes are "the consequence of aggressive militarism rather than genocide."[19] The effectiveness of this information aligns with chief prosecutor Robert Jackson's legal argument, which hinged on building a case for extraordinary military aggression (war crimes) rather than the more nebulous and novel crimes against humanity. Despite the fact that evidentiary rules of the proceedings were laxer than those of a traditional legal proceeding, the prosecution still had to circumscribe the events within a known legal framework in order to assure the culpability of those on trial. In this chapter, the approach taken in this first turn to evidence is widely expanded and updated by WITNESS for the digital age. In much of their video advocacy work, adjudication hinges less on graphic or extreme imagery and more on framing specific images and the legal case in a particular way to ensure justice. In partnership with local groups in affected areas, WITNESS adapts and creates applications, platforms, and advocacy strategies that will be most impactful in the legal and policy contexts of a particular collaboration.

In 1992, the Rodney King trial demonstrated that a single instance of video evidence, no matter how affectively potent, in and of itself does not guarantee accountability or justice, as the image is always subject to a variety of competing interpretations and racist frames of reference. George Holliday surreptitiously captured the beating of King by LAPD officers on video, which was shown countless times on broadcast and cable television and used as the key piece of evidence in the trial. This video clearly seemed to show the use of excessive force by the officers, and both the prosecution and the defense used it in the trial. In defiance of the apparent clarity of the evidence, the officers were acquitted of any wrongdoing. This verdict, a gross miscarriage of justice, sparked outrage and indignation around Los Angeles, leading to days of looting and rioting at the end of April 1992. Despite the verdict, the case revealed both the powerful potential impact of visible evidence and its volatile interpretive instability.[20] While the video possessed undeniable affective power in court and in the media, it was slowed, frozen, and overanalyzed, which negated its emotional impact. King's status as a victim was not in question; rather, he was cast as aggressive and animalistic in court—the only debate concerned how much force was required to properly subdue him.

In recent years, despite a deluge of visible evidence, cases of police abuse and killings are often adjudicated with light sentences, if they are adjudicated at all. The erasure of Black men and women as victims continues, often with the same strategies used against King, as in the killing of forty-three-year old Black man Samuel DuBose by University of Cincinnati police officer Ray Tensing during a July 2015 traffic stop. The video, taken from Tensing's body camera, seemed to show an unjustified homicide. When prosecuting attorney Joe Deters charged Tensing with murder and voluntary manslaughter, he stated on television that the incident arising from a "chicken crap" traffic stop over a missing front license plate was "asinine" and "without question a murder."[21] Yet during the trial, the visible evidence became open to interpretation. The trial became more about Tensing's state of mind and the alleged threat proposed by DuBose. Two different juries failed to convict Tensing, and the charges were later dropped.

As Jackie Wang notes, the trial "lays bare the fallacy of believing that body cams will curb anti-black policing" because "the footage captured by body cams will be used against the people who are being policed and not against the officers who are *legally* given discretion to shoot people."[22] In addition, minority groups, particularly Black people, are often policed so heavily that they live in a state of near constant surveillance by technologies such as body-worn cameras, drones, facial/tattoo recognition devices, and automated license plate readers—many of which were originally developed for US military operations.[23] In this way, in many minority communities in the US, like in Palestine and other areas under military occupation, the police act as an occupying force engaged in near total surveillance of the people residing there. Thus, potential digital active witnesses and the police are all concerned with capturing, archiving, and instrumentalizing documentary media, yet the latter have access to military-grade technologies and are given enormous deference in the media and in legal proceedings. It is an arms race for evidence and narrative framing, but it is not a fair contest.[24] In this chapter, many of these same concerns are reflected in B'Tselem, as much of their work looks to prove the everyday violence Palestinians contend with at the hands of the Israeli Defense Forces (IDF), police, or aggressive settlers and use this accumulated militant evidence to argue for the abolition of the occupation. In direct partnership with Palestinians, B'Tselem uses a strategy that will be most impactful in legal, policy, or media contexts of a particular situation and seeks justice for the victims through the Israeli court and police, military, or government systems less than sympathetic to Palestinian complaints.

In the late 1990s, Jane Gaines argued that the King video raised fundamental questions about the meaning of documentary reality, coining the productive term "visible evidence," which incorporated both the visual and public broadcast impact of the tape as well as its juridical status.[25] She argues forcefully against the old *Cahiers du Cinéma* and poststructural critiques posit that reality outside of cultural signs does not exist—the idea being there is no "real" to record. Gaines, though, makes an interesting and persuasive move when she contends that documentary reality never lies in the image itself but in the discursive field surrounding it, a necessary consideration to understand the failures of the King tape to produce justice. The tape was affectively powerful but subject to racist frames of reference in the courts and the media, enervating its force and rendering it ineffective in manifesting justice.

The routine police violence uncovered by the King tape has only increased, and despite a massive accumulation of visible evidence, convictions still rarely occur. Further, media activists often put too much faith in individual instances of visible evidence and the affective power of realism, despite its lack of success in engendering accountability. The Nuremburg trial and the King tape are thus important flashpoints within documentary history and also specters that haunt media activism. The affective power of the visible evidence in both cases is often considered, but the actual effects are much more crucial to understanding its true impact. Both instances underscore the importance of context, venue, and purpose when deploying visible evidence. They also help to conceptualize a more militant notion of evidence that conceives of the camera not as a gun but rather a type of productive force, that can produce militant evidence as a weapon of intervention and community-based activism. This lays the foundation for a more open purview capable of considering the slow work of accountability and justice and the resilience of occupied and oppressed peoples within larger ecologies of media activism. While digital communication and emerging technologies have enhanced their power, the concepts of militancy and evidence, as well as nascent forms of transmedia advocacy, have existed since the beginnings of radical documentary practices in the early 1920s. The partial genealogy offered below roots the idea of militant evidence and effective radicality in contemporary practices.

Rooting Militant Evidence: "Fists Made of Facts"

Writing in 1981, William Alexander, whose landmark monograph *Film on the Left* helped cohere the historiography of radical filmmaking in the United States, touches on a primary concern when attempting to codify "radical documentary" into a subgenre; namely, the vast heterogeneity of practices. He writes, "Their goals were sometimes complementary and sometimes even conflicting, but all are part of a viable leftist film tradition, a usable past."[26] What these practices do have in common, particularly in the early years of transnational radical documentary, are five main features: a multitude of professional and personal exchanges; unyielding militancy on behalf of political and/or social causes; a concern with the capture and militant presentation of facts; the use of on-the-ground witnesses and evidence; and, as seen in the writings of many documentarians, a host of wishes and recommendations for the uses of documentary that often exceed the capabilities of available technology. These features form a "usable past" for a consideration of the effective radicality of contemporary transmedia advocacy. Similarly, German artist and filmmaker Hans Richter, writing in the late 1930s, sees promise in the ability of technology to bring the world so close that the most remote "documented facts" can gain significance and affect us. "Technology," he contends, "overcoming time and space, has brought all life on earth so close together that the most remote 'facts,' as much as those closest to hand, have become significant for each individual's life ... Everything that happens on earth has become more interesting and more significant than it ever was before. Our age demands the documented fact."[27] Richter, who began his career firmly in the modernist avant-garde era, turned his attention from formalist concerns, like a number of European artists in the 1930s, to an engagement with the question of how to develop an oppositional ("progressive") cinema as a mode of counterpractice against bourgeois film and political intervention. He saw vast potential in his ages' demand for the documented fact when marshalled to fight insidious forces. Our current digital age, immersed in more information than we could possibly fathom, demands the accumulation, targeting, and strategic use of documented facts; *Radical Documentary and Global Crises* explores this militant evidence deployed around the globe. This section examines a partial genealogy of radical documentary practices, antecedents to the effective radicality function of militant evidence that evolved between Richter's time and today in regard to the development of form, content, spectatorship, and intent on the part of the filmmakers. While each phase was short-lived and context specific, the contributions examined shape the transnational emergence of radical documentary since the 1920s and root the study of how versions of these practices re-emerge, evolve, blend, and/or are discarded in contemporary projects that deploy militant evidence in global crises.

Film and media makers in the radical tradition from the 1920s to the beginnings of the digital revolution profess a desire for more cameras to document and amass images, faster and wider means of distribution, and more potential spectators to view their work. They put a great emphasis on the concepts of witness, testimony, and evidence as means of persuasion. Their approaches also involve an avant-garde style to form and/or content, a militant political and/or ideological stance, and an openness to and wish for new technologies to further their experiments in filmmaking and political interventions. They also, importantly, wish to capture, accumulate, and deploy visible evidence as counterinformation against mainstream narratives and, as such evidence accumulates, to produce counterarchives that can be further mined and weaponized. More recently, in light of the multitude of documentary images and digital "global archives of suffering," which have chronicled all manner of abuses, wars, genocides, and occupations in recent years, Bhaskar Sarkar and Janet Walker have urged documentary media scholars to consider the larger networks of official policy and law, particularly with documentary media produced by subjects directly, where witnessing and testimony are used as forms of visible evidence.[28] To bridge the gap between radical documentary history and the expanded purview outlined by Sarkar and Walker and demanded by the proliferation of images in the digital age, the instrumental intentions, effects, and uses of historical radical documentary practices are explored. Here, a combination of artists, activists, and amateurs capture visible evidence in an effort to transform the world.

Undergirding this approach was a radical reconsideration of the representational possibilities of cinema; a new cinematic language of revolution and class expression extolled by Dziga Vertov as a way to concretize and spread Bolshevik ideology, revolutionary fervor, and new ways of seeing the world in the wake of the 1917 Russian Revolution. Vertov conceived of this new cinematic language as a locus for forming visual bonds between people throughout the world based on the idea of the "kino-eye," or camera eye, a fusion of man and technology. He argued that "kino-eye means the conquest of space, the visual linkage of people throughout the entire world based on the continuous exchange of visible fact, of film documents."²⁹ The opposition to traditional modes of fictional cinematic production and a visual linkage of people throughout the world is also premised on the existence of an alternative network of production and distribution that fosters this continuous exchange of visible facts. While the form is new, the content of such films is constructed from the documentary material captured by cameramen, what Vertov calls a "film fact."³⁰ He argues that these film facts must be stored and cataloged in an archive or museum where they can be easily accessed and used by film editors—raw material to construct new montages. This raw material, which Vertov refers to as "data," can then be deployed for a variety of purposes.³¹ He later advocates for the "urgent necessity for immediate centralization of all types of nontheatrical, non-acted film. The storing of newsreels, the production of Soviet film-magazines, the production of *Kino Pravda*, animation rooms, of major kino-eye films" in what he calls a "factory of facts."³² In this factory, the mass of information produced and stored can be weaponized as "fists made of facts." He writes, "Filming facts. Sorting facts. Disseminating Facts. Agitating with facts. Propaganda with facts. *Fists made of facts* . . . Lightning Flashes of facts . . . Mountains of facts . . . Hurricanes of facts . . . And individual little factlets."³³

Here, fact is anthropomorphized and becomes an appendage of the body. Much like the concept of the kino-eye, the accumulation of facts and the ability to weaponize them endows man with a nearly supernatural ability to capture aspects of the world and then wield them, like a force to nature, to intervene within it—a radical and democratized view of the means of representation and agency. The individual fact ("little factlet") in Vertov's formulation has been diminished, yet mountains of facts (i.e., their accumulation) are a source of immense power, an idea that only intensifies with greater technology in the proceeding decades. While the kino-eye is an analogy for the merger of humanity and instrument, engendering a new way a seeing, fists made of facts amalgamates a militant approach with the capture of evidence, a tendency that gains momentum in the networked digital age with the concept of militant evidence.

Vertov wished for many of the developments that have come to fruition today, arguing that the *kinoks* must have "quick means of transport . . . more sensitive film . . . small, lightweight, hand held cameras . . . a staff of lightning-fast film reporters . . . (and) an army of kinok-observers."³⁴ These items are technologically based and rely on the concepts of speed, efficiency, and ubiquity. As technology becomes more advanced, the spectator gains access to a greater number of facts in more pockets of the world. To properly record such facts, Vertov proposed a group of fast and omnipresent cameramen eagerly observing the world around them. In addition, he thought, cameras should be "interconnected," "compact," and "electrically self-sufficient" during shooting. Vertov saw further limitations to developing and training "creative cadres" devoted to film and the revolution.[35] Thus, he proposed a set of objectives, including staff training, the development of mobile filming and editing equipment, and a systematized information base for an accumulation of film "documents" to be preserved and reused for other films. Vertov's approach has influenced radical documentary practices across the globe and many contemporary documentary-based media activist practices. Thus, while the kino-eye changes a conception of vision, fists made of facts change the way we intervene in the world—in Vertov's fantasy, an army of kinok-observers who glean facts that accumulate, strengthening the power of their militancy.

While Vertov's more radical, aesthetically based ideas eventually fell out of official Soviet favor, his conceptions about the militant use of facts saw an expanded realization in the development of the practice of factography, which became the dominant mode of Soviet cultural representation and information. There is not one particular style of factography, as the approach ranged from aesthetically innovative compilations in the work of Esfir Shub to more dry and mundane examples like the photo-essay. Devin Fore argues that factography was not understood "as a static genre, but as a mode of praxis."[36] The process or mode of production of factography was intended to make new facts or novel ways of conceiving history and the present through a constructed Soviet lens. In this way, there was a reorientation from the formalism of Vertov to artistic practices that allowed factographers to more aptly engage and produce "collective social knowledge and networks of communication."[37] As Joshua Malitsky contends, there was power and unity in factography's accumulative practices. Through "multimediality and immediacy," they were able to transform the "subjectivities and social imaginaries of Soviet citizens," where citizens could locate their individual productive efforts as part of the larger collective Five-Year Plan.[38] Here, militant, revolutionary, and aesthetic fervor gives way to a careful, persistent, and accumulative project of building the Soviet nation.

A version of fists made of facts sees an initial manifestation outside of the Soviet Union in developing militant workers' and labor rights advocacy movements in the United States during the Great Depression. The Workers Film and Photo League, founded in New York City in 1930, was sponsored by Communist International and produced a variety of documentary-based film and media in support of workers' rights and strong unions. The League helped spread the energy of communism, socialism, class consciousness, and revolution to the working classes, realizing some aspects of Vertov's vision in America while also modeling radical transmedia efforts that would develop in later years. They did this in the service of constructing revolutionary subjects and actively engaged camera-wielding witnesses from members of unions and the unemployed. The League was a fulcrum for the emergence of radical documentary in the United States, as it made a series of militant films and served as a distributor and exhibitor of radical works from abroad. The group initially started as the American chapter of the *Internationale Arbeiterhilfe* (IAH), a section of the Workers International Relief (WIR) organization. IAH's primary purpose was to provide support for labor strikers and their families, but its influence extended throughout the twenties, and it organized drama groups, dance troupes, and a WIR film group, "Friends of Soviet Russia," which distributed documentaries demonstrating the non-Hollywood version of the Soviet Union.

While the League had obvious affiliations with the Communist revolution in the Soviet Union and a familiarity with their filmmakers, the style of the films produced were more firmly rooted in actuality than the radical experiments with montage favored by Vertov. They were also seen as an alternative to conventional newsreels in the United States and were shown in conjunction with Soviet feature films. As William Alexander argues, these initial attempts at a social documentary form in the United States, which focused on issues of unemployment, strikes, breadlines, union activity, and civil rights "tended to be formally unsophisticated relying for their effectiveness on the *fact* of the event, on the basic power of sheer documentation."[39] The power of the documented fact is not based on the simple mechanical reproduction of reality that had enthralled spectators at the turn of the century a few decades prior. Rather, the power is embedded in the documented fact's ability to lay bare images not in line with the broader capitalist imagination—counterimages that could disrupt the established visual order—essentially a more radical version of Progressive Era social realist photography.

In the early years, as Seymour Stern wrote in the journal *The Left* in his 1931 manifesto "A Working-Class Cinema for America?" the League was squarely focused on a radical practice that relied heavily on the instrumentalization and weaponization of the documented fact. He writes that the League conceived of "a cinema attacking with supreme fury, vehemence, and passion the mightiest and most vicious capitalism, the most brutal class-exploiting 'society,' the world has ever known. No other instrument has the same capacity to present the class struggle of the ages in such *concentrated perspective*, so that what was separated vastly in time and space is united, and what was externally minute but intrinsically significant can be *magnified* in the cinematic scale of relative dimensions."[40]

Stern argues for a militant, instrumental cinema that would weaponize the everyday capture of violence—a "fists made of facts" for the United States. This everyday violence, magnified in importance through projection on a large screen, concentrated the attention and outrage of the audience and brought far off events of class struggle directly into the audience's purview. As Russell Campbell argues, the films "aspired to the status of accurate documents of the class struggle . . . to convey a spirit of militancy while retaining its documentary status, whereby they seized on concrete issues . . . to dramatize abstract notions of class injustice and racial oppression." Further, they filmed and projected images of everyday workers, "miners, agricultural laborers, longshoremen, cab drivers," who took place in strikes, marches, and demonstrations alongside the unemployed, fighting for benefits so audiences could easily identify and empathize with people much like themselves.[41]

Beyond the anticapitalist and proworker content of the images captured by League cameramen, the power of the League's films also derived from a combination of the class-conscious people filming, the technology they deployed, and the ways the films were framed for audiences. For instance, the film *Hunger 1932* presented footage of a march of unemployed workers from New York to Washington, DC, and included images of rampant police brutality.[42] Writing in regard to his experience as one of the cameramen for the film, writer and League filmmaker Samuel Brody stresses both the importance of the camera's presence and its evidence gathering ability:

> This evidence is totally unlike anything shown in newsreels taken by capitalist concerns. Our cameramen were class-conscious workers who understood the historical significance of this epic march for bread and the right to live. As a matter of fact, we "shot" the march not as "disinterested" news-gatherers but as actual participants in the march itself. Therein lies the importance of our finished film. It is in the viewpoint of the marchers themselves . . . our worker cameramen, working with small hand-cameras that permit unrestricted mobility, succeeded in recording incidents that show the fiendish brutality of the police towards the marchers.[43]

Brody's invocation of the term *evidence* paired with his characterization of the cameramen as active and not disinterested is particularly notable. This relay between the filmed point of view determined by a class-conscious participant in the events being documented and the mobility allowed by the small handheld cameras shapes the evidence portrayed from dry objective facts to a viscerally engaging spectacle for viewers. Campbell argues that this form of "participant camerawork," which is characterized by "hand-held, close-range cinematography of street actions . . . must have struck spectators with great novelty and force."[44] The cameramen could intermingle within active demonstrations allowing them to witness and embody abuses of power, such as police brutality, and then relay those affects to their comrades when the images were projected. Beyond the intensity and immediacy such images convey, they are also deliberately framed for maximum impact on spectators. This framing takes place within the space of the film itself through the careful placement of pithy intertitles but also gains momentum through a combination of lectures, cartoons, and newsreels that buttress a typical film. This immediate framing is then further reinforced by a comprehensive alternative media structure of union and activist periodicals that connects political ideas to everyday material realities and class consciousness. In the digital age, there exists plenty of engaging, handheld, participant camera work from cell phones, documenting strikes, protests, direct actions, police killings, wars, occupations, and human rights abuses. What it lacks is the comprehensive alternative media structure for legibility or clear avenues for targeted dissemination or adjudication for militant evidence to realize its effective force.

Continuing with these effective dimensions, and beyond the instrumentalization of documentary for propaganda purposes during World War II, radical documentary practices re-emerge after the war with a renewed emphasis on evidence and its use in the urgent spread of information and the use of documentary for creating and sustaining revolutions as well as in service of solidarity, particularly Third World anticolonial struggles and anti–Vietnam War activism. One of the most influential developments to emerge in this period in regard to using cinema in an effective and instrumental way toward revolutionary ends was the theorization of Third Cinema by Argentinian filmmakers Octavio Getino and Fernando Solanas. Their groundbreaking essay, "Towards a Third Cinema," first appeared in the journal *Tricontinental* in October 1969 in its original Spanish, accompanied by simultaneous translations in English, French, and Italian.[45] Subsequent revisions, updates, and improved translations have both helped to recontextualize the contribution and give a more fully formed view of Third Cinema and its internal category, militant cinema, as processes that continue to transform, grow, and adapt to present circumstances.[46] "Toward a Third Cinema" is meant as a companion piece for Getino and Solanas's epic, three-part *Le Hora de los Hornos / The Hour of the Furnaces* (1968).[47] The film is part political, pro-Peronist treatise and part avant-garde documentary produced under the auspices of the Grupo Cine-Liberación, which, according to Robert Stam, "revives the historical sense of avant-garde as connoting political as well as cultural militancy."⁴⁸ The film does this by deploying a range of historical and direct cinema-style footage punctuated by constant headlines, advertisements, captions, and title cards that situate the images within the broader context of history, ideology, culture, and economic struggle in Argentina. Getino and Solanas seek to merge theory (the manifesto) with praxis (the film) while engaging the spectator to fulfill the obligation of continued political struggle, exhorting the audience to continue the work of the film.⁴⁹

Like their radical predecessors, Getino and Solanas view the camera as a gun, a weapon for social and political struggle. They advocate a form of cinema that has three main functions. The first is to speak directly to the concerns of a localized audience by providing information and an ideological perspective not available from the mainstream media—films they regard as "indigestible" by the dominant system. Second, when politically engaged films are screened (in most cases clandestinely), they serve as a locus for people to come together, share the experience of the film, discuss and debate the issues presented, and ideally, take up the cause of revolutionary engagement. Finally, while the issues presented in such films are location and context specific, the films also function as means of dialogue between other revolutionary movements and contexts throughout the world.

Yet, not just any genre of film can draw spectators and contain an effective revolutionary message. Getino and Solanas posit that documentary is the most effective avenue with which to achieve this synergy. They contend that "every image that documents, bears witness to, refutes or deepens the truth of a situation is something more than a film image of purely artistic fact; it becomes something which the System finds indigestible."⁵⁰ Getino and Solanas argue that "testimony about a national reality is also an inestimable means of dialogue and knowledge on the world plane," where successful revolutions demand "a mutual exchange of experiences among people."⁵¹ Testimony, in this sense, is not merely an expression of prior witness but a call for recognition and a provocation to discussion, forming the basis for shared experience across national boundaries. To achieve this mutual exchange, they contend that any documentary-based, revolutionary expression can be effective: "Pamphlet films, didactic films, report films, essay films, witness-bearing films—any militant form of expression is valid, and it would be absurd to lay down a set of aesthetic norms."⁵² Whatever form film takes, revolutionary cinema cannot passively document, "rather, it attempts to intervene in the situation as an element providing thrust or rectification."[53] In this way they conceive of a weaponized cinema: the camera, a "rifle," and the "inexhaustible expropriator of image-weapon," the projector, "a gun that can shoot 24 frames per second."[54] In "The Cinema as Political Fact (1973)," Getino further refines the claims elucidated above by defining his conception of "militant cinema." He argues that "militant cinema is that cinema that is taken entirely as instrument, complement, or support of a specific political goal, and of the organizations that carry out any number of diverse objectives that it seeks: counter information, raising consciousness, agitation, training of cadres etc."[55] In this way of thinking, documentary media serves a utilitarian function. Getino also makes reference to the importance of specificity and context; a militant film in one country does not necessarily work in the same way in another, as militant cinema, always a collective practice, must intervene in a specific political situation.[56]

Noticeably absent from the prescriptive gestures toward a theory and practice of militant cinema is any codification of specific aesthetics. The cinema-event (*cine-acción*) of the screening, where spectator and film come together to catalyze political action within the process of liberation, is not compelled, in their estimation, solely by what is on the screen. Both content and aesthetics are determined via specific historical moments, places, and political situations. Further, the political efficacy of militant cinema is not found in its intended purpose or its makers but rather the specific ways it is received by, affects, and activates its targeted spectators. In a similar way, the work of WITNESS and B'Tselem examined in this chapter find the efficacy of their transmedia advocacy in how it not only affects and activates its targeted spectators but also what those spectators do in the space for action provided by the relevant context the militant evidence is received in.

By the late 1980s in the United States, radical documentary practices gained a more subjective and issue-focused advocacy lens rather than the more rigidly ideological or revolutionary-based focus of previous iterations. One influential manifestation of this shift is seen through the self-representation, testimony, and direct actions from groups not usually found in previous iterations of radical practices: namely a diverse group of gay, lesbian, bisexual, transgender, and other individuals living with HIV and AIDS. ACT UP was founded in 1987 in New York City among the ever-expanding spread of HIV and ensuing AIDS panic that gripped the United States. ACT UP and its scores of affiliate groups, including the video activist cohort DIVA TV, participated in militant, direct, and collective action "at an astounding rate."⁵⁷ The diverse, multicity actions included street protests, leaflets, posters, stickers, public access television programming, die-ins, and demands for more funding for research and treatment. Art historian and activist Douglas Crimp contends that AIDS was not simply a scientific problem whereby the correct "facts" about the disease were simply not widely known among the public, and if they were, a rational response would ensue; rather, AIDS, in his view, is a problem of representation whereby the disease exists among discourses of homophobia and racism that posit gay, bisexual, transgender, and racialized individuals and IV drug users as disposable others whose lives lack value. This crisis of representation also involves expectations for art that emerges from the assumptions that cultural producers can only respond to the epidemic in two ways: raising money for research or by documenting the graphic human suffering of those with HIV/AIDS around them.⁵⁸ New facts had to be created and circulated within public consciousness. Crimp argues that narratives and practices of meaning-making about people with HIV or AIDS must be controlled by activist cultural producers as a form of "cultural activism," whereby they disseminate highly attuned self-representations and counterinformation in both form and content that challenge expectations while providing urgent education about the disease and the lack of government and medical establishment responses.

Cultural activism is the group of militant practices that accurately represent the dynamic energy and heterogeneity of those amid the crisis, resists commodification, disseminates accurate information about protection and prevention, and directly confronts the lethargic response of government and medical institutions.⁵⁹ Within this form of activism, video practices, particularly those by DIVA TV, were the fulcrum of intervention for artists and amateurs in the fight against AIDS. The work of DIVA TV within ACT UP gains much of its power and meaning from its imbrication with ACT UP's other practices of representation and direct action. It is also situated within a larger boon in film and video (particularly documentary) that includes work produced during this time by Gay Men's Health Crisis, the Video Data Bank "Video Against AIDS" series, and scores of independent filmmakers. Within these contexts, Ann Cvetkovich taxonomizes four different kinds of video activism: the use of video in educational institutions, in activist groups, within mainstream cultural institutions, like museums, and as a site of alternative representation.⁶⁰ The first two reorients the space of and participants in the political, while the second two work to redefine and circumvent the dominant culture. In addition, because much of the representation of AIDS has been disseminated via television, counter–video practices (music videos, education tapes, etc.) have contested such representations through the same medium. Video offered its practitioners the ability to portray an array of information and access to VCRs and cable television in one's home, dispersing spectators from spaces of collectivity in public to private—singular spaces in front of personal screens.

In the digital age, transmedia advocacy is a new form of media activism, rooted in documentary, that privileges on-the-ground digital active witnesses and deploys militant evidence in the service of concrete legal, policy, and community goals. Groups like B'Tselem and WITNESS, with their quantifiable successes in the realm of human rights and reliance on militant evidence in seeking justice, accountability, and other material improvements in the lives of everyday citizens, stand as the current culmination of the generative transmedia legacy of "fists made of facts." In a world of cameras everywhere and wide circulation and reception of images of spectacular brutality and trauma, WITNESS and B'Tselem work to slowly and persistently wield militant evidence and generate effective radicality in ethical and generative partnerships with digital active witnesses in a variety of legal, political, and media ecologies, providing trailblazing models of generating effective radicality in the realm of human rights.

B'Tselem and WITNESS

In the aftermath of the King tape and the steady spread of consumer-grade camcorders—and eventually cell phones with cameras—models of partnership-centered, bottom-up human rights interventions have been emerging over the last thirty years that deploy documentary video, witnessing, and testimony in a targeted way. These new models allow for a unique intervention into human rights discourses, letting individuals living in those situations speak for and represent themselves while partnering with organizations in a position to execute successful transmedia advocacy campaigns to end various human rights abuses throughout the globe. WITNESS and B'Tselem successfully challenge a broadcast model of distant suffering in favor of smart narrowcasting and direct-action strategies using targeted audiences of local citizens, lawmakers, government officials, international relief organizations, and a host of others. In each specific case, the choice of audience depends on context in all of WITNESS's projects, while B'Tselem's are squarely targeted at the Israeli public and its global allies. Both groups' use of militant evidence relies on highly contextualized strategies within larger transmedia advocacy projects, catalyzing effective radicality through official forms of justice as well broader jurisgenerative and sociogenerative effects while forming communities and creating spaces of active participation.

The WITNESS and B'Tselem projects are made in partnership with on-the-ground human rights groups and shot by local people intimately connected to the issues. Here, a video or other documentary-moving image used as militant evidence, whether it be in a traditional form of witnesses telling their stories within a constructed narrative or a brief moment of action caught on a camcorder or cell phone, is aligned within specific networks, narratives, and contexts. While the campaigns and advocacy projects are all locally centered, they are globally informed and financed and work in a variety of legal, governmental, and global media ecologies.

A collection of lawyers, journalists, academics, and Knesset members formed the Israeli human rights advocacy organization B'Tselem in 1989.[61] The mission of the organization is fourfold: to document and disseminate evidence of human rights abuses and violence in Israeli-occupied territories in the West Bank and the Gaza Strip; to educate the Israeli and international public about previously unseen abuses; to change policy toward Palestinians through legal and governmental channels; and to ultimately end the occupation. B'Tselem, like WITNESS, is not concerned with simply raising awareness of human rights issues. Instead, the group engages in a multifaceted strategy focused on accountability. As the organization argues, there exists a "systematic lack of accountability for ensuring the rule of law that endangers the well-being of the population" in the Occupied Territories "and undermines Israel's image as a country guided by the rule of law."[62] To stymie this lack of accountability, the group produces scores of thoroughly researched and documented reports about abuses ranging from illegal searches and seizures, unlawful detainments, and land expropriation to unjustified killings of Palestinian civilians by police and the IDF. They use these reports to brief members of the Knesset in an attempt to offer concrete policy solutions and garner official reactions from Israeli police and the IDF on acts deemed detrimental to Palestinian human rights. In early 2007, B'Tselem added a video advocacy component to their work. Initially dubbed "Shooting Back," the project is now known under the less militant name "The Camera Project." To date, the project has distributed cameras to over two hundred Palestinian families with a focus on areas of the Gaza Strip and the West Bank, which B'Tselem has identified as most prone to violations.

The logic of the project has three components. First, it works as a tool of empowerment for Palestinians, giving civilians the ability to document abuses as they happen and performing a form of "citizen journalism," which produces evidence of abuse in areas unseen by the Israeli media and public.[63] As the ubiquity of cameras and their documentations of abuse have increased, the camera itself has acted as a deterrent for unseemly behavior.

Project director Oren Yakobovich asserts that "undoubtedly, when they carry a camera, they suffer less violence, because a camera is a deterrent. There are even some who go around with a broken camera, just so that people won't come near them."[64] Second, the raw footage captured by Palestinians is turned over to B'Tselem and is repurposed in varied contexts. At times, B'Tselem then distributes to Israeli print and televisual media, producing new knowledge for Israeli citizens and policy makers. It is also used as a form of visual evidence in legal complaints filed with Israeli authorities. Diala Shamas, a B'Tselem researcher, argues that "the project started as response to the need to gather evidence. We were constantly filing complaints to no avail on the basis of lack of evidence . . . Now we are going back and forth with our video-cassettes to Israeli police station begging them to press rewind, freeze . . . it is the bulk of our work."[65] Finally, the thousands of hours of footage are stored in a vast video archive available to the public and used by academics, students, filmmakers, lawyers, and journalists who hope to glean the perspective of Palestinians living under occupation. Both the archive and the participation of Palestinians recording the abuses around them has increased greatly with the spread of cell phones with cameras—so much so that Israel has sought to restrict the recording of IDF forces.

The ability of Palestinians to record police and the IDF, digitally archive, and distribute militant evidence of abuses is constantly under threat. Recently, constraints on video recording in the Palestinian territories have tightened, underscoring the power and threat of the camera and militant evidence. For example, in May 2018, the Israeli parliament introduced a bill to ban the photographing of IDF soldiers with punishments beginning from five years in prison for the act of filming, with an additional five years possible for the "intention to harm."[66] In addition, protestors have encountered lethal counterforce. During the Great March of Return protests, also in May, the IDF openly fired on Palestinian journalists, clearly marked as "press," killing Yaser Mutaja and Ahmad Abu Hussein as well as unarmed civilians.[67] A number of groups, including B'Tselem, challenged IDF rules for use of weapons and force all the way to Israeli supreme court. The court, however, sided with the military, arguing lethal force was justified because Hamas is in armed conflict with Israel in Gaza.[68] Moreover, beyond the hampering of media and intentional killings, there was also purposeful maiming of Palestinian bodies. As Jasbir Puar says, Israel asserts a fundamental "right to maim" as a form of both biopolitical control and debilitation of protest movements in addition to the larger digital occupation controlling data in and out of Palestine via Israeli-owned servers.[69] Palestinian transmedia advocacy in partnership with B'Tselem and other groups adopts a different notion of weaponry, where the camera allows generative shooting to intervene, archive, and communicate across the globe. This is a collective project of preserving and capturing militant evidence, which is deployed primarily in legal and governmental settings within Israel as way to engender accountability for IDF soldiers and justice for Palestinian citizens working to end the occupation.

B'Tselem's slogan, "A Camera Changes Reality," acts on a number of levels in this context. First, as mentioned previously, there was and is a sense among the participants in the camera project that the mere presence of the camera has acted as a deterrent for illegal behavior on the part of Israeli settlers, police, and IDF soldiers. The success of the project over the past twelve years at exposing violations by these groups has forced them to alter their actions for fear of being prosecuted and/or exposed to the public at large. Similarly, as the project was once called the more militant "Shooting Back," the camera functions as a nonviolent weapon for those living in the occupied areas. It is a tool of empowerment that allows for the active documentation of the tribulations, indignities, and illegal acts encountered on a daily basis. Like in the WITNESS model, their partnership with the resources of B'Tselem allows digital active witnesses' videos to be properly accumulated, contextualized, and deployed as militant evidence within larger advocacy projects to adjudicate many of the situations captured and bring Palestinian lives and stories into Israeli and international consciousness.

B'Tselem also expresses the notion of bringing the perspectives of Palestinians into mainstream consciousness by producing more traditional documentary texts. In 2010, they produced *Gaza: An Inside Look*, a compilation of various scenes of everyday life shot by young Palestinians.[70] In 2011, they teamed up with the United Kingdom–based newspaper *Guardian* to produce the web-based documentary series *Living in East Jerusalem*, which featured video diaries of three Israeli and three Palestinian children who recorded aspects of their daily lives living in East Jerusalem.[71] Further, B'Tselem has expanded their partnerships and engagement with emerging technologies. For example, their recent interactive documentary project, *The Invisible Walls of the Occupation* (coproduced with Canadian digital studio Folklore) is an immersive guided tour of the ordinary, occupied West Bank town of Burqah and the tribulations and indignities faced in daily life by residents there.[72] The interactive documentary was based on an extensive B'Tselem report on life under occupation in the area. Finally, B'Tselem has partnered with a wide variety of allied groups and media artists, such as Zohar Kfir, whose interactive documentary using videos from the archive, *Points of View* (2014), will be analyzed in the next chapter. In all their work, B'Tselem does not seek to reform or simply lessen the effects of the occupation. Rather, their massive work of documentation, media making, and legal cases, works to end the occupation in direct collaboration with Palestinians living under Israeli control. By exposing the full scale of the repressive apparatuses and violence faced, B'Tselem and a multitude of digital active witnesses are able to militantly erode the legitimacy of the occupation within Israel and internationally while holding the government legally accountable internally.

The use of documentary for similar radical and activist purposes has an illustrious recent past for Palestinians, as a cadre of filmmakers for the Palestine Liberation Organization (PLO) documented the Palestinian national liberation movement between 1968 and 1982, hoping to catalyze solidarity from Arab audiences outside Palestine and international audiences through the global festival circuit. As Nadia Yaqub contends, the films, mostly documentaries, "treated Palestinian encounters with violence, militant response[s] to that violence, and difficulties related to Palestinians' status as a stateless people"[73] Yet, after the 1982 Israeli invasion of Beirut and the PLO's move from Lebanon, both the nascent revolution and the film archive that had been assembled were both eradicated.[74] B'Tselem's work in Palestine does not reflect the levels of violence in the Palestinian revolutionary period from 1968–1982, but it is a part of growing, loosely affiliated groups of on-the-ground Palestinian, Israeli, and collaborative organizations, such as Active Stills, Yesh Din, Visualizing Palestine, and Al-Haq, which all fight the occupation on a number of fronts while securely archiving and deploying militant evidence.

Since its inception three years after B'Tselem in 1992, WITNESS has harnessed the power of both video evidence and transnational partnerships with on-the-ground groups and digital active witnesses, having partnered with 570 organizations in 135 countries and directly trained more than 11,000 people. Their many publicly available digital resources have been accessed by over one million people in 2020 alone.[75] Although this chapter aligns the approach of WITNESS with the discussion of the Nuremburg trial earlier, the founding of the group actually arose directly in the wake of the King tape. The tape demonstrated to its founders, musician Peter Gabriel and the Lawyers Committee for Human Rights, "the power of video cameras in the hands of a bystander/witness," which they felt could be harnessed by human rights activists in various corners of the globe.[76] The initial impulse to harness the power of video evidence captured by well-informed activists and advocates draws from two complementary vectors. First is a belief in the power of the image itself to reveal an unbiased view of the act of abuse, which would be both necessary and sufficient for exposing and adjudicating it properly. Second is the reliance on an engaged, properly trained, digital active witness who is aware of the vagaries of the situation on the ground and is able to effectively use the camera to capture violations. As this logic goes, the video evidence would then be shared with the international community, who would act to stop the violations. But WITNESS soon realized that the mere exposure of abuses and the shame model of accountability were doing little to spark lasting changes.

The WITNESS approach, unlike the approach of many human rights organizations, does not merely wish to shine the spotlight on abuses in order to shame governments and groups into accountability and action. Rather, their "theory of change is rooted in the research and experience showing that catalyzing long-term and sustainable change within societies relies on those societies having a vibrant, independent, and diverse civil society."[77] In other words, WITNESS seeks not just to uncover and expose human rights abuses but also form cohesive and lasting publics comprising engaged and vigilant citizens, much like their radical forbearers wished for early in documentary history. As they argue "video always provides a 'space for action' by the audience, encouraging them to participate in solving the problem."[78] In addition, "video has a candid authority that the written word lacks and its serves as a powerful evidentiary tool," but only when it is contextualized and part of a broader, targeted advocacy campaign and within a defined narrative framework that explains the visible evidence and offers ways to act.[79] They contend that there are three types of videos that can be used as militant evidence for human rights issues: advocacy video (created by WITNESS and local partners), witness documentation, and perpetrator video. The creation of advocacy videos composes most of the groups' work, such as those that will be considered in this chapter. These videos make cogent appeals and marshal forms of militant evidence for various types of targeted interventions. WITNESS argues that such videos work to "change the vernacular of human rights advocacy, to make space for voices from the outside, and to push a new way of communicating around rights abuses."[80] The dominant model of human rights advocacy historically followed a top-down, broadcast "we speak about them to you model."[81] Central to the WITNESS mission is to change this orientation to one of empowering people directly affected by abuses to tell their stories in order to direct appeals to law and policy makers in a position to help—or smart narrowcasting.

As program manager Sam Gregory notes, "We're in a world of a billion potential observers to the Rodney King incidents" of the future and that has radically increased the participation of digital active witnesses, but it "raises significant questions of agency, action, and audience."[82] The idea of smart narrowcasting or "speaking to a particular audience at a particular time, and seeking a distinct change in policy, behavior or practice" attempts to ameliorate the nonspecificity and spectacle of mass media while directing militant evidence to the most impactful avenues for justice, accountability, and action.[83] WITNESS works primarily with and within evidentiary and quasijudicial settings, like the United Nations, direct to decision-making contexts, on-the-ground community activist and mobilizing campaigns, and organizing within virtual communities via the internet and digital networks. In 2006, McLagan noted the WITNESS model of change had evolved to one of "brokering relations between partners, audiences, and decision makers," which demonstrates "a new hybrid model of advocacy" that is attuned to the particularities of official adjudication and governmental policy in specific contexts but also cognizant of how militant evidence circulates within lager local and global media ecologies.[84]

The work of WITNESS can be broken down into five main components: technology and advocacy, where the groups partner with technology companies and develop their own tools to aid digital active witnesses; video as evidence, where WITNESS provides a host of resources to partner organizations, and activists deploy and heighten the evidentiary value of militant evidence; the WITNESS Media Lab, which addresses the sourcing, verifying, and contextualizing of militant evidence, as well as cases studies and other resources; and finally, archiving and training, where the group trains activists and organizations how to properly preserve and store militant evidence and how to deploy it successfully as transmedia advocacy. The specific needs and situations of partner organizations determines all of their work and often involves many aspects of WITNESS. For example, in 2009, WITNESS collaborated with Healthy Options Project Skopje (HOPS) in Macedonia to provide video advocacy training in how to conduct and produce concealed identity interviews in order to launch a campaign against law enforcement officers, who often committed violent acts against local sex workers and failed to properly enforce the law when such violence was done by others. WITNESS and HOPS produced the short documentary *You Must Know about Me: Rights Not Violence for Sex Workers in Macedonia* (2009), which included direct testimony and other forms of evidence of violence and was shown to police academy students and distributed to the media, members of the judiciary, and within sex worker communities. While the campaign was not targeted directly for specific prosecutions and legal venues, it had wide jurisgenerative effects, including an increased monitoring of and accountability for police that has significantly lessened violent offenses and increased successful prosecutions of other violent crimes against sex workers. In terms of sociogenerative effects, sex workers have seen a more sympathetic and positive portrayal in local media and within the community.

In New York, state law prohibits public access to the records of police officers, yet, especially in New York City, the police often systematically target and harass minority communities. The WITNESS collaborative project "Profiling the Police: El Grito de Sunset Park" sought to explore and render visible systemic police abuse and then keep a secure, community-based archive of the abuses.[85] WITNESS partnered with El Grito de Sunset Park, a community-based organization in the Sunset Park section of Brooklyn. Due to years of "broken windows" and "stop and frisk" policing in New York, the mostly Latinx residents of the area have faced routine harassment and abuse. Beginning in the early 1990s, El Grito emerged to train citizens how to legally and properly film police activity while also de-escalating situations between the police and community members. The captured militant evidence has been used in the courtroom to prosecute offending officers and in the media to pressure local police officials and the mayor's office. In the "cameras everywhere" age, the group has received a massive amount of new militant evidence from digital active witnesses armed with their cellphones. WITNESS and El Grito have collaborated to organize, analyze, and preserve the footage in an effort to render visible and expose patterns of surveillance, harassment, and violence at the hands of police. They created an ad hoc, community digital archive about police misconduct that is secure, growing each year, and an important source of information about bad police officers, who may have a long record of harassment that is usually shielded from public view. The groups have created an unofficial resource for accountability reinforced by a properly trained and vigilant population of digital active witnesses who harness and archive militant evidence in the slow pursuit of justice.

Despite WITNESS' many successes, persistent challenges remain. First, human rights activists and digital active witnesses work in extremely dangerous areas that often lack rule of law. These unstable situations often thwart efforts of on-the ground groups to document abuses, execute an advocacy strategy, or disseminate their evidence. In turn, some of the worst human rights abuses go largely unreported. Second, they face the challenge of how to "capitalize on emerging technology opportunities (to) make sure that the people who could potentially benefit the most from these tools are not left out due to inequities in access,"[86] which has become a bit easier with the increased presence of cell phones with cameras and video-recording capability in previously unnetworked areas. Finally, WITNESS is very cognizant of the potential ethical questions and hurdles it faces by disseminating and promoting videos of other survivors of abuses and other horrors. The group has "emphasized a model that relies on helping people who film and are filmed to understand the worst case scenario consequences for their safety . . . 'informed consent' is genuinely informed."[87] They work diligently to ensure that in the "survivor-centered human rights model" there is no revictimization or exploitation of survivors, a goal certainly made easier through targeting specific audiences within a strictly defined campaign.[88] While both groups deploy video in a number of contexts and produce positive sociogenerative and jurisgenerative effects, as outlined above, the case studies analyzed below focus primarily on their use of militant evidence in legal and governmental settings. The concept of the evidentiary function of media in these contexts hinges on varied modalities of evidence and of witnessing and testimony. The legal venue, whether it is local, national or transnational, determines the rules of evidence. Each body has its own interpretations and parameters governing how, when, and in what context video evidence can be used.

There are three main categories with which video evidence is deployed. The first is as direct evidence. In this instance, the video directly portrays some element of the crime being adjudicated. For example, if one were on trial for stealing a computer and the prosecution entered into evidence a store security camera clearly showing the defendant putting the computer in a bag and walking out of the store without paying, it would directly prove the charge of theft. The second category comprises the use of circumstantial evidence in which the video evidence indirectly proves a facet of the crime committed. In the case of the theft described above, if there were no direct video evidence of the crime being committed but prosecution had offered instead a video of the defendant clearly showing they were in possession of the item said to have been stolen, that would act as circumstantial evidence. Circumstantial evidence can also be used to corroborate and contextualize witness testimony. Finally, video evidence can be used as rebuttal evidence and comprise either the force of direct or circumstantial evidence. For example, if the prosecution had used the aforementioned security footage showing the defendant putting the computer in the bag and walking out of the store, the defense could rebut this evidence using a cell phone video shot by the defendants' friend showing him paying for the item at the register.[89] WITNESS often works with evidence that is circumstantial in nature, constructing videos that seek to lead the viewer, often a judge or prosecutor, to bring a case based on a reasonable inference that a crime occurred and the defendant had been aware of and/or directly participated in it. They also produce many videos from witnesses and survivors that contextualizes and narrativizes direct video evidence of crimes and abuses being committed. On the other hand, B'Tselem works more often in direct evidence, distributing videos that directly prove that had violations occurred.

For both groups, the video evidence encompasses the use of witnesses and testimonies and constructs itself as witness and testifier in the context in which it is shown. In the case of WITNESS, the actual events being adjudicated, such as widespread child-soldier conscription, are, like the Holocaust, simply too large to represent adequately. There generally exists scant video or photographic evidence of the actual events. Thus, WITNESS must rely on the representation of direct witnesses giving testimony to their experience of trauma to corroborate the charges being brought. In these videos the invocation and representation of past trauma manifests on the body of the victim, in their recounting, and in the mind of the spectator, who must actively reconstruct, picture, and assemble the images evoked into coherence. This inversion of spectacle in a relay from the witness giving testimony to the receiver/spectator necessarily involves internalizing the event in the body and mind of the targeted spectator, hopefully moving them to act.

In the case of B'Tselem, witness and testimony are deployed in a different register with similar goals. In a sense, there are two witnesses. The digital active witnesses, embodied by the local Palestinians, who see rights violations occurring in their daily lives and who use the camera to intervene. And the mechanical witness, in the form of the camera itself, which records the abuse. The testimony is also twofold. The resulting video evidence testifies to the crime in its showing, while the active witness who captured the video testifies (either directly in court or indirectly through affidavits) to the conditions surrounding its making, helping to shape the discourse of its reception. In the B'Tselem cases, the proof is often obvious; it is only the limits of IDF power that is adjudicated. How much violence, in other words, is legal. Many of the images captured in the B'Tselem project are disturbing and are meant to shock. While the WITNESS approach is born of necessity in the sense that many of the human rights abuses they document are either too large or have already occurred, the B'Tselem approach is one of circumstance, tactic, and strategy. The interventions made by B'Tselem occur during an active occupation of Palestinian territories by the Israeli government. Second, part of their strategy, beyond bringing cases against the specific instances of violations documented, is to represent visually the effects of occupation to Israeli citizens, who are generally unaware of the details of the arduous nature of daily life in the occupied territories. In this way, theirs is a strategy of accretion.

While the short-term goals involve the adjudication of violations, the longer-term goal is to accumulate so much militant evidence that it changes public sentiment and official Israeli policy. In this sense, they strongly shape the discourses in which the current and future visible evidence gathered by Palestinians will be received while harnessing militant evidence to end the occupation.

The potential effective radicality of the transmedia advocacy of WITNES and B'Tselem relies on contextualizing and catalyzing militant evidence produced by digital active witnesses through global advocacy networks. As Sam Gregory argues, "Video footage is mobilized as visual evidence . . . and the camera is an instrument at the start of global advocacy chains."[90] Margaret Keck and Kathryn Sikkink argue that these advocacy chains are enmeshed within "transnational advocacy networks," which, powered by digital media and cameras everywhere, enable "nontraditional international actors to mobilize information strategically to help create new issues and categories and to persuade, pressure, and gain leverage over much more powerful organizations and governments" emphasizing that outcome.[91] Digital active witnesses gain greater agentive force when their captured militant evidence is harnessed by partner organizations that have access to transnational advocacy networks that provide resources, access, legibility, and space for positive action and movement building. Further, digital active witnesses often depend on partnerships with transnational organizations in order to realize the potential force of the militant evidence they produce.

Case Study: WITNESS and the Campaign to End Child-Soldier Recruitment

The Democratic Republic of Congo (DRC) first achieved independence as a nation in 1960 after decades of Belgian colonial rule. The years of colonization brought mass human rights abuses, particularly during the reign of King Leopold, and in 1890, the first documentation and transnational circulation of human rights abuses occurred. As Sharon Sliwinski discusses, after traveling to the Congo in 1890 and witnessing widespread and violent injustices, George Washington Williams wrote an "Open Letter to King Leopold II of Belgium," which was published in the *New York Herald* in July 1890. The letter, a "public accusation armed with measured and detailed testimonial accounts" laid out twelve specific charges, including arson, rape, and massacring whole villages, though it did little to stop the violence.[92] However, by 1903, enough humanitarian pressure had built that the British House of Commons passed a resolution calling for the humane treatment of "natives" and sent Roger Casement to the Congo to produce an investigative report. His report, released later that year, included a number of graphic photographs of maimed and mutilated Congolese people and "set off an explosion in the public realm" while serving as the antecedent for the use photography as "forensic evidence for alleged acts of atrocity."[93] It also led to the birth of the Congo Reform Association (CRA) in 1904, which sought to disseminate information about the atrocities in the Congo to build a popular reform movement—both photographs and accumulated evidence were part of this strategy. As Sliwinski argues, through traveling lantern-slide lectures and other public gatherings, photographs and discourses of distant human suffering provided "the spectator with a heady illusion of her ability to intervene in distant suffering." They did so with the use of the aforementioned atrocity photographs, which combined with verbal appeals to "provoke spectators affect" and then transform this heightened state "into meaningful action."[94] While these tropes have become common though ethically fraught aspects of many humanitarian appeals, WITNESS works to ensure that targeted spectators are in a position for meaningful action while avoiding spectacular imagery or nonspecific, dehumanizing appeals to distant suffering.

Between 1994 and 2003, the DRC (formerly Zaire) was involved in a number of military battles. In the first Congo War, in 1996, forces from Rwanda and Uganda, who sought to overthrow Joseph Mobutu and take control, invaded the country. The second Congo War began in 1998 and lasted until 2003, resulting in five million deaths. Two rebel movements from within the DRC along with the remaining Rwandan and Ugandan troops waged war against the DRC army. During this time, Thomas Lubanga Dyilo served as a militia leader and president of the Union of Congolese Patriots (UPC), which represented the Hema ethnic group from the northeastern Ituri region of the DRC. Lubanga and groups like his were some of the worst offenders of employing child soldiers, some as young as eight, in various armed conflicts. Especially in the eastern section of the DRC, tens of thousands of child soldiers were recruited and deployed in various warring factions.[95] WITNESS teamed with the local human rights organization Association des Jeunes Pour le Développement Intégré—Kalundu/Projet Enfants Soldats (AJEDI-Ka/PES) to produce the video *A Duty to Protect* (2005), which was aimed at the International Criminal Court (ICC) and US policy makers. When WITNESS met with the Office of the Prosecutor (OTP) for the ICC, they screened both *A Duty to Protect* and *On the Frontlines* (2004). The prosecutor requested all of the unedited footage and initiated an in-depth investigation. In April 2005, the video was screened in New York to audiences of UN representatives and other advocacy groups. This screening garnered national media attention and led to further screenings at The Hague and in private meetings between AJEDI-Ka/PES and the ICC. In addition, a video was made specifically for local villagers. Throughout 2006, AJEDI-Ka/PES traveled throughout the DCR with *On the Frontlines* (2004). The video served as a powerful and efficacious tool of information and urgent education in a largely illiterate culture and significantly decreased child recruitment efforts.

A Duty to Protect tells the stories of Mafille and January, two girls who were recruited into the military at thirteen and ten years of age respectively. Mafille is a demobilized child soldier whose experience of violence and sexual exploitation cause her deep psychological scars. Halfway through the video, she recounts being raped: "Before . . . I didn't know men. My first experience was being taken by force. I am still in shock; I cry whenever I think about it." The sequence ends with a tight close-up of Mafille's eyes as she wipes away tears. The sexual exploitation of girls was just one of the many atrocities being committed by the warlords, yet it is the main thrust of the appeal being made to the international community in this video. This is not to say the video does not touch on other problems, such as rampant drug use among children in the army camps and the horrendous living conditions children faced there. Yet, the appeal made focuses almost solely on a call to the international community to step in and end the rampant sexual violence against young girls.

The film relies heavily on the presence of a narrator who guides the audience through the abuses exposed in a measured, sober, and informed way. Nothing is sensationalized, and the images paired with the testimony are far fairly mundane. Yet, the pain of trauma exudes from the faces of the girls and their families. The video lays out a concise yet powerful case for international intervention. The structure and logic behind the choice of this specific approach have to do with positioning both the atrocities and the testimony within the dominant tropes of human rights discourse in relation to the DRC, which focuses on sexual violence against women and individual stories.[96] As the activist group Peace Women contends, "The scope of sexual violence in the DRC is a well-known reality that has been documented and reported by media, NGOs, international institutions and States.[97] Amnesty International characterized the fighting in the DRC as a "war against women," where women and girls were raped *en masse* by forces on all sides, particularly the Congolese armed forces—wrecking families and communities.[98] In addition to having suffered during the year and a half she spent in the military, Mafille also recounts the stigma she faced upon returning

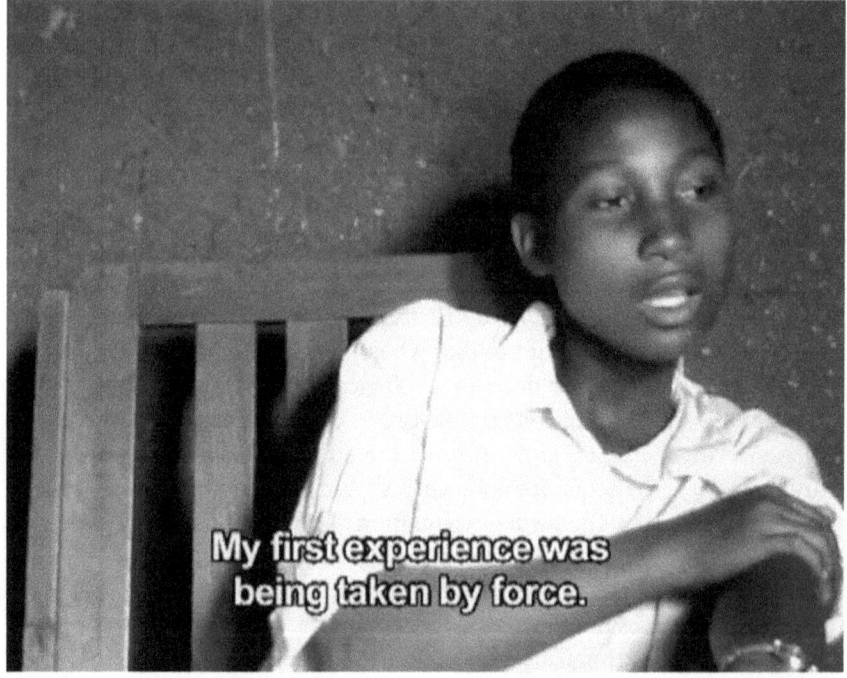

Figure 1.1 Mafille recounting her rape at the hands of soldiers in *A Duty to Protect*.

to civilian life and the constraints in seeking medical attention without financial resources. In this way, the use of the two girls as the centerpiece of the appeal aligns the conflict and its horrid abuses squarely into what has become common knowledge in the human right community, allowing intensely personal stories of rape and abuse to be contextualized within a broader, international framework.

A Duty to Protect was launched in New York and Washington, DC, in April 2005 to audiences of civil society organizations, UN representatives, and congressional staffers, among others. The campaign and the problem of child-solider recruitment garnered brief media attention in the United States on "NOW with David Brancaccio" (PBS), "American Morning" (CNN), "The Leonard Lopate Show" (WNYC), and internationally on the German television series "Kulturzeit" and "Voice of America" radio and television programs broadcast in countries throughout Africa. In November 2005 and 2006, the video was screened at a public event in The Hague during the Assembly of State Parties to the Rome Statute and in private meetings between AJEDI-Ka/

PES and key personnel at the ICC, such as the Office of the Prosecutor, the investigations team for the DRC, and the Office of the Registrar.

While *A Duty to Protect* was made for policy makers and the ICC, *On the Frontlines* was made specifically for villagers in the DRC. The video advocates for the cessation of voluntary recruitment of child soldiers in eastern DRC and was the first film produced by AJEDI-Ka/PES in collaboration with WITNESS. The video features powerful footage shot between 2003 and 2004 of the military training of children in several militia camps in South Kivu and compelling testimony from demobilized child soldiers recounting the horrifying memories of life as soldiers. The film has been screened to more than thirty thousand villagers across eastern DRC to raise awareness and debate about the issue of child soldiers and to discourage enlistment in local armies. Since the screenings began, AJEDI-Ka/PES has noticed a significant decrease of voluntary recruitment of child soldiers in many parts of eastern DRC. Because of its local audience, the film is structured to be more affective and personal than *A Duty to Protect*. It relies heavily on direct testimony from a group of boys who had been forced or voluntarily recruited into service. The testimony is graphic and focuses on the "behind the scenes" life of what it is really like to be a child soldier. In the particularly disturbing opening sequence, a young demobilized child soldier named Byaombe recounts his arrival at a training camp: "When I arrived at the camp, I went to see the commander. I explained my worries to him. He told me they would show me how to kill the enemy. When we capture an enemy, we must make him suffer. We must take out his eyes and remove his heart and cut his ears and feet."

The testimony of other young, male, demobilized soldiers is intercut with experts from Amnesty International and the Transcultural Psychosocial Organization making appeals to the villagers about both the illegality of child-soldier recruitment and the deep, scarring effect life as a soldier has on children. Added to this are grainy videos captured by the AJEDI-Ka/PES that show young boys high on various drugs and living in squalor as they fight on the frontlines. The video ends with the emotional appeals of former soldiers, urging their friends and neighbors not to join any of the warring factions. The jarring opening testimony and appeals from experts all work to counter the discourse of honor, sacrifice, and monetary rewards promised to parents and children by the warlords. *On the Frontlines* does not rely on a narrator to guide the audience's reaction. Instead, it makes a direct appeal from one local villager to another, engaging in a common vernacular and drawing on similar experiences. Both videos, however, forge links to either a transnational or a local discourse working to affect change on multiple levels without the use of graphic images. As John Tomlinson argues, "Access to

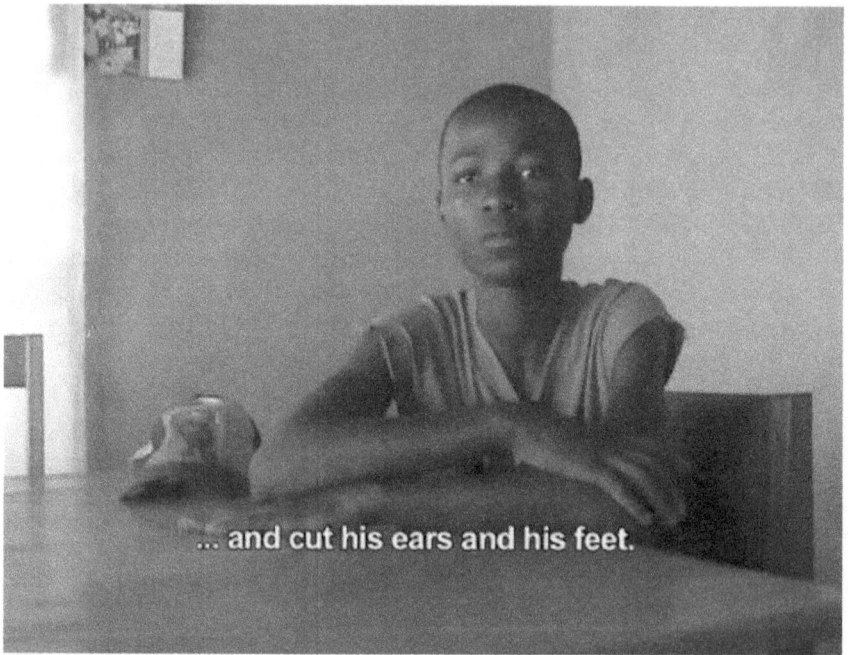

Figure 1.2 Byamobe recounts torturing a fellow child soldier in *On the Frontlines*.

discourse is *always* linked to material—meaning in a capitalist global order, economic—power."[99] The notion of localization in transnational partnership with larger structures with access to capital, power, and influence allows for localized interventions that are committed to achieving a quantifiable impact on a specific problem while strengthening communities and partnerships on human rather than purely state-centered structures, concerns, and policies. In this case, *A Duty to Protect*, as part of a larger advocacy campaign and the work of many on-the-ground groups, was able to spur an international war crimes trial, while *On the Front Lines* spread urgent information and sparked a cessation in families sending their children to fight.

Since WITNESS' initial screening for the ICC, the OTP spent nearly three years collecting evidence, including a mass of video evidence. On March 23, 2006, the ICC arrested Lubanga for his alleged involvement in the commission of war crimes, namely enlisting and conscripting child soldiers. The arrest warrant followed the major advocacy drive by AJEDI-Ka/ PES and WITNESS with *A Duty to Protect* at the core of the campaign. On January 29, 2007, the Pre-Trial Chamber I of the ICC confirmed the charges against Lubanga as presented by the prosecutor on the basis of individual criminal responsibility with three war crimes: (1) enlisting children under the age of fifteen, (2) conscripting children under the age of fifteen and (3) using children under the age of fifteen to participate actively in hostilities. At Lubanga's Confirmation of Charges hearing, twelve clips of video evidence were played for the judge to prove that Lubanga enlisted and conscripted child soldiers. He ordered Lubanga to stand trial, which began January 26, 2009, in The Hague.[100] Video evidence was used as the centerpiece of the prosecution's case to implicate his complicity in war crimes and, importantly, to show some of Lubanga's soldiers were under fifteen years old. In the absence of live witnesses, official birth certificates, or a medical exam, such information is difficult to determine, but the video evidence proved sufficient to the task. Much of the video was shot by AJEDI-Ka/PES during field missions from 2003–04, and it plainly shows many instances of children at a very young age engaged in combat and training. More importantly it shows Lubanga on site supervising and leading activities. In addition to the video, the testimony of live witnesses added substantially to the case. A number of children came forward to testify at the trial to the abuse they suffered at the hands of Lubanga and his deputies. On March 14, 2012, the ICC convicted Lubanga on all three counts of war crimes with which he was charged. He was sentenced to a total of fourteen years in prison, but since he has been detained since 2006, he will be released in 2020. While the two films made by WITNESS in partnership with AJEDI-Ka/PES were not the videos that operated in court, they were successful at spurring the investigation that led to the conviction. Militant evidence was used in various ways at different stages of the process and demonstrates the flexibility and attention demanded by each aspect of transmedia advocacy strategy.

Case Study: B'Tselem and the Shooting in Ni'lin

On July 7, 2008, Palestinian activist Ashraf Abu Rahma was protesting against the construction of a separation fence, along with members of the International Solidarity Movement, in his West Bank village of Ni'lin located near Ramallah. Rahma, a frequent participant at protests in the West Bank, was arrested by IDF soldiers, blindfolded, and placed in a military jeep. "They held me in the sun for a long time," asserts Rahma. "I recall hearing a conversation about how to shoot me. What I recall is the words rubber bullet, rubber bullet."[101] While Rahma was detained and contemplating his fate, a seventeen-year-old Palestinian girl named Salam Kannan was readying her B'Tselem supplied camera. The short video begins with a blurry long shot of Rahma standing in front of a small group of protestors holding a Palestinian flag in his right hand while holding up the fingers of his left hand in a "peace"

Figure 1.3 Palestinian activist Ashraf Abu Rahma protests in a B'Tselem video.

sign. The video then cuts to a medium shot of Rahma sitting on the ground in front of a separation barrier flanked by an IDF soldier and military jeep. His arms are handcuffed behind his back; he is blindfolded. Next Rahma is shown in a medium shot standing with his back to the camera in front of a military jeep. Two IDF soldiers on the right, one of which holds his arm to flank him. To the left, another soldier aims a gun directly at him. He is still blindfolded and handcuffed. The soldier holding the gun fires at close range; a loud boom is heard on the video, and the camera quickly pans left and to the floor. The next image depicts Rahma lying on the ground as he is tended to by group of soldiers, who hover above him. The rest of the framing in the video is jumpy, as Kannan's camera focuses on the aftermath of the shooting and then abruptly ends. Fortunately, Rahma was not seriously injured, sustaining only a minor wound on his foot. Yet, the brazen brutality and carelessness with which the IDF treated a detainee worked as both evidentiary proof of wrongdoing in the military court system as well as affective proof of Israeli state violence and the suppression of dissent for the larger viewing public.

Digital Active Witnesses and the Limits of Visible Evidence | 71

Figure 1.4 Palestinian activist Ashraf Abu Rahma after being shot in a B'Tselem video.

After receiving a copy of the video from Kannan, B'Tselem turned over the evidence to the Israeli Military Police Investigative Unit and demanded a full investigation of both the soldier who fired the shot, Staff Sergeant Leonardo Corea, and the soldier who held Rahma during the shooting, Lt. Col. Omri Borberg. The military, however, did not initially open an investigation. They opted for a less formal and less public internal "operational debriefing" and took no action against the soldiers. It was not until B'Tselem publicly released the video on July 20 that the military investigators decided to pursue the matter more aggressively. After the Judge Advocate General (JAG) office reviewed the case and the investigators findings, the two officers were formally charged with the relatively minor charge of "conduct unbecoming."

Unsatisfied with this outcome, Rahma, along with B'Tselem, the Association for Civil Rights in Israel, and the Public Committee Against Torture in Israel appealed the JAG decision to Israel's High Court of Justice, claiming that the charges were insufficient to the offenses clearly shown to have been committed on the video. The petition was successful, and the High Court sent the case back to the JAG office so that they could reconsider the charges. On November 4, 2008, JAG Officer Brig. Gen. Avichai Mandelblit came to the decision not to change the indictment, and the case was placed back before the High Court. Some months later, on July 1, 2009, the High Court ruled that "the military prosecution's decision to charge the battalion commander and the soldier with unbecoming conduct will be cancelled, as it is extremely unreasonable" and ordered the JAG to change the charges to "adequately reflect the facts and the nature of the acts in the indictment."[102] The indictment was thus changed and Borberg was charged with threats and conduct unbecoming an officer and Correa was charged with unlawful use of a weapon and conduct unbecoming, charges that carry a maximum three years of prison time and a criminal record. On July 15, 2010, a special military court convicted the men on all charges. Interestingly, Borberg's lawyers argued during the sentencing phase of the trial that the key piece of evidence, the video made by Kannan and distributed by B'Tselem, had somehow been tampered with and altered to give an untrue impression of the events. With B'Tselem's intervention, the Kannan family turned over the original tape to the forensics department of the Israeli police. After examination, they found the tape to be genuine and devoid of any tampering or editing. Shortly after this matter was cleared up, on January 27, 2011, the court sentenced Borberg to a suspended jail sentence and barred him from serving as a commander for one year. Corea was demoted in rank from staff sergeant to private.

After the convictions and sentencing—three years after the video first reached public consciousness—the militant evidence took on a second life as part of Emad Burnat and Guy Davidi's documentary *Five Broken Cameras* (2011). The film, shot and narrated by Burnat, a Palestinian living in the occupied West Bank village of Bi'lin, premiered at the International Documentary Festival Amsterdam on November 23, 2011. It subsequently appeared in a number of other international festivals, including Sundance and the Jerusalem Film Festival and was nominated for an Academy Award for best documentary in 2012. Though not the central component of the film, the footage of Rahma being shot is endowed with layers of context for a viewer, whether in Israel or internationally, that lacks a proper frame of reference for the violence portrayed. The film is narrated in the first person by Burnat and begins in 2005 with his purchase of a simple consumer camcorder in order to capture and preserve images of his recently born fourth son, Gibreel. Around the same time, IDF forces move into the village, bulldozing Palestinian land and erecting razor wire fences as construction began on massive high-rise apartments for settlers on the seized land. In addition to filming Gibreel, Burnat also begins to film the ensuing nonviolent protests by villagers against the new wall and apartment construction. As viewers witnessed

Gibreel growing, the intensity and size of the protests also increased. While B'Tselem's Camera Project seeks to bring the ubiquity and structural violence of occupation to light by documenting the countless daily violations that take place, *Five Broken Cameras* helps to reinforce this typicality while embedding it within a familial narrative that is easily relatable to a wider swath of viewers.

Emerging Technologies, Human Rights, and Digital Active Witnesses

In the many years since the start of the cases analyzed above, there have been three major developments that have further enhanced the power of the digital active witness: a marked increase in the number of people with cell phone and digital cameras worldwide; the expanded use of technologies in the service of ending human rights abuses in specific contexts; and an accelerated turn toward accumulating, measuring, and visualizing human rights data for advocacy and adjudication. A variety of emerging digital tools have aided the production and dissemination of such data to maximize efforts of accountability, archiving, and effectiveness. For example, open source applications have been designed or re-engineered for human rights documentations, such as Amnesty International's Citizens Evidence Lab, which allows activists and amateurs to crowdsource, verify, and analyze evidence,[103] Ushahidi, an open-source tool originally developed to map violence in the wake of the 2008 elections in Kenya,[104] and eyeWitness to Atrocities, a closed source mobile application for digital active witnesses to capture and store verifiable footage, including metadata, in a secure cloud-based archive.[105] In Syria, Visual Forensics and Metadata Extraction (VFRAME), a group and collection of open-source computer vision tools has partnered with Syrian Archive, an organization of digital active witnesses dedicated to documenting war crimes and human rights violations in the current Syrian civil war, to aid them in their work.[106] Specifically, VFRAME is developing tools to aid Syrian Archive with detecting evidence of illegal weapons, filtering graphic content, searching for specific visual media in large caches of videos, and producing a web-based annotation platform.[107] The sheer amount of militant evidence produced by digital active witnesses every year across the globe requires new tools capable of analyzing massive visual datasets. There is also a great deal of power in the accumulation itself. As Todd Landman and Edzia Carvalho argue, the accumulation and measurement of human rights documentation "can serve as the basis for the continued development of human rights policy, advocacy, education, and political dialogue" and are important advocacy tools in a world where governments and legal venues expect legible, verifiable visual data.[108] The accumulation of documentation adds to the force of each piece of militant evidence and leads to wider jurisgenerative and sociogenerative effects.

But, this level of accumulation and dissemination brings persistent challenges. Notably, the mass of digital active witnesses and widely circulated media has raised new and urgent issues regarding ethics and representation and participation in the public sphere, particularly when dealing in images emerging from spaces of conflict and protest that have arisen in recent years and fueled by social media. Sam Gregory and Elizabeth Losh, writing in the wake of multiple forms of media produced by digital active witnesses during the Arab Spring in 2008, argue that this digital-media environment of widespread footage capturing, streaming, and uploading, should undergird our consideration of ethics and the image. They assert that "an image uploaded, blue toothed or shared is an image that can circulate and move and be reshaped, and all ethical assumptions should be based on this."[109] Here, one must be mindful of issues of consent, privacy, respect for human dignity grounded in empathy, the preservation of individual agency, and how to generate a "responsibility to act" when media is shared widely across popular platforms like YouTube and/or remixed and recontextualized by other individuals and groups. Gregory and Losh also raise a host of issues, including dignity, agency, and grounding in the communities and contexts of origination that will be analyzed in chapter 4 in discussions of the Syrian film and activist collective Abounaddara and the production and training organization Bidayyat. In their documentary practices, Abounaddara articulates a broader and more radical notion of an ethics of the use of images, especially from spaces of war and conflict, as well as a fundamental "right to the image"—the innate right of all to control and produce their own representations, while Bidayyat funds, educates, and promotes a new generation of Syrian filmmakers.

The idea of the right to the image is based on Article 19 of the UDHR and is particularly relevant for the digital age of cameras everywhere. Article 19 states that "everyone has the right to freedom of opinion and expression: this right includes freedom to hold opinions without interference and to seek, receive, and impart information and ideas through any media regardless of frontiers."[110] While not every country recognizes this right, the United Nations recently upheld the "right to record," specifically in regard to citizens filming law enforcement and military members with cell phones and other personal devices.[111] Palestine and its citizens are thus in a unique situation as visual media is increasingly precarious to capture and subject to surveillance. Whether or not this right is officially recognized by a given state, there is a deluge of images of atrocities of all sorts, making claims for human rights and the concept of humanity, a terrain that, according to Randall Williams, "has increasingly come to define 'the political' in this age of advanced capitalist globalization."[112]

Yet, appeals to the concept of humanity and human rights have come under productive scrutiny. Didier Fassin argues that humanitarian interventions, from recording evidence of abuse to full-scale military operations, engage in a "politics of life," which categorizes and places value judgements of lives to be saved and lives to be risked, leading to "the inequality of lives."[113] Part of this inequality stems from the idea that humanitarian interventions to gain support depend on the production of "public representations of the human beings to be defended . . . by showing them as victims rather than combatants and by displaying their condition in terms of suffering rather than the geopolitical situation."[114] Historically, one way to theoretically foster ethical representation came from the idea of the participatory documentary, where the camera is given to the "other" so they can document their humanity.

Pooja Rangan refers this form as a "humanitarian media intervention" to critique the participatory documentary, which requires individuals, already in perilous circumstances to perform and represent their abject humanity in highly proscribed and ideologically fraught ways, using immediations or tropes that reinforce their status as other.[115] She advocates for a reconsideration of the radical potentiality of human rights discourses, articulating more open and inclusive models of representation and reception of humanitarian media. These arguments point to a vital way forward for rethinking documentary representation and reception, and I expand their purview to consider the important work being done to bring forth effective radicality in acute situations that depend on the militant evidence captured. In addition, in the rapidly shifting globalized digital age, the concept of humanity is a site of protean political struggle. Millions around the globe are asserting their right to the image within an interstitial space between the state and the digital, the legal and extralegal, the archive and the forgotten, the witness and the testifier, and the border and the open space.

Witnessing, and testimony in particular, retain vast political potency in in the epoch of cameras everywhere. As Wendy Kozol suggests, "Eyewitnesses and survivors today retain powerful cultural authority as embodied witnesses."[116] That said, there are many ethical considerations, particularly in regard to the use of footage and testimony from survivors and witnesses. This mass of evidence can be conveyed widely and in a variety of contexts, which raise a host of concerning questions about the right to one's image and its dissemination. WITNESS, B'Tselem, and groups like them work in this space and necessarily deal in the currency of images and stories, victims and perpetrators, and witnesses and testimonies. But they do not simply spread images of widespread suffering captured without full consent. Rather, they work through active partnerships with on-the-ground digital active witnesses and groups to amplify their causes and properly deploy their militant evidence. As Tamar Ashuri and Amit Pinchevski argue, "Witnessing is a field in which various forces, resources, and agents compete. In other words, witnessing is to be regarded as subject to constant struggle, and hence as a genuine political arena."[117] Human rights–based media activism, witnessing, testimony, and strategically deployed militant evidence have come to define how genocides and other large-scale abuses have been adjudicated and understood. Testimonial narratives in these circumstances, as McLagan asserts, "hinge on the presentation of victim's bodies, which elicits sympathy from the audience . . . putting them into relationship with one another in such a way that obligations are put into play and communities of solidarity are formed."[118] This sentiment has been true since photographs were used to prove atrocities in early conceptions of human rights and remains a potentially ethically problematic position.

To function politically and foster radical changes, the practice of employing human rights–based militant evidence must work toward some common features in regard to ethics, context, and the ability to quantify the effects of various campaigns. First, it must intimately involve the participation of the people whose rights have been violated and/or have recorded militant evidence. These digital active witnesses must give consent, be fully aware of the possible perils of their participation, and be actively involved in the campaign. Second, the images, testimonies, and other information gleaned must be used in the context of targeted campaigns regarding a specific set of abuses. Third, the effects of the partnership must be quantifiable in the sense that, after the intervention, the lives of real people have been positively affected and structural changes have been or are being implemented. And fourth, in principle and practice, the projects must be firmly against the use of dehumanizing imagery. In the same way, they must not construct the people in these situations as helpless victims in need of rescue. Rather, they are digital active witnesses, partners in the capture and dissemination of militant evidence for activism and survival. Here, documentary practices move beyond the participatory documentary model as digital active witnesses reclaim the agentive force of representation by exercising their fundamental right to the image. When their images function as militant evidence that engender effective radicality, the power of the digital active witness is amplified by partnership with other groups actively working to transform the material conditions and experience of everyday life.

Whether in the courts, international bodies, or local communities, the practice of deploying militant evidence can work as an effectively radical practice with materially significant, quantifiable impacts and a host of jurisgenerative and sociogenerative effects beyond them. With transmedia advocacy, the radical power of documentary media lies not directly in its singular instance as an object of either art of evidence but in how effective it is at moving targeted spectators into a space for action within the specific ecologies in which it is circulated. In this way it can function effectively as militant evidence, a conduit to justice and accountability. Nichols takes historical radical documentary projects to task for a peripatetic accounting of injustices that disperse and disable the power of sustained productive action. He argues that "the Left's political strategy has paralleled the repetition and forgetting that characterize media news. We hurdle from one indignity to another, from one crisis to the next, less intent on discharging outrage in radically transformative action than on keeping conscience and witness barely alive."[119] Examining WITNESS and B'Tselem in light of these credible charges, it is productive to think through how their use of transmedia advocacy campaigns ameliorate some of these concerns. On the one hand, WITNESS intentionally limits the number of local groups it will partner with, while B'Tselem is solely focused on ending the Israeli occupation. Both groups target specific situations and areas where they can have the most transformative impact and work for years to create and sustain positive gains. Further, because of the targeted and collaborative nature of their efforts, witness and conscience are removed from life support and placed squarely at the center of their campaigns. In a world saturated by images and abuse, new ways of thinking, documenting, and adjudicating such horrors, via the collection of militant evidence, must be deployed. It is no longer sufficient to create documentary film and video projects that raise awareness of an issue; there is simply too much to be aware of. The many global crises faced demand multifaceted transmedia advocacy practices that collaboratively attack systemic issues with sustained, nonviolent militance on every possible level to bring forth effective radicality.

Groups such as WITNESS and B'Tselem, through partnerships with digital active witnesses, realize many of the aims of radical documentary pioneers by targeting specific audiences and quantifying the impact of their transmedia advocacy. In collaborative frameworks, among constellations of other groups and individuals, they also pursue the slow work of justice and accountability while building resilient communities. WITNESS and B'Tselem work within larger ecologies of activism and media where impact involves targeting militant evidence for specific spectators in the ideal venues for adjudication. In addition, they provide a framework for an emerging common politics of human connection, previously silenced voices, and vigilance outside of official media apparatuses, which will be explored in later chapters, in regard to the further analysis of media activism in Palestine, as well as in Iraq, Syria, and the prison system in the United States. The allied media activist practices explored work in many effective and affective registers simultaneously, collecting, shaping, and wielding militant evidence in effectively radical ways for varied platforms, audiences, and venues. In all of these instances, the concepts of visibility, digital community archival practices, and resistance are fraught and constantly shifting. Yet, these practices continue to emerge and grow in many iterations across the globe. They are a conduit for various effective and affective radicalities among everyday people in fights against occupation, incarceration, and all manner of injustices in pursuit of a radically different world. These emerging practices demand new frames of reference and modes of analysis. This chapter has examined the use of militant evidence in bringing forth effective radicality within various ecologies of impact as they have manifested throughout radical documentary history and within today's current practices of transmedia advocacy. The next chapter also looks to radical documentary history but turns to questions of form, affect, and aesthetics to explore how accumulated documentary media can be used by contemporary media artists as tools for activism, engendering an "affective radicality" for their viewers/users through interactive media projects that deploy militant evidence.

Notes

1. John Durham Peters, "Witnessing," *Media, Culture and Society* 23, no. 6 (November 2001): 707.
2. See Sameer Padania, Sam Gregory, Yvette Alberdingk-Thijm, and Bryan Nunez, "Cameras Everywhere: Current Challenges and Opportunities at the Intersection of Human Rights, Video and Technology," WITNESS, 2011, http://www.ohchr.org/Documents/Issues/Opinion/Communications/Witness_1.pdf.
3. Jay D. Aronson, "Preserving Human Rights Media for Justice, Accountability, and Historical Clarification," *Genocide Studies and Prevention* 11, no. 1 (2017): 82–99.
4. Sasha Costanza-Chock, *Out of the Shadows, into the Streets! Transmedia Organizing and the Immigrant Rights Movement* (Cambridge, MA: MIT Press, 2014), 5. Costanza-Chock is drawing on Henry Jenkins's concept of "transmedia storytelling" as well as Lina Srivastava's idea of transmedia activism.
5. Ibid., 14.

6. Seyla Benhabib, *Dignity in Adversity: Human Rights in Troubled Times* (Cambridge, UK: Polity Press, 2011), 14.

7. As defined by WITNESS: "'Video advocacy' is the process of integrating video into an advocacy effort to achieve heightened visibility or impact in your campaign. 'Advocacy' is the process of working for a particular position, result or solution." See Sam Gregory, Gillian Caldwell, Ronit Avni, and Thomas Harding, eds., *Video for Change: A Guide for Advocacy and Activism* (London: Pluto, 2005), 3–4.

8. Leshu Torchin, *Creating the Witness: Documenting Genocide on Film, Video and the Internet* (Minneapolis: University of Minnesota Press, 2012), 144.

9. Louis-Georges Schwartz, *Mechanical Witness: A History of Motion Picture Evidence in U.S. Courts* (Oxford: Oxford University Press, 2009), 105.

10. Sam Gregory, "Cameras Everywhere: Ubiquitous Video Documentation of Human Rights, New Forms of Video Advocacy, and Considerations of Safety, Security, Dignity and Consent," *Journal of Human Rights Practice* 2, no. 2 (2010): 193. Gregory adopts this term from Megan McLagan, "Making Human Rights Claims Public," *American Anthropologist* 108, no. 1 (2006): 1.

11. Peter Gabriel, "Video Will Bring Us Justice in the Long Run," *Time*, May 16, 2017, http://time.com/4781418/peter-gabriel-video-justice.

12. Liz Miller, "The Shore Line and the Practice of Slow Resilience," *Frames Cinema Journal*, 2018, http://framescinemajournal.com/article/the-shore-line-and-the-practice-of-slow-resilience.

13. "Charter of the International Military Tribunal," The Avalon Project, Yale Law School, http://avalon.law.yale.edu/imt/imtconst.asp.

14. Ibid.

15. Two similarly produced films, *The Nazi Plan*, screened December 11, 1945, and *Original Eight Millimeter Film of Atrocities against Jews*, screened December 13, 1945, followed.

16. Lawrence Douglas, "Film as Witness: Screening Nazi Concentration Camps Before the Nuremberg Tribunal," *Yale Law Journal* 105, no. 2 (November 1995): 451–452.

17. Torchin, *Creating the Witness*, 76.

18. After the title screen, the film opens with three successive images of statements. The first is an intertitle informing the viewer that the film presented was made by military photographers under orders from General Dwight D. Eisenhower. Two authenticating documents followed in the form of sworn affidavits presented in their original form on screen and read by a narrator. The first is from Lieutenant Colonel George Stevens, Hollywood filmmaker and director of the film, attesting that the images are a "true representation" and have not been altered in any respect. To further verify these claims, a second affidavit is presented in the same manner from Lieutenant E. R. Kellogg, also from Hollywood, who was employed by Twentieth Century Fox as a "director of photographic techniques." He certifies that he has inspected the images and they have not been "re-touched or distorted or otherwise altered" and adhere completely to the original copies of the films. These documents are further verified by images of Eisenhower himself, flanked by US congressmen, in part three of the film at the Ohrdruf concentration camp. The narrator informs us Eisenhower told them as they viewed corpses scattered around the campgrounds, "Nothing is covered up; we have nothing to conceal."

19. Douglas, "Film as Witness," 477.

20. For excellent writing on the Rodney King case in terms of the use of video, see Vivian Sobchack, *The Persistence of History: Cinema, Television, and the Modern Event* (London: Routledge, 1996); Ron Burnett, *Cultures of Vision: Images, Media, and the Imaginary* (Bloomington: Indiana University Press, 1995); Marita Sturken, *Tangled Memories: The Vietnam War, the AIDS Epidemic, and the Politics of Remembering* (Berkeley: University of California Press, 1997); and Regina G. Lawrence, *The Politics of Force: Media and the Construction of Police Brutality* (Berkeley: University of California Press, 2000).

21. John Minchillo, "Ohio Prosecutor's Comments in Fatal Traffic Stop Shooting of Sam DuBose Draws Critics," *Chicago Tribune*, August 7, 2015, http://www.chicagotribune.com/news/nationworld/ct-ohio-fatal-shooting-samuel-dubose-20150807-story.html.

22. Jackie Wang, *Carceral Capitalism* (South Pasadena, CA: Semiotext(e), 2018), 94.

23. See Electronic Frontier Foundation, "Street-Level Surveillance: A Guide to Law Enforcement Technology," 2018, https://www.eff.org/issues/street-level-surveillance.

24. For a further discussion of the King tape and recent viral images of Black death and their relation to the concept of militant evidence, see Ryan Watson, "In the Wakes of Rodney King: Militant Evidence and Media Activism in the Age of Viral Black Death," *The Velvet Light Trap* 84 (Fall 2019): 34–49.

25. See Jane Gaines, "Introduction: The Real Returns," in *Collecting Visible Evidence*, edited by Jane Gaines and Michael Renov (Minneapolis: University of Minnesota Press, 1999), 1–18.

26. William Alexander, *Film on the Left: American Documentary Film from 1931 to 1942* (Princeton, NJ: Princeton University Press, 1981), 296.

27. Hans Richter, *The Struggle for the Film: Towards a Socially Responsible Cinema* (New York: St. Martin's, 1986), 42.

28. Bhaskar Sarkar and Janet Walker, "Introduction," in *Documentary Testimonies: Global Archives of Suffering*, ed. Bhaskar Sarkar and Janet Walker (New York: Routledge, 2010), 1–3.

29. Dziga Vertov, "From Kino-Eye to Radio-Eye," in *Kino Eye: The Writings of Dziga Vertov* (Berkeley: University of California Press, 1985), 87–88.

30. Dziga Vertov, "The Same Thing from Different Angles (1926)," in *Kino Eye: The Writings of Dziga Vertov* (Berkeley: University of California Press, 1985), 57.

31. As Vertov argues, "In a film archive, a storehouse, or museum where footage from current newsreels is kept in numbered chronological order, all the necessary data can be appended to each box of negative, such as a detailed description of each film-fact, relevant newspaper clippings, biographical and other data. This is necessary so that a film editor in constructing a film-object on a given theme will not make errors and mix up the facts in time or space. In those films in which space is overcome by montage (for example, 'workers of one country see those of another') it's all the more essential that the editor take into account all data on the film footage to be organized. But this does not in any way mean that the editor has to set forth all this data in the picture in the form of an information supplement to each shot shot or group of shots. This data only represents cover documents, as it were, for the editor, a kind of guide to the correct 'editing route.'" Ibid.

32. Dziga Vertov, "The Factory of Facts (1926)," in *Kino Eye: The Writings of Dziga Vertov* (Berkeley: University of California Press, 1985), 58–59.

33. Ibid., 59–60. Emphasis mine.

34. Dziga Vertov, "Kino-Eye," in *Kino Eye: The Writings of Dziga Vertov* (Berkeley: University of California Press, 1985), 74–75.

35. Dziga Vertov, "On the Organization of a Creative Laboratory (1936)" in *Kino Eye: The Writings of Dziga Vertov* (Berkeley: University of California Press, 1985), 137–141.

36. Devin Fore, "Introduction: Soviet Factography," *October* no. 118 (Fall 2006): 5.

37. Ibid., 6.

38. Joshua Malitsky, *Post-Revolution Nonfiction Film: Building the Soviet and Cuban Nations* (Bloomington: Indiana University Press, 2013), 188.

39. William Alexander, *Film on the Left: American Documentary Film from 1931 to 1942* (Princeton, NJ: Princeton University Press, 1981), 33. Emphasis mine.

40. SS (a.k.a. Seymour Stern), "A Working-Class Cinema for America?," *The Left* 1, no. 1 (Spring 1931): 71. Quoted in Russell Campbell, *Cinema Strikes Back: Radical Filmmaking in the United States, 1930–1942* (Ann Arbor: University of Michigan Press, 1982), 108.

41. Ibid., 111.

42. Similarly, members of the Detroit League filmed what came to be known as the "Ford Hunger March" on March 7, 1932, capturing a massacre where police opened fire on demonstrators, killing four.

43. Samuel Brody, "The Hunger March Film," *Daily Worker* (December 29, 1932): 4. Quoted in Russell Campbell, "Radical Documentary in the United States: 1930–1942," in *Show Us Life: Toward a History and Aesthetics of the Committed Documentary*, ed. Thomas Waugh (Metuchen, NJ: Scarecrow, 1984), 75–76.

44. Ibid., 75.

45. Octavio Getino and Fernando Solanas, "Towards a Third Cinema," in *Movies and Methods*, ed. Bill Nichols (Berkeley: University of California Press, 1976), 44–64. After initial publication in *Tricontinental*, the essay was republished in English in the West throughout the 1970s in the journals *Afterimage* (1971) and *Cineaste* (1970/71) and in Bill Nichols's influential anthology *Movies and Methods* (1976).

46. See Jonathan Buchsbaum, "A Closer Look at Third Cinema," *Historical Journal of Film, Radio and Television* 21, no. 2. (2001): 154. See also Teshome Gabriel, *Third Cinema in the Third World* (Ann Arbor: University of Michigan Press, 1982). See also Jonathan Buchsbaum, "One, Two . . . Third Cinemas" *Third Text* 25, no. 1 (2011): 13–28.

47. Section one: "Notes and Testimonies on Neocolonialism, Violence and Liberation;" Section two: "Act for Liberation;" Section three: "Violence and Liberation." Among these three sections, the 208-minute film is divided into fourteen chapters: 1. Introduction, 2. The History, 3. The Country, 4. Daily Violence, 5. The Port City, 6. The Oligarchy, 7. The System, 8. Political Violence, 9. Neoracism, 10. Dependence, 11. Cultural Violence, 12. Models, 13. Ideological Warfare, and 14. The Choice.

48. Robert Stam, "The Two Avant-Gardes: Solanas and Getino's *The Hour of the Furnaces*," in *Documenting the Documentary: Close Readings of Documentary Film and Video*, ed. Barry Keith Grant and Jeannette Sloniowski (Detroit, MI: Wayne State University Press, 2014), 271. *Grupo Cine Liberación* ("The Liberation Film Group") was founded by Solanas, Getino, and Gerardo Vallejo as an effort to produce collective, politically revolutionary films concerned with the struggle for Third World liberation

49. At the end of the film, they say, "Now it is up to you to draw conclusions to continue the film. You have the floor."

50. Getino and Solanas, "Towards a Third Cinema," 46.

51. Ibid.

52. Ibid.

53. Ibid., 47.

54. Ibid., 49, 50. Emphasis in the original text.

55. Octavio Getino, "The Cinema of Political Fact (1973)," trans. Jonathan Buchsbaum and Mariano Mestman *Third Text* 25, no. 1 (2011): 41.

56. Ibid., 43.

57. L. A. Kauffman, *Direct Action: Protest and the Reinvention of American Radicalism* (London: Verso, 2017), 110.

58. Douglas Crimp, "AIDS: Cultural Analysis / Cultural Activism," *October* 43 (Winter 1987): 3.

59. See Deborah B. Gould, *Moving Politics: Emotion and ACT UPs Fight Against AIDS* (Chicago: University of Chicago Press, 2006) for an excellent account of ACT UPs varied militant practices.

60. Ann Cvetkovich, "Video, AIDS, and Activism," in *Art, Activism, and Oppositionality: Essays from Afterimage*, ed. Grant Kestor (Durham, NC: Duke University Press, 1998), 185.

61. B'Tselem in Hebrew literally means "in the image of" and is also used as a synonym for human dignity. The word is taken from Genesis 1:27: "And God created humans in his image.

In the image of God did He create him." It is in this spirit that the first article of the Universal Declaration of Human Rights states that "all human beings are born equal in dignity and rights." "About B'Tselem," *B'Tselem.org*, http://www.btselem.org/about_btselem.

62. "About B'Tselem," *B'Tselem.org*.
63. Ibid.
64. Youval Azulay, "B'Tselem Cameras Pay Off for Victims of Settler Attacks," *Haaretz*, June 17, 2008, http://www.haaretz.com/print-edition/news/b-tselem-cameras-pay-off-for-victims-of-settler-attacks-1.247973.
65. Peter Beaumont, "Palestinians Capture Violence of Israeli Occupation on Video," *Guardian*, July 30, 2008, http://www.guardian.co.uk/world/2008/jul/30/israelandthepalestinians.
66. Harriet Agerholm, "Israel Considering Law to Ban Photographing or Filming IDF Soldiers," *Independent* (UK), May 27, 2018, https://www.independent.co.uk/news/world/middle-east/israeli-knesset-ban-photographing-filming-idf-soldiers-recording-journalists-robert-ilatov-a8371426.html.
67. "Video: Israel Targets Journalists in Gaza," *Electronic Intifada*, May 24, 2018, https://electronicintifada.net/content/video-israel-targets-journalists-gaza/24431.
68. "Israeli Supreme Court Rejects Challenge to Open Fire Rules," *Associated Press*, May 24, 2018, https://apnews.com/da582f11ad4443ddbf44ea6f2fc72c3a?__twitter_impression=true.
69. Jasbir K. Puar, *The Right to Maim: Debility, Capacity, Disability* (Durham, NC: Duke University Press, 2017), 128–129.
70. "News," Ynetnews, http://www.ynetnews.com/home/0,7340,L-8111,00.html.
71. "Living in East Jerusalem–A Video Interactive," *Guardian*, June 8, 2011, http://www.guardian.co.uk/world/interactive/2011/jun/08/east-jerusalem-israel-palestine-interactive.
72. See http://theinvisiblewalls.btselem.org.
73. Nadia Yaqub, *Palestinian Cinema in the Days of Revolution* (Austin: University of Texas Press, 2018), 17.
74. Ibid., 3.
75. "Our Impact," WITNESS, https://witness.org/about/.
76. Gregory, "Cameras Everywhere," 192.
77. Gregory et al., eds., *Video for Change*, 38.
78. Ibid., 39–40.
79. Ibid., 38.
80. Ibid., 39.
81. See Bill Nichols, *Speaking Truth with Film: Evidence, Ethics, Politics in Documentary* (Berkeley: University of California Press, 2016).
82. Gregory, "Cameras Everywhere,"193.
83. Ibid.
84. Meg McLagan, "Making Human Rights Claims Public," *American Anthropologist* 108, no. 1 (2006):191–195.
85. See https://elgrito.witness.org/.
86. Gregory et al., eds., *Video for Change*, 50.
87. Ibid., 57.
88. Ibid., 58.
89. Ibid., 214–218.
90. Ibid., 195.
91. Margaret E. Keck and Kathryn Sikkink, *Activists Beyond Borders: Advocacy Networks in International Politics* (Ithaca, NY: Cornell University Press, 1998), 2.
92. Sharon Sliwinski, *Human Rights in Camera* (Chicago: University of Chicago Press, 2011), 62.
93. Ibid., 67.

94. Ibid., 81.
95. The two main factions are the Mai-Mai and the Hutu.
96. See Michael Ignatieff, *Human Rights as Politics and Idolatry* (Princeton, NJ: Princeton University Press, 2003). Here, Ignatieff discusses the importance of common human rights language and bottom-up rights campaigns that focus on individuals as representative of the effects of systematic abuses.
97. See http://www.peacewomen.org/node/91733.
98. See https://www.amnestyusa.org/press-releases/congo-order-to-attack-village-in-january-resulted-in-the-rapes-of-more-than-35-women/.
99. John Tomlinson, *Cultural Imperialism* (London: Pinter, 1991), 16.
100. For an excellent account of both the background on the case and the current developments, see the Coalition for the International Criminal Court website devoted to this case: http://www.iccnow.org/?mod=drctimelinelubanga; see also the WITNESS site devoted to the trial: http://hub.witness.org/Lubanga-Trial.
101. Peter Beaumont, "Palestinians Capture Violence of Israeli Occupation on Video," *Guardian*, July 30, 2008, https://www.theguardian.com/world/2008/jul/30/israelandthepalestinians.
102. "The Army Must Internalize the Gravity of the Ni'lin Shooting Incident," *B'Tselem.org*, January 27, 2011, http://www.btselem.org/firearms/20110127_nilin_shooting_sentence.
103. See https://citizenevidence.org/.
104. See https://www.ushahidi.com/.
105. See https://www.eyewitnessproject.org/.
106. See http://syrianarchive.org and http://vframe.io.
107. See https://vframe.io/.
108. Todd Landman and Edzia Carvalho, *Measuring Human Rights* (New York: Routledge, 2010), 5.
109. Sam Gregory and Elizabeth Losh, "Remixing Human Rights: Rethinking Civic Expression, Representation, and Personal Security in Online Video," *First Monday* 17, no. 8 (August 2012), http://firstmonday.org/ojs/index.php/fm/article/view/4104/3279.
110. https://www.un.org/en/universal-declaration-human-rights/.
111. Dia Kayyali, "The Right to Record Recognized at the United Nations," *WITNESS*, August 2, 2018, https://blog.witness.org/2018/08/the-right-to-record-recognized-at-the-united-nations/.
112. Randall Williams, *The Divided World: Human Rights and Its Violence* (Minneapolis: University of Minnesota Press, 2010), xv.
113. Didier Fassin, "Humanitarianism as a Politics of Life," *Public Culture* 19, no. 3 (2007): 499, 520.
114. Ibid., 501.
115. Pooja Rangan, *Immediations: The Humanitarian Impulse in Documentary* (Durham, NC: Duke University Press, 2017), 11.
116. Wendy Kozol, *Distant Wars Visible: The Ambivalence of Witnessing* (Minneapolis: University of Minnesota Press, 2014), 6.
117. Tamar Ashuri and Amit Pinchevski, "Witnessing as a Field," in *Media Witnessing: Testimony in the Age of Mass Communication*, ed. Paul Frosh and Amit Pinchevski (New York: Palgrave Macmillan, 2009), 135.
118. McLagan, "Making Human Rights Claims Public," 193.
119. Bill Nichols, *Blurred Boundaries: Questions of Meaning in Contemporary Culture* (Bloomington: Indiana University Press, 1994), 20.

2. Prisons, Palestine, and Interactive Documentary

THIS CHAPTER TURNS to an analysis of the uses of militant evidence by contemporary media artists and considers two interactive documentary projects: Sharon Daniel's *Public Secrets* (2006) and Zohar Kfir's *Points of View* (2014), which represent the lives of women in prison in California and Palestinians living under Israeli occupation, respectively. This chapter also explores how and why militant evidence is used in an affective mode by Daniel and Kfir, who draw on the legacies of radical documentary practices in their utilization of the interactive documentary form. This form, in concert with a radical political stance and in direct collaboration with digital active witnesses and/or larger activist organizations, is a locus for the representation of viewer/user critical engagement with broad systemic problems while rendering visible hidden structures of violence and power. Moreover, this engagement and the militant evidence used in each project generates an "affective radicality," that moves viewers/users into larger ecologies of activism and political discourse.[1]

To explore the development of the antecedent affective dimensions of spectator engagement in radical documentary, this chapter turns to a brief analysis of the work and writings of Jean Vigo and Joris Ivens in the 1930s; the documentary practices of the left wing film collective Newsreel in the United States in the 1960s; Third Cinema and the role of the spectator for radical work in the 1970s in the construction of the revolutionary subject; and the activist and artistic practices of the "new documentary" movement in the 1980s with an analysis of Martha Rosler's video *A Simple Case for*

Torture (1983). An exploration of these antecedents reveals affective forms of radicality mobilized for a variety of audiences and deployed as a catalyst for education, intervention, solidarity, and revolution. The intersection of documentary, new media, and emerging technologies is part of this longer history that has shaped the aesthetic, technological, and political parameters of global radical documentary practices. The interactive nature of recent documentary projects is a contemporary manifestation of the subgenre's larger investments in active and engaged spectatorship. This chapter explores how the interactive documentary form facilitates a productive and multifaceted affective encounter with a range of subjects and evidence for viewers/users.

In documentary studies, particularly with radical political documentaries, affective power is tied to the concepts of indexicality and evidence. Jane Gaines argues, "Indexical privilege contributes something to one of the forks of the radical cause—the *evidence* of material conditions."[2] The power of documentary often relies on the capture of a certain kind of fact—what Gaines calls a "pathos of fact."[3] This sort of fact relies on the generation and reception of affect for its impact, but in Gaines's formulation it is limited to the linear unfolding of information, images, and narratives that define traditional documentary exhibition. Yet, as Adrian Miles argues in regard to the interactive documentary form, the reception of accumulated and curated examples of the aforementioned pathos of fact can lead to a type of "affective knowing," which "allows for the agency of knowledge that is documentary's currency."[4] He aligns the interactive documentary within the tripartite structure of perception (the viewer/user notices the images and sounds presented), affect (the viewer/user moves toward deciding), and action (the viewer/user clicks to explore more). The affective and effective quality of the viewer/user experience is thus rooted in the "depth of material that is to be found" in a given project.[5] Affect, for Miles, is premised on a virtual encounter between subjects and information and the viewer/user who moves beyond the passivity, collectivity, and narrative linearity of traditional cinematic viewing. It is provoked by the activity on the part of the viewer/user within a singular experience in front of a "deep" screen interface consisting of a nonlinear superfluity of data, stories, and possible experiences.

Technological developments, vast digital storage capability, and a plethora of cameras have led to a mass of transnational digital active witnesses and countless hours of testimonies, stories, footage of atrocities, and other forms of media. To succeed in advocating for a particular cause and activating their viewers/users, media artists seeking to intervene in or represent global and/or systemic crises can present this multimedia documentary evidence tactically and strategically while employing the logic of amassing such evidence as a radical intervention. In interactive documentaries that critically engage with radical political movements, the impact of the evidence presented, both affective and effective, is amplified due to its accumulation and can potentially work more forcefully on the viewer/user in the service of engagement with the political claims presented. Affective radicality is created through accumulated and curated forms of militant evidence that reveal affective forms of knowledge, empathy, and witnessing to move viewers/users into broader activist movements and practices of resistance.

The first project examined, Daniel's *Public Secrets* explores the prison industrial complex and the struggles of female inmates at the Central California Women's Facility (CCWF) in Chowchilla, California, the largest female correctional facility in the United States. *Public Secrets* eschews the photographic (cameras are explicitly prohibited in the prison) and relies instead on an effective mixture of sound, text, and minimal graphic design. The second project analyzed, *Points of View*, was created by New York–based, Israeli video artist Zohar Kfir and maps a selection of the Palestinian video-advocacy footage created for and/or disseminated by B'Tselem.[6] Whereas *Public Secrets* eschews imagery, *Points of View* foregrounds conventionally shot, short documentary videos—the type of images produced by digital active witnesses in Palestine examined in the previous chapter. While these projects are very different in their approach and aesthetics, they both engage with two seemingly intractable and urgent situations that are difficult to capture in their scope and complexity in traditional forms of documentary; they are made by female media artists—a group underrepresented in documentary studies; and the occupation of Palestine and the prison industrial complex in the United States share an overlapping set of systemic challenges, despite their geographic distance.

Prisons and Palestine

Black abolitionist critics, such as Angela Y. Davis, have explored the intersectional struggles and attendant basis for global solidarity between the struggle of the Palestinian people and those incarcerated within the prison industrial complex in the United States. Davis contends that "it is important to insist on the intersectionality of movements. In the abolition movement, we have been trying to find ways to talk about Palestine so that people who are attracted to a campaign to dismantle prisons in the US will also think about the need to end the occupation in Palestine."[7] Davis's investigation of G4S, a global "security" firm that is the world's third largest private corporation, makes the linkage particularly clear. Davis contends that "G4S is especially important because it participates directly and blatantly in the maintenance and reproduction of repressive apparatuses in Palestine—prisons, checkpoints, the apartheid wall, to name a few."[8] Beyond Palestine, G4S, argues Davis, "characterizes the profit-driven motives of transnational corporations associated with the rise of mass incarceration in the US and the world."[9] The carceral structures of occupation and the prison industrial complex are ones of enclosure, partition, and exclusion composed of criminalized people whose subjugation is purposeful, punitive, and often profit generating.

The idea of the prison industrial complex refers to the vast array of structural connections between prisons, the legal system, and the needs of capital and business, all of which detain and marginalize staggering numbers of people of color, undocumented migrants, the poor, and other vulnerable populations. Despite the vast number of people locked in cages each year within this system and the wide ownership of cell phones and digital cameras, the public rarely hears from prisoners themselves while they are in prison due to the many rules, which vary by jurisdiction and/or state, that prisoners are subjected to regarding communication. In addition, prisoners suffer solitary confinement, all manner of abuses, forced work for meager pay, and other forms of modern-day slavery and often have few means of seeking justice. Using smuggled cellphones, inmates have produced images of these barbaric conditions and direct testimonies of their experiences, sparking widespread prison strikes and outside activist work. In Alabama in September 2016, for example, Bennu Hannibal Ra-Sun (a.k.a. Marvin Ray) began the Free Alabama Movement and helped catalyze the largest prison strike in US history by using a contraband cell phone to disseminate footage from his solitary confinement cell. The strike, which spanned twenty-four states and over twenty-four thousand prisoners, demanded higher wages for prison labor, more sanitary conditions, better food, and access to legal aid.

Media artists are also employing emerging technologies, such as virtual reality and interactive digital forms, in order to provide viewers/users with an immersive experience that attempts to mimic the feeling of being in prison. For example, David Deufresne and Philippe Brault's interactive work *Prison Valley*, which began as a traditional television documentary, was released by Arte TV in 2010.[10] The cross-platform interactive documentary focuses on Freemont County, Colorado, a section of the state containing thirteen prisons with more than seven thousand inmates—a main source of jobs for locals. *Prison Valley* is anchored in the town of Cañon City, where the viewer/user begins their journey, which functions as a quasiroad movie touring the carceral matrix of the county. The project highlights the overlaps between the many prisons and the small community of people living in the area, who cycle through three main roles: inmate, guard, and resident. After completing a registration process, the viewer/user is taken to a virtual hotel room where they have a menu of items to explore from a large multimedia archive: film clips, animations, photos, and interviews. The project also features "interactive zones" built into the interface where one can engage with other viewers/users who are also logged in at the same time. This array of media allows the viewer/user a self-paced, nonlinear, and immersive experience both inside and outside the cells in Cañon City and provides subjective points of view from various positions while rendering a more fully formed and representative view of the totality of effects wrought by the local carceral economy.

Other interactive documentaries and virtual reality works, such as *The Deeper They Bury Me: A Call from Herman Wallace* (2015) directed by Angad Singh Bhalla and distributed by the National Film Board of Canada and *6 x 9: A Virtual Experience of Solitary Confinement* (2016) directed by Francesa Panetta and Lindsay Poulton for the *Guardian*, attempt to immerse the viewer/user in the experience of solitary confinement.[11] *The Deeper They Bury Me*, which is based on Bhalla's 2013 documentary, *Herman's House*, uses audio recordings of interviews with political prisoner Herman Wallace, a former Black Panther and member of the "Angola 3," paired with renderings and replicas of his cell, his prison block, and his "dream" bedroom. Wallace was placed in solitary confinement in 1972 after being framed for the murder of a prison guard during a riot at the Angola prison in Louisiana. He spent every day of his life in solitary from 1972 until his release in 2013. When exploring the project, the viewer/user is limited to just twenty minutes of interaction to convey a brief temporal semblance of what it is like to have communication with the outside world severely restricted. Furthering the immersive experience, the virtual reality project *6x9* plunges viewers/users into a 360-degree model of a solitary confinement cell, providing a brief but affective sense of enclosure and a glimpse of the immediate psychological stress and acute claustrophobia an inmate endures when placed in such barbaric conditions. As they spend time in their cells, the viewers/users can listen to the stories of six men and one woman who share their experiences of spending twenty-three hours a day locked away, alone. With an estimated one hundred thousand people in the United States currently enduring solitary confinement, it is a widespread practice of legal torture that is rarely discussed in mainstream discourses.

Much like the case of prisoners in the United States, the Palestinian cause receives scant attention in mainstream Western news media. This is partly due, as Gil Hochberg argues, to the Israeli control of Palestinian bodies, which is based on an unequal access to visual rights. Israel maintains a stultifying security state of massive surveillance and the "militarized gaze" of checkpoints while they also have vast digital control over what can be seen and heard from within Palestine to the outside world.[12] The effect of this constant gaze and digital occupation renders Palestinians both hypervisible and invisible at the same time. On the one hand, Palestinians are made hypervisible for two purposes: to play the role of the terrorist for media accounts or by being forced to represent the violence around them in order to gain recognition by Western media and humanitarian organizations—to make "the conditions of living under military occupation *visible* to others."[13] On the other hand, Israel successfully masks their own violence and the humanity of the Palestinians in two ways: first, by diffusing the security state into all aspects of Israeli life with constant checkpoints, bag screenings, and young, conscripted Israeli soldiers in uniform (with weapons) walking among the crowds—all of which contributes to a sense of normalized and routine violence and constant threat. And second, due to their economic power and alliance with the United States, Israel dominates the public relations war, always able to frame the occupation as necessary for self-defense in media accounts despite their massive military advantage. Further, and to an even greater degree than seen in the policing of poor and minority neighborhoods in the United States, Israel deploys cutting edge surveillance, including the widespread use of drones, the control of networked servers used by Palestinians, and other means of digital occupation so pervasive that it engenders "*a new mode of visualization*: one that eliminates the possibility of witnessing, while rendering those who are subjected to live *under the drones* completely invisible despite their hypervisibility."[14] Here, invisibility does not describe a lack of being seen; rather it defines a state of living in a body rendered disposable, anonymous, and without value.

While witnessing is in serious peril, it nevertheless persists against the odds on a variety of fronts. New technologies and modes of communication and visualization, in addition to global collaborations and partnerships, have allowed innovative modes of witnessing and resistance to emerge even as Israel has tightened its strangulation of Palestinians in Gaza and the West Bank. Many of the projects, particularly interactive documentaries aimed at international audiences, involve accounts of everyday life under occupation. For example, B'Tselem's recent interactive documentary *The Invisible Walls of Occupation* brings viewers/users on a virtual tour of the Palestinian village of Buqah, outside of Ramallah.[15] Interactive maps of the village highlight the oppressive infrastructures that residents must overcome each day: road closures, checkpoints, and expanding Israeli settlements on stolen land. When the viewers/users enter the digital village, they have the option of pursuing various narratives from the point of view of the residents, including a farmer, teachers, doctors, and village elders, who relay their subjective experiences of how the occupation deeply affects even the most mundane tasks of daily life. Al Jazeera's *Palestine Remix* takes a wider view of the occupation, providing viewers/users with a selection of twenty-three short documentaries from Palestinian, Israeli, and international media makers.[16] The films include Ashraf Al-Mashharawy's *Hunger Strike* (2014), which explores the use of hunger strikes as a form of protest by Palestinians languishing in Israeli jails and Rawan Damen's *Al Nakba* (2008), a lengthy four-part look at Palestinian history since 1799, particularly the expulsion of Palestinians in the wake of the 1948 establishment of the State of Israel. Viewers/users can watch each film individually or "remix" the films to create a one of a kind montage of scenes from each.

While most media activist groups base their works in documentary footage, other groups, such as Forensic Architecture, focus on visualizing the built environment and both creating and contextualizing militant evidence through image and data compositing, mapping Palestine with technologies to envisage the architectonics of occupation and the domination by Israel of the built environment. Forensic Architecture also conducts counter-forensic investigations of images, official narratives, and state produced visual content. As group founder Eyal Weizman argues, their work and efficacy are fueled by the vast "proliferation of new sources of evidence, leaks, data, and user-generated images" that have circulated in the digital age.[17] Forensic Architecture leverages their work in a variety of art spaces and legal settings as a way to provoke the opening of closed legal cases. They conceive of their practice as firmly in the realm of the effective radicality of militant evidence that seeks to spur concrete actions in the cause of justice. The group foregrounds the "the evidentiary dimension of art and its truth value."[18] This practice manifests in novel deployments of a variety of data, visual and otherwise, that Forensic Architecture uses to create three-dimensional (3D) models, interactive digital projects, installations, and evidentiary exhibits for legal proceedings. Architectural-based compositing allows Forensic Architecture to "build and enter into a space and that allows us to move from one image to the next, from one-time frame to the next, to compose something from it and compare it to the disruption or interruption we find within the image or the flow of images or data," generating new dimensions for activism

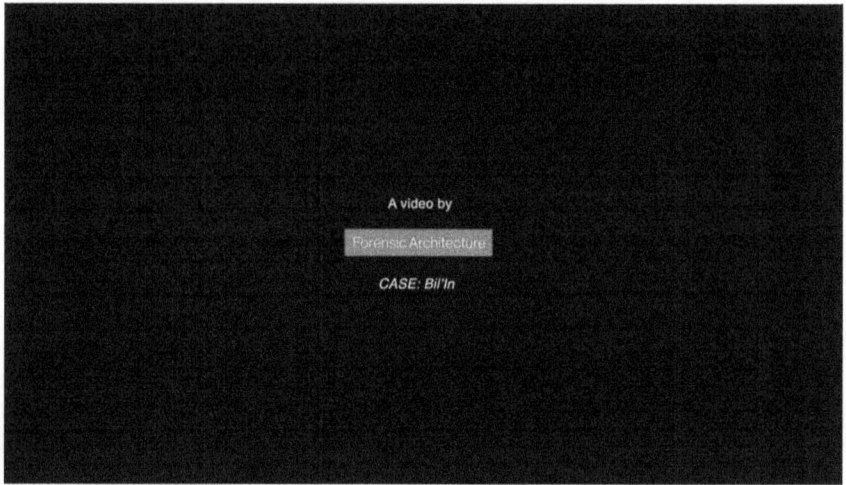

Figure 2.1 Still from *Bil'in: The Killing of Bassem Abu Rahma*.

and evidence.[19] For example, the groups' recent project *The Gaza Platform*, a collaboration with Amnesty International, allows viewers/users to interact with a plethora of data, mapped onto Gaza, that contextualizes, documents, and narrates the hundreds of Israeli attacks in the area between July 8 and August 26 in 2014. In another recent project, the video *Bil'in: The Killing of Bassem Abu Rahama*, documents Weizman and the Forensic Architecture team reconstructing the death of Bassem Abu Rahma, referenced in chapter 1, using 3D modeling to demonstrate that the IDF shot was meant to kill. While the case made it to the Israeli High Court in September 2018, based on the reconstruction, to date no one has been held criminally responsible for the death.

Visualizing Palestine, another activist group, has taken a less photo-realist approach; instead the group renders a visual account of the occupation through infographics and interactive maps.[20] Working at the intersection of design, digital storytelling, and data science, the group produces slick, modern-looking infographics reminiscent of advertisements to quickly communicate digestible and understandable instances of systematic Israeli oppression. For instance, in November 2018 in partnership with the groups Human Rights Watch and Kerem Navot, Visualizing Palestine disseminated the infographic "Airbnb Benefits from Israeli Rights Abuses," which shows the overlap between Palestinian communities and over 139 Airbnb rentals in Israeli settlements. Their infographics mainly circulate on social media, working to counter Zionist myths while historicizing and visualizing the

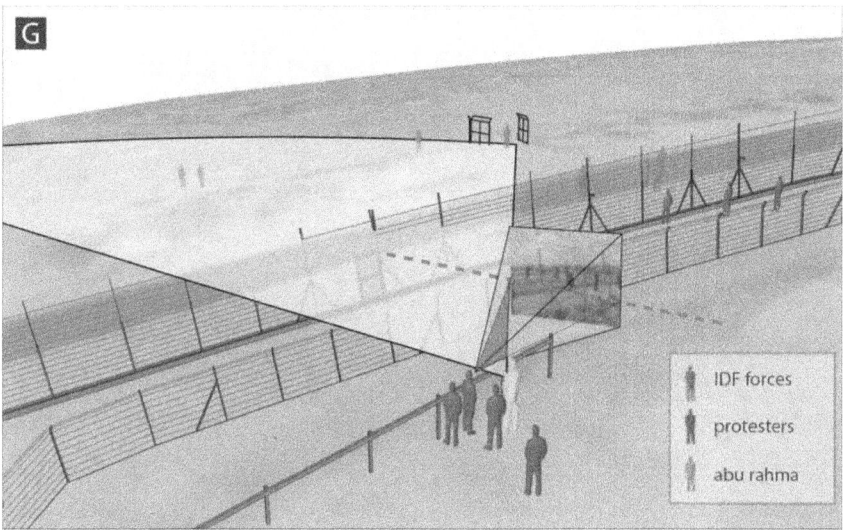

Figure 2.2 Still from *Bil'in: The Killing of Bassem Abu Rahma* showing the lines of sight of various witnesses at the killing.

plight of the Palestinians through a common and popular way of receiving a condensed rendering of information. Like Forensic Architecture, Visualizing Palestine works to bring about effective radicality, deploying militant evidence in novel and strategic ways for specific purposes and outcomes within larger advocacy projects while often partnering with other organizations.

Public Secrets and *Points of View* work in a different mode that generates affective radicality. Here, the force and political potentiality of the militant evidence emerges from the accumulation and affective deployment of individual witnesses and subjective testimonies, along with a host of other media, contexts, and discourses and in direct collaborations with digital active witnesses and lager activist organizations. In both projects, the subjects, who are often hidden from public view, move from invisibility to visibility and from a lack of voice to an expansive platform for communication. This platform, coupled with an accumulation of other stories, media, and contexts, allows the affective intensities of the subjects and the militant evidence to be unleashed amid a move from hiddenness to openness. Though no longer hidden as they had been before, the criminalized Palestinians living under occupation and incarcerated female prisoners in California examined here are still ensnared within carceral structures. Thus, the relay of affect, in this specific context, resonates with Melissa Gregg and Gregory Seigworth's contention that "affect arises in the midst of *in-between-ness* . . .

94 | Radical Documentary and Global Crises

Figure 2.3 "Airbnb Benefits from Israeli Rights Abuses," *Visualizing Palestine* infographic.

an impingement or extrusion of a momentary or sometimes more sustained state of relation."[21] The sense of in-between-ness certainly applies here, as both occupation and incarceration imply living in a state between life and death, freedom and bondage, humanity and barbarity; these bodies are neither here nor there, existing for a moment and receding. "Affect," they posit, "is in many ways synonymous with *force* or *forces of encounter* . . . and "*accumulates* . . . becoming a palimpsest of force encounters."[22]

The idea of force is directly related to Massumi's definition of *affect* as "intensity." Affect, in its emergence and intensity, has two sides, the virtual and the actual: "Affect is this two-sidedness as seen from the side of the actual thing, as couched in its perceptions and cognitions. . . . the autonomy of affect is its participation in the virtual. Its autonomy is its openness. Affect is autonomous to the degree to which it escapes confinement in the particular body whose vitality or potential for interaction, it is."[23] The intensity, or force of the encounter, and the affect relayed are amplified via the accumulation inherent within the interactive documentary form. This form is not structured like an archive or narrative but something in-between—cinematic and arranged, though open and interactive. The accumulation of stories, evidence, and testimonies in interactive projects become a palimpsest of force encounters, rendering visible hidden, yet systemic, structures of violence and power through the accumulation of affective encounters with subjects under occupation and incarceration. While these situations are extreme, part of the affective radicality of the projects is generated in their relatability and ordinariness, rooted in the individual, subjective stories. As Kathleen Stewart argues, there can be a potent politics of ordinary affects "where the "potential that a something [is] coming together . . . can be seen as . . . the trajectories that forces might take if they were to go unchecked" and thus where ordinary moments and subjectivities can be reclaimed as powerful potential forces.[24] In the project examined in this chapter, these ordinary affects are engaged in a form of micropolitics while, as Massumi contends, "chipping away at the macro problems."[25] "Micropolitics" he argues, "makes the unimaginable practicable."[26] This is seen in *Public Secrets* and *Points of View* through the accumulation of ordinary affects, testimonies, and stories—microcosms and microhistories of the systemic effects of incarceration and occupation. The potential affective radicality of the interactive documentary is premised on the logic of amassing. The move from the virtual to the actual and back again referenced by Massumi and based on the perception of the viewer/user is where the potential for political change exists. To feel the affective accumulation and engage the claims of the subjects presented buttressed by a great depth of information, arms the viewer/user with a plethora of affective and effective evidence and knowledge that is acquired in the virtual world to (hopefully) be redeployed in the actual world. The interactive documentary form engenders an expansive, deep, and transformative witnessing: an affective knowing that demands action.

Kfir's project intervenes on two registers. First, it disseminates the work of B'Tselem to a wider audience, thereby promoting their advocacy work while giving Palestinian voices and stories a global platform. Second, it accumulates and structures years of affectively potent video evidence, testimony, and stories to present and map a view of the Israeli-Palestinian conflict as one of long-standing, systematic oppression on the part of Israel, rather than discrete conflicts and skirmishes one might see in Western news accounts.

In a similar spirit, Daniel's work gives a voice to incarcerated women who have a paucity of means for communicating with the outside world. She relies on a large corpus of audio-based testimonies from inmates buttressed by philosophical, legal, and theoretical texts. The archive of testimonial accounts, much like in Kfir's project, makes a convincing case for systemic abuse while the addition of the texts aligns the women's experiences within a broader framework of human rights and political discourse. These projects participate in the traditions and aspirations of the radical documentary. However, they do so while engaging and deploying new forms of narrative arrangement and viewer/user engagement. Both *Public Secrets* and *Points of View* present a mass of militant evidence endowed with the depth of affect that seeks to move the viewer/user from the position of active engagement with the project (in a virtual space) to critical engagement with the situation itself (in an actual space)—in other words, to convert virtual engagement into real world activism.

The idea of producing activist or revolutionary spectators through the generation of affect emerges as a main concern among filmmakers in the transnational radical documentary tradition. This chapter next explores a few moments from this historical genealogy to demonstrate how and why these filmmakers considered affect a key force in producing spectators who would further an ideology and spread revolutionary knowledge; empathize and feel solidarity with those seen on screen; participate in an emerging revolution; or rectify a systemic injustice. Global documentary practices, rooted in their use of documentary evidence, develop as key instruments in affectively producing revolutionary or activist subjects throughout the twentieth century.

Rooting Militant Evidence: Affect and Audience

Jean Vigo stands as another important catalyst in developing radical documentary practices across the globe, particularly in an affective register, through his theorization and practice of "social cinema." On June 14, 1930, before a screening of his documentary *À propos de Nice* (1930), Vigo gave an introductory lecture entitled "Toward a Social Cinema" at the Théâtre du Vieux Colombier ciné-club in Paris. The lecture was a brief yet powerful manifesto that exhorted the audience to rethink the nature of cinema in terms of spectator engagement and in conjunction with its deployment as a powerful means of social commentary. It was a declaration of rebellion against a modernist emphasis on form and aesthetics in the face of pervasive social inequity. As Siegfried Kracauer argues, "Vigo was a rebel on two counts: against the screen formulas and, even more intensely, against the established order of things. He used the camera as a weapon, not an anesthetic."[27] Vigo argued that cinema based solely in aesthetic absorption forged an unproductive "listlessness" in the viewer.[28] To stymie this listlessness, Vigo advocated a form of cinema that would "stimulate echoes" and cultivate a new form of vision, "something more than one's everyday eye."[29] A social documentary, in short, "should open our eyes." This all entails a "kick in the pants," argued Vigo, something that must come about through the affective force of the subject matter presented.

The aim of social cinema was to deal with "proactive subjects, subjects that cut into the flesh."[30] Even more precisely, social cinema should portray a clearly articulated, "documented point of view."[31] As Steven Ungar notes regarding this point of view, "Vigo used it as a means to describe the capacity of social cinema to express a vibrancy not found in films grounded in realist concerns."[32] Similarly, Dudley Andrew asserts that "Vigo valued the situation he staged before the camera, cared about its integrity, and let it play itself out in the guise of 'a document' rather than something confected for consumption."[33] Vigo's documentary style was one to be read and felt in order to awaken the viewer to a world beyond spectacle while focusing on the material conditions and inequity of France in the 1930s. Ungar contends that Vigo's manifesto "was not answered until twenty to thirty years later, in post–World War II films by Alain Resnais, Chris Marker, Jean Rouch, Agnès Varda, Georges Franju, and lesser-known filmmakers such as Eli Lotar and René Vautier."[34] Yet while the force of Vigo's call is not fully answered in France during the interwar period, it is Ivens, whose film *Misère au Borinage* (1934), discussed briefly below, who most ardently continues, expands on, and spreads the ideology of social cinema after Vigo's death in 1934.

Vigo's all-too-brief career existed at a point of confluence in both film and the dynamism of shifting economic and social conditions.[35] In the world of cinema, sound synchronization had recently become possible, and Grierson had just coined the term *documentary* in 1926, catalyzing a distinct, socially engaged genre. Within the European avant-garde, filmmakers such as René Clair, Hans Richter, Jean Cocteau, and Marcel Duchamp explored surrealist sensibilities in the cinema. In Russia, Vertov and Shub, along with filmmakers Sergei Eisenstein, Vsevolod Pudovkin and others, experimented with the powerful effects of montage. Further, as James Chapman notes, "Vigo . . . provides a stylistic link between the avant-gardes of the 1920's and the 'Poetic Realists' including Jean Renoir and Marcel Carné, who showcased marginalized characters and a heightened aesthetic sensibility."[36] While grounded, the poetic realism of Renoir and Carné lacked the direct, militant social commentary favored by Vigo, particularly that which could be achieved through documentary. Yet, the documentary genre as it is understood today was inchoate in the 1930s. In this period, a steady relay existed between socially conscious artists in the modernist avant-garde, who worked in painting and experimental film, and documentary—a melding of innovative form with real world content. In his discussion of the influence of the modernist avant-garde on documentary film forms, Nichols invokes Peter Wollen's notion of "the two avant-gardes," arguing that "individuals such as Buñuel, Vigo, Vertov, Richter, Louis Delluc, and Joris Ivens moved readily between a stress on the effects of form itself . . . and a stress on social impact, in keeping with the documentary impulse."[37] Given his frequent ciné-club going and his association with Vertov's brother, Boris Kaufman, who served as cameraman on *À propos de Nice*, Vigo was not only familiar with these movements, he took up the concerns and structures from these emerging practices in the pursuit of his own unique form of socially engaged, cinematic language. While Vigo sought to jar spectators from a complacent listlessness, he still had to get their attention. His images and representations are both familiar and provoke thought and sensation beyond the expected.[38]

À propos de Nice was Vigo's first film under the social-cinema mantle. The film has been more generally categorized as both a city-symphony and a travelogue. While its approach and aesthetics have an obvious relationship with these forms and subgenres, it counteracts the usual symmetry of people and places seen in the city-symphonies. Rather, it presents a discordant asymmetry that undercuts the traditional erotics of desiring a set in foreign locales portrayed in the travelogue with a scathing indictment of bourgeois excess. The main tenets of the film's critique reside in three themes: the ways in which the urban environment is organized, the ways in which space is occupied based on class, and the ways in which time is used. As Ungar observes, "*À propos de Nice* could thus be seen as an exercise in the rhetorical possibilities of silent film grounded in attention to physical scale, point-of-view, framing and editing."[39] After Vigo's death in 1934, Ivens's film *Misère au Borinage* takes up the social-cinema mantle.

Misere au Borinage was made by Ivens and Henri Storck under the auspices of *Club de l'Ecran*, the film club of Brussels. Just prior to production on the film, Ivens had returned from the Soviet Union, where his views on art as a political weapon had been refined. Ivens wrote that he "had learned to work with the socialist realist method . . . having put behind . . . the flawed abstract theories regarding the function and formalist tendencies of art."[40] In addition to this transformative visit, the confluence of economic, social, and cinematic changes in Europe outlined earlier also had a profound effect on

Ivens, who, like Vigo, made a transition from an artist thoroughly enmeshed within the modernist avant-garde, to one who came to value and promote a vision of social cinema. As Bill Nichols argues, "Ivens exemplifies the avant-garde filmmaker turned leftist documentarian who offered relentless opposition to the bourgeois-democratic state."[41] In his 1931 essay, "Notes on the Avant-Garde Documentary Film," Ivens posited that "the documentary film allows the avant-garde filmmaker to work in a positive way. Being a representative of the masses, a mouthpiece of the people that are represented through him."[42] Ivens's early documentaries, which fit the aesthetic forms of cubism, futurism, and constructivism, appear to be lyrical meditations on the interplay between humanity and machine, often visually "converting machinery into art."[43] But, these works lacked a committed authorial presence. As Ivens argued: "It was not long before we felt that as artists we had to take part in the social life, in the economic life of our country; that we were dead in the water if we remained on the abstract side of aestheticism."[44] This was corrected with *Misère au Borinage* (1934), which engendered a further radicalization of both politics and filmmaking ethos for Ivens and his codirector, Storck.

Borinage portrays the chaotic and sorrowful aftermath of a revolutionary coal-miners' strike that occurred in the Borinage area of Belgium in 1932, which was known for militancy and class struggle among its workers. In making the film, Nichols notes, "Ivens came to realize that capturing 'life unawares' was not enough: one also had to guard against the artistic norms that might color a filmmaker's perspective and diminish his political voice."[45] Aesthetic innovation and experimentation had been completely drained from Ivens and Storck's intent; they wanted to portray the life of the workers in all its grimness. "Our aim," Ivens asserted, "was to prevent agreeable photographic effects distracting the audience from the unpleasant truths we were showing."[46] There would be no anesthesia, no room for a listless spectator. The film, a compilation of (mostly) re-enactment, was coupled with newsreel footage and filmed newspaper headlines. Despite some objections in documentary scholarship to the efficacy and representational effect of re-enactment, Nichols argues that this film (and the people depicted) actually benefited from such a strategy. "Ivens had no desire," he writes, "to be reflexive and draw attention to the problems of representation ... the workers regained their sense of militancy" because "the intensity of emotion during reenactment blurs the distinction between history and recreation."[47]

This intensity marks the entire film, notably in the opening, which begins with a fierce exhortation via intertitle: "Crisis in the capitalist world. Factories are closed down, abandoned. Millions of proletarians are hungry!"

The wasteful nature of the capitalist system soon confronts the spectator. In newsreel footage from Wisconsin, milk is poured from trucks, while later shots portray coffee dumped into the sea and corn being burned. Ivens goes back to the United States briefly to show an Ambridge, PA, miners' revolt. As the miners stand in solidarity, hordes of policemen appear, wielding clubs and guns. They beat and shoot at the crowd indiscriminately. By depicting American capitalism run amok, Ivens and Storck made a convincing statement for systemic failure, rather than small, isolated pockets of injustice. In the preceding shot, we see an intertitle that reads, "In the Borinage, we have had enough!" Vigo's wish for a "kick in the pants" had finally come to fruition. "The documentary film," argued Ivens, "has to stimulate lingering activities to evoke reactions."[48] This intense inequity remains a constant theme throughout the film, especially in terms of food, housing, and fuel. Without adequate pay, workers found it impossible to keep up with rent, buy fuel, or provide food for their families. Ivens and Storck depict the horrid conditions this perverse set of circumstances brings forth. Families are crowded into ramshackle tenements, old pigsties, and shack-like barracks, all while a church is being built nearby for over three million francs. Four million tons of coal sits by, rotting and fenced off, while workers scavenge the slag piles hoping to find some usable fuel.

Thinking back to Vigo's manifesto "Toward a Social Cinema," there is no doubt that this affective parade of misery has represented subjects "that cut into the flesh" of the spectator. As Ivens argued, *Borinage* is not a detached discourse; rather, its distinct, documented point of view emerges from a sense of anger—a necessary effect for a socially engaged cinematic practice: "the filmmaker must be indignant and angry about the waste of people before he can find the right camera angle on the dirt and on the truth. I wanted the spectators of the finished film to want to do more than send these worker's money. The films required a fighting point of view. It became a weapon."[49] The camera lens no longer recorded events passively and objectively; rather, it took aim, fashioning itself and the films it created as weapons. At the end of the film, this militancy is in full force: an intertitle makes a stark call for "the dictatorship of the proletariat and the realization of socialism." A shot of a small newspaper cutout of Lenin, hanging in the house of a worker, buttresses these words. As spectators, we have slowly become accomplices, as Vigo contended, in a revolutionary solution. This relay between visible evidence and affect comes to define the ways that radical documentary is conceived of as having a force to move others into empathy, anger, or action. Further, it was a way to highlight, with stark clarity, the lives of others beaten and broken by the capitalist cause. In these ways,

Ivens and Vigo viewed the camera and the affective forces generated by radical documentary as weapons that could be aimed at improving the material conditions of life for people across the globe, a trend that persists in different iterations in the digital age.

The impetus to improve the lives of people, both home and abroad, while combatting larger political and global forces gathers and grows in the wake of World War II and in the midst of the development of lighter, more mobile cameras and synch-sound recording. Ivens, truly a radical Pied Piper, as Thomas Waugh has meticulously chronicled, had continued to make films throughout the war period and became a role model, collaborator, and teacher for the emerging militant filmmakers in France, Cuba, and other locations throughout the world.[50] Ivens's writings after the war concerned militant documentary and the promises of technology. Writing in the 1960s, Ivens argued that "a militant documentary film has to reach further." To do so, the film must inform and move the audience, and "it should agitate—mobilize them to become active in connection with the problems shown in the film."[51] Further, he argued that radical documentarians "should not be modest in our demands for technical progress," because documentary filmmakers "daily face reality with their cameras" and should "have the best tools known to men."[52] With the emergence of synch-sound recording, Ivens noted his excitement in giving the audience "the chance to hear the people *in* the film speak for themselves" and providing them with another level of closeness to the subject presented.[53] In addition, the advent of television, for Ivens, was seen as positive development as it "sharpened the powers of its viewers to absorb a quantity of images, and this increased visual capacity," yet it has also, in his view, occluded the need for documentary to engage in "news interpretation and information" in favor of the "complicated, deeper aspects of the events we depict."[54]

As William Alexander argues regarding Ivens's conception of militant cinema, "Viable social change can only rise from the particular conditions and perceptions, past and present, of an exploited people themselves . . . the role of artist and educator is to help people define their situations in their own images and language to facilitate their discovery of workable methods for improving their conditions."[55] Here, the filmmaker is conceived of as a facilitator or guide, collaborating with people in oppressive and precarious situations in order to rectify various societal ills. This facilitation and guidance manifests as providing training, material support in the forms of cameras and film, access to networks of circulation and distribution, and audiences of potential allies and collaborators. Yet, while this sort of collaboration was often welcomed and necessary, the wider access to filmmaking equipment and radical documentaries from around the globe seen in the 1960s and 1970s gave rise to the concept of Third Cinema and a variety of localized filmmaking practices in service of Third World liberation and inchoate revolutionary movements. Further, in the digital age, many media artists working in radical documentary modes provide context and curation rather than content, instead partnering with amateurs, activists, and others on the ground in the midst of global crises.

In Argentina, Getino and Solanas were less concerned with improving or reforming conditions and more concerned with sparking a revolution among the nonelite classes. In this instance, the filmmaker is also conceived as a facilitator or guide but to local citizens and about the unseen truth of the national reality. In this way the filmmaker works to uncover the causes of oppression and domination and activate viewers rather than simply documenting the effects of those circumstances. They promote a militant cinema, producing decolonized media, information, and entertainment that is wholly committed, politically and ideologically, to an emerging class-based revolution. Getino and Solanas's idea of militant cinema is conceived through the larger category of Third Cinema as a collective and instrumentalized form of tactically deployed cinema. The political efficacy of these tactics depends on the specific ways the films are received by and move spectators through their discussions and engagements with the film. To work affectively, the film must spur the viewer to participation and engagement in the action of the cinematic event and then the filmmaker hopes it engenders a more lasting, affective attachment to an emerging revolution or political movement—a dictum that is still present today with new and emerging digital representational technologies rather than just film. Context is especially important as well. In Argentina in the 1970s, "the mere viewing of a militant film was a clandestine activity punishable by incarceration or worse," notes Julianne Burton, where "each spectator becomes an accomplice, a co-participant"[56] Yet, despite the danger, the cinema itself was a kind of weapon the people could arm themselves with, as well as a transformative political force. Solanas and Getino view the camera and projector as guns, a decolonial act "of 'turning the guns around': using the arms of the dominant system in order to destroy or subvert it."[57] With the cinema, the projector shoots images at the dominant classes and fascistic regimes and the spectator transforms into an accomplice in an activating and revolutionary act of affective viewing and collective participation.

In the United States, despite being in a vastly different political and media context, the filmmaking collective Newsreel employed similar tactics as Solanas and Getino but in pursuit of ending the Vietnam War, solidarity with Third World movements, and building the student movement. Newsreel was the major Left-affiliated filmmaking group in the United States during the 1960s and first emerged from the perceived shortcomings of the mainstream media's coverage of the war in Vietnam and the movements mobilized to oppose it. Founded in New York City in December 1967 by Norm Fruchter and Robert Kramer, Newsreel formed in response to the biased and scarce coverage the massive October 21, 1967, antiwar protest at the Pentagon received in the mainstream news media. In particular, the group targeted the media's failure to show the military police's brutal treatment of protestors—an impulse to provide counterinformation. In the United States, there was a paucity of politically engaged filmmaking in the period directly after World War II. As Nichols notes, "Newsreel stepped into a vacuum ... Left film culture in America withered away in the late thirties and early forties with the demise of the Film and Photo League and Frontier Films."[58] As Newsreel grew, a sister organization called California Newsreel was founded in San Francisco in 1968 that provided a bicoastal base for production and distribution.

Newsreel supplied a visual point of reference and distillation for the emerging New Left in the United States. "Newsreel occupied a crucial position," argues Michael Renov, "in the largely unconscious construction of a political imaginary for the New Left," as they effectively "covered" the emerging cultural, political, and social unrest in ways the mainstream media would and could not adequately represent.[59] During the late sixties and early seventies, Newsreel was also at the forefront of distributing films from the Third World that "helped draw the American Left into Third World struggle."[60] Newsreel eschewed the making of fictional films of any sort, focusing instead on short, weekly newsreels, long-form documentaries that analyzed events, and more tactical films meant to intervene in ongoing conflicts or spur direct action. A sense of urgency underscored by low-quality film stock, shaky handheld cameras, and a lack of dynamic editing characterized early Newsreel films, such as *Columbia Revolt* (1968), the first and most widely distributed film by the New York group, and *Black Panther* (1969) and *San Francisco State on Strike* (1969) by the California group. For Newsreel, however, aesthetics and sober reflection were really beside the point. Newsreel members characterized their grainy images as "battle footage" serving a propagandistic function akin to guerilla warfare.[61] The political and affective *use* and force of the films was the most important thing. This emphasis on efficacy and affect manifests itself in the Newsreel principle, never fully implemented, that films should be disseminated to and screened widely by activists on campuses and other venues throughout the United States. Each screening was to be followed by a discussion to further engage the audiences toward both analysis and action, very much in the model of Third Cinema. To engender an informed discussion, Newsreel members were assigned the role of facilitating pre- and postscreening discussion sessions. When the discussion-screening format developed, the "structure of the screening had as much priority as the structure of the film."[62] The affect generated by the films was a way to engender discussion and raise consciousness.

After the failures of 1968, the idea of militance begins to fray, veering into affective extremity on the left while it is also slowly co-opted by reactionary forces. Some filmmakers, like Jean Luc-Godard and his *Groupe Dziga Vertov* (Dziga Vertov Group) in France and filmmaker Masao Adachi in Japan, ventured into the nexus of militant filmmaking and armed struggle in Palestine, much like Ivens had in the beginning of the 1960s in Cuba. Here, we begin to see the death knell of militant films that use evidence of militancy as radical intervention. Godard and the Vertov Groups' *Ici et Ailleurs* (*Here and Elsewhere* (1976)) for instance, is the result of a failed project in the Middle East—specifically, a film that never came to fruition titled *Until Victory* (*Jusqu'a la Victoire*). Between 1969 and 1970, in Jordan, Lebanon, and the West Bank, Godard and his collaborator, Jean Pierre Gorin, filmed the armed Palestinian struggle. Two years later the project had been abandoned. Eventually, in collaboration with Anne Marie Miéville, Godard and Gorin end up releasing *Ici et Ailleurs* in 1976, a fascinating and frustrating film that combines 35 mm footage shot for *Until Victory* of militant, armed Palestinian struggle with footage of a French family shot in the town of Grenoble as well as experimental sequences shot in Godard and Miéville's Sonimage studio. In the context of this investigation, the film is of interest because it is a prime example of the "evidence of militancy" tendency in 1970s radical filmmaking circles.

In a similar vein, films like Masao Adachi's *Red Army/PLFP: Declaration of World War* (1971), coedited by the Red Army (Red Army Faction of Japan Revolutionary Communist League) and PFLP (Popular Front for the Liberation of Palestine), also represent the Palestinian struggle. Adachi, who would later take up arms and join that struggle in 1974, gained access, in 1971, to Palestinian training camps through Japanese ex-patriots and Red Army members Fusako Shigenobu and Mieko Toyama. In a particularly jarring sequence at the beginning of the film, inaugurating a "declaration of war," hijacked planes are blown up in an unnamed desert. As a radical documentary, these images push conceptions of Leftist militance to the extreme. Even if this were an effective tactic, its usage, the idea of representing "evidence of militancy," was later co-opted by religious extremists from various parts of the Middle East and North Africa. This trend began in the late 1970s with suicide bombings and plane hijackings and remains a favored tactic of modern, media-savvy terrorist organizations, like al Qaeda and ISIS. The use of images of the evidence of militancy, such as literal armed struggle, may be highly affective for some but not likely productive. The idea also has other hazards in the digital age, namely the use of video evidence against activists for allegedly committing unlawful acts.

In the 1980s, radical documentary begins to recover more productive uses of its affective power. In addition to the video and multimedia advocacy deployed by ACT-UP and other organizations, and within the larger turn to identity and subjectivity in the 1980s, there emerged what has been called "new documentary" in the art world. The movement focused particularly on documentary photography and was pioneered by Martha Rosler and Allan Sekula. They argued against Progressive era social realism seen in the work of Jacob Riis and Lewis Hine with their discourses of exposure and top-down benevolence. They argued for practices centered on politically focused, ground-up forms of documentation that intervene in the world. They advocated for and defended activist forms of documentary practice that examine the root causes of injustice and, when those causes had been located, that solutions and/or representations emerge from people in afflicted groups themselves.[63] Those practicing new documentary attempted, through a variety of formal strategies, to dislocate documentary images from the space of the gallery and museum. While these strategies had mixed results, and like many counterpractices were co-opted and eventually became markers of more conventional types of photography, the reorientation of representation back to the spaces where it could intervene is a main concern with the radical uses of documentary in the digital age.

Another highly relevant practice can be seen in other works in the new documentary mold exemplified by Rosler's video *A Simple Case for Torture, or How to Sleep at Night* (1983). Her tactic and strategy can be characterized as bombardment by fact, an analogue to the conception of militant evidence prior to the digitally networked age. The video is framed as a response to a 1982 Newsweek column by philosophy professor Michael Levin, in which the author posits an "ends justify the means" argument for torture, invoking the red herring of a "ticking time-bomb" scenario. As Rosler recounts, as she skimmed the magazine, she was startled by the article: "The title? 'The Case for Torture.' I was shocked, and I was meant to be, for this article was a provocation. The belligerent, rhetoric-spouting president, Ronald Reagan, was ratcheting up the Cold War, smashing what remained of Jimmy Carter's détente by planting nuclear- armed Cruise missiles in Western Europe . . . and some obscure nut had made his way onto *Newsweek's* front page arguing for the United States to torture people."[64]

The sixty-two-minute video is unrelenting. A constant, monotone voice-over reads Levin's column as well as snippets of facts, stories, statistics, and other information while the image track shows a hand, layering cut out news articles one upon the other, nearly nonstop. While the disjunction between image and soundtrack is purposeful and a barrier to paying close attention, it is also clear by reading the headlines of the aforementioned articles that Rosler is mercilessly and militantly backing up her critique with evidence while steadily undercutting the argument of her opponent. The tendency of artists and activists to deploy militant evidence in a radical way has only gained potency and currency as documentary continues its imbrication with the possibilities of emerging technologies. Militant evidence is harnessed as a practice of resistance and catalyzing force by artists in activist struggles across the globe.

Writing in the mid-1980s and reflecting on the plethora of radical documentary work in the 1960s and 1970s, Chuck Kleinhans offered a cogent assessment for the direction of a relevant radical documentary practice that continues to resonate with the current media environment and the use of militant evidence. Concerning function, or what can such work "do," Kleinhans posits the idea that radical documentary can be distilled into two basic tasks: "witnessing and affecting."[65] No matter how advanced technology becomes, or how instantaneous the communication and dissemination of media within the global sphere, radical documentary practices will work to capture visible evidence and represent subjective experiences while moving spectators on an emotional level toward a larger political critique or space for action. Beyond meeting these basic criteria, an effective radical documentary or media project must interpret and analyze. He argues that "to witness, move, and interpret is not enough. We must produce radical documentaries which deal with why things are the way they are and how they might change and be changed."[66] But to continue an effective practice while seeking an engaged audience, Kleinhans contends that documentary film and media makers must "embrace a variety of forms which depend on context, audience, intention, and other concerns for effect. We can also be open to using new forms, mixing and creating forms appropriate to new political forces, and new voices within the progressive coalition."[67] This is a particularly important sentiment as the networked digital age consists of a dynamic technological environment with ever-changing platforms and audiences receptive to politically engaged projects.

Consequently, any theorization of emerging documentary practices must be fully open to new forms, modes, makers, and voices. As Nichols posits, "New modes partly arise in response to perceived deficiencies in previous ones, but the perception of deficiency comes about partly from a sense of what it takes to represent the historical world from a particular perspective at a given moment in time."[68] Though many of the problems, questions, and overall aims of radical documentary remain vital, the old models, though highly informative and generative, are no longer operative in a media-saturated, corporate platform–dominated world of curated and screened social realities that disguise massive material inequities, brutal wars and occupations, and all manner of human rights abuses. The plethora of stories, evidence, and systemic problems combine in the digital age to present an exigent conundrum of abundance. On the one hand, there is a wide access to the means of representation and the ability to capture and disseminate militant evidence. On the other, this has produced a massive global flow of information and documentary images, from the mundane to the grotesque, and inundated audiences with images and videos from spaces of global crises. In addition, there is limited potential audience attention for long-form, traditional documentaries.

Further, as Patricia Zimmermann and Helen de Michiel have persuasively argued, new and emergent digital technologies have exploded staid notions of radical documentary practices and spectatorship. They theorize the idea of "open space" documentary, which can accommodate the dynamism, fluidity, and various iterations that documentary-based media operate within today while encompassing new modes of spectatorship of convenings, dialogue, and collaborative authorship. In the realm of open-space documentary, they posit that "media practitioners and exhibitors become *context providers* rather than *content providers*, creating scenarios that facilitate dialogue, participation, collaboration, shared experience and, interconnections across boundaries" that are attuned to "human scaled, localized social agency."[69] But, how does this work in practice? How can a media artist affectively move and activate the viewers/users when they are routinely inundated with a deluge of images, appeals, stories, and demands for their attention? In addition, how can they catalyze action, participation, and collaboration in the real world when viewers/users of their work engage with it in a singular and often private environment? A partial answer comes from catalyzing interaction with the work through a strategy that generates affective radicality within the interactive documentary form.

The interaction and combination of documentary with emerging media and technologies is a new topic of research for scholars from a variety of fields. Yet, there is no consensus on what such a practice should be called.[70] This chapter uses the term "interactive documentary" as it best conveys the changing relationship between documentary makers and their audiences as well as functioning as an analog for the subject position of the activist or revolutionary spectator to historical radical documentary practices. There, successful viewing required interaction, affective and critical engagement with the work to further political and social change. Interactive documentary is "characterized by the presence of distinctive recurring elements, including intuitive menus, maps, timelines, video clips, hyperlinks, and direct connections to social networks."[71] Further, interactive documentaries function as "cross-media products" that engender a nonlinear viewer/user experience within a global, connected network of other users.[72] It is not the case that every interactive documentary will contain all of these features, but all contain some of them. Hart Cohen offers a similar conception and addresses another aspect: namely, the importance of archives and databases. Cohen contends that this form of documentary practice relies on "access to an archive or other sources of knowledge and information" whereby the documentary maker "is closer to a curator or designer" by providing a structured, though open, experience for the viewer/user.[73]

Such an open experience implies a high degree of interactivity, yet the simple promise that one can "interact" with a work of art does not automatically make it affective or effective. According to Massumi, "Interactivity can make the useful less boring and the serious more engaging" but simply saying "'you may interact with the work' is not enough."[74] But, when interactive art "works" affectively on the viewer/user, it can "take the *situation* as its 'object' . . . it can take a situation and potentially 'open' the interaction it affords."[75] This idea of "openness" is analogous to de Michiel and Zimmermann's concept of the open-space documentary and is particularly relevant to the projects examined in this chapter because the subjects and situations presented are precisely those of enclosure, where representation (self or otherwise) is severely curtailed. Massumi argues that "this is precisely what makes art political in its own way. It can push further to the indeterminate but relationally potentialized fringes of existing situations, beyond the limits of current framings."[76] In the interactive documentaries analyzed here, the current framings place criminalized people within carceral structures. Each project seeks to break down and open the space of the frames of crime and punishment to represent occupation and incarceration as unjustified, systemic problems of enclosure and hiddenness that can be more holistically and affectively rendered.

As Lev Manovich notes, technologies of representation have produced, over the last 150 years, "an unprecedented amount of media materials: photo archives, film libraries, audio archives."⁷⁷ While an earlier generation effectively weaponized the camera in the capture and dissemination of previously unseen images, unheard sounds, and unrepresented bodies, the task of the radical documentarians of today is a bit more complex. They must not only continue to reveal the unseen and unrepresented, they must also produce and/or contend with a vast audiovisual, testimonial archive—procuring and curating affective militant evidence while providing deeper contexts and access to new networks, discourses, and modes of participation.⁷⁸ Further, they often partner with and thus amplify the work of activist organizations in the cause of social, political, and economic justice. Spectatorship of documentary or any other form of traditional filmmaking involves the discreet task of allowing a narrative line and/or argument to unfold as the director sees fit. Interactive documentaries function nonlinearly, as archival interfaces. They are a guide to viewer/user experience and a structuring device for militant evidence. The viewers/users of interactive documentary projects find a greater burden placed on their engagement: they must actively navigate through these projects by making decisions, synthesizing disparate information, and creating connections between multiple forms of media. Further, as Kate Nash argues, the concept of interactivity allows the expansion of the notion of the voice within authorship, moving it from a single unified voice to one of polyvocality and a form of social participation.⁷⁹

To define the potential political efficacy of digital media, Jessica Clark and Patricia Aufderheide have theorized the concept of "Public Media 2.0" to think through how media makers can engender a sense of a collective public that the viewer/user can act to effect, despite the fact a viewer/user is likely interacting with the work in a noncollective setting. They offer five types of engagement within their conception that constitutes media activist political action in the networked age:

> creation: producing original and remixed content to offer views outside of mainstream news channels
> collaboration: crowdfunding, crowdsourcing journalism, and circulating petitions
> choice: audiences actively seeking out alternative media sources
> conversation: using comment sections and discussion boards
> curation: aggregating and sharing information and content across platforms ⁸⁰

As Daniel Marcus argues, "These actions can reinforce a sense of collective activity moving toward shared goals through the dispersal and retrieval of information" and "promote interest in more embodied movements."[81] Earnest engagement with interactive documentaries, particularly those aligned with broader activist movements, facilitates all the forms of participation outlined above. Further, Mandy Rose contends that collaborative and open-ended interactive documentaries that engage social change "can be a platform for a convening through which an audience becomes a public—a group conscious of itself and its shared sense of purpose."[82] In addition, when media artists partner and collaborate with digital active witnesses, activist organizations, and other groups, the work becomes a fluid and emerging act of co-creation that engenders multiple forms of authorship and agency. As Rose observes, "Within a context of interactive documentary, co-creation can be a route to convening dialogues that can provide significant resources in . . . processes of change."[83]

Both *Public Secrets* and *Points of View* use the interactive documentary form and strategically curated militant evidence to provoke affective radicality across platforms and spaces of exhibition and engagement, moving viewers/users into expanded political and activist ecologies and collaborative actions. The combination of interactivity, data visualization, mapping, and open-ended narratives employ interfaces that can be manipulated on a variety of screens in a multiplicity of settings: public spaces like galleries, advocacy spaces, and classrooms and private spaces like personal screen devices within peoples' homes. These dynamic possibilities for exhibition and reception reimagine the idea of the public while challenging older models of documentary spectatorship and participation. The viewers/users also bring their own experiences, interests, and proclivities to bear on a wealth of material. Thus, the notion of authorship is further challenged and expanded, as Daniel and Kfir encourage engagement with a heterogeneous array of voices, opinions, and theories, all of which have a claim to structuring the meaning of the viewer/user experience. Finally, by partnering with outside organizations, both Daniel and Kfir strategically position their work to operate within broader activist and political ecologies.

Public Secrets

Daniel's work as a media artist involves both installation and interactive projects that are based in documentary but rarely utilize photorealist images. In addition, she directly collaborates with the subjects portrayed, who are often in precarious and/or oppressive situations. Daniel produces works that can operate in a range of contexts—from interactive documentary projects that function as affective interfaces for an array of testimonies and stories, to large installation pieces that immerse the viewer in fragmented narratives, striking visual displays, and forms of militant evidence. This militant evidence is then deployed in various combinations, depending on the context and space of the exhibition, to intervene in larger social, political, and legal discourses. As Daniel asserts, it's "been an intentional strategy for me to try to create works that are either flexible or variable enough to address different audiences and reach different kinds of publics."[84] The audiences and publics range from policy makers, activists, and museum patrons to law students, nonprofit staff, and social workers. Daniel has long been interested in having her work directly affect both policy and viewers/users. She consciously strategizes "how best to address a certain issue and how to create a public record or archive around that issue that might have political potency in the policy arena."[85] In much of Daniel's work, political potency emerges from the affective radicality of militant evidence that she employs. This consists of compelling individual testimonies and narratives as well as historical, medical, governmental, and other discourses and texts that, when read together and/or visualized, reveal larger structural inequities and oppressions. In her previous project, *Blood Sugar* (2010), Daniel employs a text-based interface of audio recordings of twenty current and former injection drug users in California state prisons and at the HIV Education and Prevention program in Alameda County.[86] Drawing on a diverse archive of medical research, critical theory, and public evidence, Daniel integrates the impactful testimonies and stories into varied discourses about biology, medicine, and desire to present a humane and comprehensive account of addiction, public health, and poverty in the United States.

In *Public Secrets*, Daniel follows a similar, polyvocal approach to represent the unseen effects and indignities of the prison industrial complex through the audio testimonies of women in prison in California. The project, which was created by Daniel and designed by Erik Loyer, was supported by the online journal *Vectors: Journal of Culture and Technology in a Dynamic Vernacular* in collaboration with Justice Now, an advocacy organization for women prisoners based in Oakland, CA.[87] The sound portion of *Public Secrets* encompasses the voices of twenty women interviewed by Daniel at CCWF. Daniel includes nearly six hundred statements displayed algorithmically from the incarcerated women, which were recorded over a six-year period.[88] It also includes the sound of a cell door clanking shut, which marks the transition between sections as the user clicks around the site. Transcriptions of the aforementioned interviews, snippets of text from various cultural, political, and legal theorists, such as Giorgio Agamben, Walter Benjamin, Angela Y. Davis, Fredric Jameson, Catherine MacKinnon, and Michael Taussig, and contextualization via excerpts from penal codes, newspapers, and other sources comprise the text portion. The format and design of *Public Secrets* is intuitive and user friendly. Each section is presented simply as various panes in black, white, and gray marked by large fonts displaying a quote from the larger text (either in written or audio form), which awaits the viewer, if they choose to click. When one scrolls a mouse over a given pane, a blue background highlights the section and invites the viewer to learn more. The bottom right-hand portion of the opening splash screen also provides a link to search the project by topic (Drug Wars, Alternatives, etc.) and a "What You Can Do" link, which provides steps toward concrete action, definitions of "decarceration," and links to a host of organizations working in the areas of prison and drug reform.

In the United States, there are more than two million people in jail or prison, and over 10 percent of that population consists of women. While that number might seem low in comparison to the percentage of men, incarcerated women in the United States account for 30 percent of all incarcerated women worldwide.[89] In fact, in the last forty years, the percentage of incarcerated women in the United States has risen by 700 percent. Often, these women are victims of assault and cycles of abuse, with more than 85 percent of incarcerated American woman reporting past physical and sexual traumas in their lives.[90] In addition, many women, particularly in California, have few means with communicating with the outside world, apart from sporadic visits from family members and attorneys. For Daniel, part of the impetus for the project stemmed from the media ban enacted by the California Department of Corrections in 1993 in the wake of damning media reports and a slew of lawsuits alleging rampant mistreatment of prisoners. The media ban applies to all prisoners who are unable to access computers, cameras, or any other form of media making equipment. It also applies to journalists, academics, and other researchers by prohibiting them from conducting face-to-face interviews, using cameras or audio-recording devices within the walls of the prison complex, or even using a pen or pencil to record notes on interviews with prison representatives.

The near total blackout of public communication effectively leaves the prisoners invisible and unable to speak. It also shields the public from an accurate representation of what happens to an individual whose crimes are adjudicated with a prison sentence. Daniel gained access to the prisoners and the ability to record their thoughts through a legal loophole—prisoners are allowed face-to-face access to "legal advocates," who are able to record their conversations.[91] As a media artist, and in this instance, a designated legal advocate through her partnership with Justice Now, Daniel views her

Figure 2.4 Page for "The Public Secret" section in *Public Secrets*, courtesy of Sharon Daniel.

role, much like DeMichiel and Zimmermann describe a facet of open-space documentary, as a "context provider ... not a content provider," whereby she does not presume to speak for others rather, she "induces others to speak for themselves ... providing the means or tools or context where they can speak and be heard."[92]

The seeming incongruity of the title of the work that melds the oppositional terms *public* and *secret* is a deliberate strategy, playing on the notions of what can be seen and heard and what we choose not to know. Daniel writes that "there are secrets that are kept from the public and then there are "public secrets"—secrets that the public chooses to keep safe from itself ... the trick to the public secret is in knowing what not to know. This is the most powerful form of social knowledge. Such shared secrets sustain social and political institutions. The injustices of the war on drugs, the criminal justice system, and the Prison Industrial Complex are 'public secrets.'"[93]

In a basic sense, the public aspect refers to the common perception of the judicial system. In this conception, citizens, either accused of crimes or simply aware that the US legal system begins with the police and ends with adjudication, believe that people "pay back" their debts to society—either through fines, community service, or a prison sentence. The secret aspect of the title refers to what happens to the person during the prison sentence, an aspect of the system essentially shielded from public view, especially in California. It also refers to the shielding of the public from the feelings and thoughts of the prisoners. Any appeals they may make to the outside world must emerge from a labyrinth of regulations designed to stultify them. These regulations mirror the material carceral infrastructure of surveillance, enclosure, and anonymity—what Ruth Wilson Gilmore calls "infrastructures of feeling," where societal beliefs and values are imbricated within the material structures that uphold US prison system.[94] Though we never see the women, the project foregrounds their affectively moving stories, accumulating them to such a degree that they are rendered both typical and overpowering; they transcend the many structures meant to quell them.

Daniel's choice of title also signals the theoretical conception of the project itself. She first provokes viewer/user engagement in *Public Secrets* around the concept of aporia, which she defines as "an irresolvable internal contradiction, between power and knowledge, between information and denial, between the masks of politics and the goals of an open society."[95] The title itself is an aporia, but each section also functions within the same sense of contradiction. Daniel structures the project around three sections: "Inside/Outside," "Bare Life/Human Life," and "Public Secret/Utopia." These section headings appear (once scrolled over) on the left side of the screen on the initial splash page for the project. "Inside/Outside" is the most theoretically straightforward of the sections, positing a spatial relation between the space of the prison as existing outside the rules, norms, and guaranteed rights of US citizens living in the world beyond the walls. The conceptions of "Bare Life/Human Life" draw heavily on the work of Agamben and suggests, as Daniel argues, that "a prisoner . . . is reduced from political life to biological life. The prisoner is kept alive, but barely, as naked life—a status that is tautologous with the deprivation of their human rights. Prisoners are thus ideologically acceptable victims of mal-treatment, neglect, and abuse"[96] Finally, the "Utopia" aspect of the "Public Secret/Utopia" section employs Jameson's conception of the "politics of utopia," an impulse to foreground utopia when it seems most out of reach within the political imaginary, and the work of Davis, which focused on prison abolition, to theorize both resistance to the prison industrial complex and a world without prisons.[97] Each section contains a selection of audio interviews (with transcripts) from the inmates. When users click to "read transcript" during the audio portion, they are also given the option to explore a personalized archive of interviews for that prisoner, allowing for a more complete conception of her thoughts and

Figure 2.5 "Bare Life" section in *Public Secrets*, courtesy of Sharon Daniel.

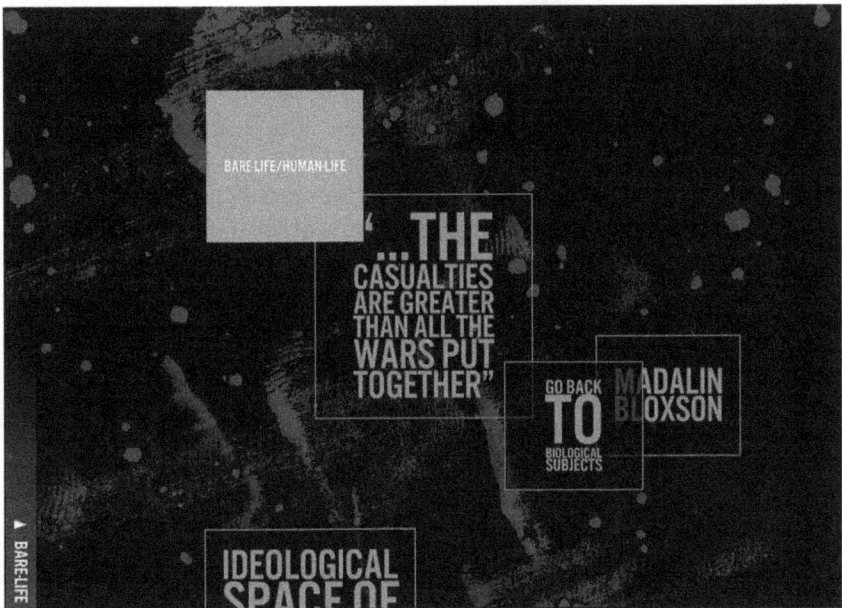

Figure 2.6 "Bare Life" section in *Public Secrets*, courtesy of Sharon Daniel.

background. Below is a brief analysis of the "Bare Life/Human Life" section to demonstrate how the viewer/user experiences the interface as well as give a sense of how the various modalities of a section interact with one another and resonate on an affective register.

Interacting with Aporias: Bare Life/Human Life and the Aesthetics of Politics

Writing about her aesthetic and design choices for *Public Secrets*, Daniel contends that "the interface design constitutes a form of 'argument' (as writing does for a scholar), and user navigation functions as a form of 'enquiry' . . . addressing the tensions and contradictions that emerge between the goals of theory and aesthetics and those of advocacy and activism."[98] She points to a number of important considerations when investigating the melding of documentary and new media in the interactive documentary form. The interface itself—the ostensible architecture of the project—exists as a form of argument in its own right, pulling documentary storytelling away from the constraints of linear narrative while employing a form that is more able to accommodate complexity, polyvocality, nonlinearity, and varied forms of media. And, the concept of enquiry is a more experiential, unfolding form of engagement and learning on the part of the viewer, which is furthered by the interactive interface.

In the "Bare Life/Human Life" section, the viewer/user can click on either the Bare Life or Human Life part, with the former occupying the top half of the interface and the latter the bottom. Whichever option is chosen, the screen is divided (in block text) by the phrase "bare life is preserved as an expression of sovereign power," appropriated from Agamben. The viewer/user is also alerted to the disconcerting notion that a prisoner's body becomes the property of the State of California and is "kept alive to represent state power—to both absorb and reflect state violence—proving that the state has the power to force the prisoner to live under any conditions."[99] This idea and its effects on the psyche of the individual is explored throughout this section. A prisoner named Jane Dorotik recalls that because the body is state property, women who have been severely sunburned during outdoor activities in the prison have been given "115s," a penal code term for disciplinary action that results from defacing state property. Zundre Johnson, another inmate, offers a heartbreaking assessment of life in prison. Recalling the suicide of another inmate's son, she argues that daily life in prison is akin to death: "They do it here every day. They just don't die. That's the cold part. They take their life everyday here . . . they just wake up in the morning and kill they self and then function dead." The constraint of only being able to hear their voices and read their words works as an aporia as well. The viewer/user must grapple with the constraint of being able to hear but not see the inmates; they exist but are unseen, alive but not fully embodied.

The wrenching personal stories and testimonies from the inmates in this section are interspersed with texts underscoring the inmate experience and broadening its contextualization by placing their thoughts within the discourses of wider systemic problems and theoretical arguments. Daniel provides more quotes from Agamben, further defining the concept of bare life as well as his concept of *homo sacer*—the "accursed man" outside the realm of the law. She also includes an excerpt from the California Code of Regulations, which governs the prison system, that states a prisoner suicide is considered the destruction of state property. These texts are supported by quotes from a *New York Times* report on Guantanamo detainees and excerpts from the Universal Declaration of Human Rights (UDHR) pertaining to prohibitions against torture and inhuman treatment. The inclusion of these texts serves a number of purposes. First, they attest to the validity of the women's testimonies. The inclusion of the specific part of the penal code defining ownership of inmate bodies, for example, gives weight to the punishment for sunburns discussed above. Second, for inmates who lack basic connections with the outside world, the inclusion of texts on torture and abuse at Guantanamo intersects with their own testimonies and experiences within a global conversation about human rights and detention. Finally, the inclusion of theoretical concepts in concert with the affective testimonials grounds abstract formulations in moving, material effects while elevating the thoughts and life experiences of the incarcerated women into the realm of academic and political discourse.

Daniel is particularly attuned to the relationship between aesthetics and the political functioning of her work within the context of the interactive documentary.[100] She turns to French cultural theorist Jacques Rancière's notion of "dissensus," a form of active political confrontation that has the potential for manifestation via art, as way to theorize her interventions.[101] Daniel argues that the politically informed and motivated interactive documentaries work to "materialize a space of 'dissensus'—not a critique, or a protest, but a confrontation of the status quo with what it does not admit, what is invisible, inaudible and othered. I do not wish to make claims of political efficacy (as commonly understood) for database documentary, but instead to identify and describe a genre and method that can function as 'politics' in Rancière's terms—a politics that I believe has the potential to circumvent the intransigence of the state."[102]

The confrontation Daniel references is of course immaterial. Notions of the state and the status quo are ideologically constructed entities with profound material effects on the bodies and lives of those subjugated by them. The political act facilitated by Daniel is the rendering audible, and thus visible in a figurative sense, the subjectivity of the incarcerated women. Their exclusion from society within the space of the prison and its attendant dehumanizing practices, procedures, and regulations strips them of any claim to agency as political subjects with rights. The political potentiality in this formulation emerges from the promise of recognition. If the state were to productively engage the (now public) testimonies and claims of the women, it may become more accommodating. But it remains unclear how such practices could circumvent the inflexibility of the state. That said, the logistics of amassing and accumulation seen in *Public Secrets* are not an end in and of themselves, and in some ways, they go beyond Daniel's alignment with Rancière. The project produces more than simply a space of potential politics—it can also be read as part of an ongoing larger political movement building consensus and a critical mass of affective and effective evidence toward the case for prison abolition. *Public Secrets* intimately fuses the personal and political, accumulating affective militant evidence against the unfeeling machinery of the prison industrial complex in California, creating an affective radicality that moves viewers/users into the realm of critique, activism, and critical engagement with the prison abolition movement.

Points of View: Mapping Palestinian Oppression

Like Daniel, Zohar Kfir's recent work has focused on interactivity, immersion, and the deployment of affective testimonials in direct partnership with her subjects and/or activist organizations. In her recent virtual reality documentary *Testimony* (2017), Kfir presents the stories of five sexual assault survivors and immerses the viewer/user in candid accounts of the assaults and the lasting effects such violence has on victims. In this first iteration of the work, Kfir uses the testimonies and virtual reality as a way to allow the public to bear witness to the silenced voices of survivors and foster courage and solidarity among those unable or unwilling to speak out. In this way, the project functions as both a digital support system for those victims who have not yet reported their assaults and as a specific site for the public to hear the subjective effects of assaults that are often obscured in the media, such as in the cases of Brock Turner and Bill Cosby.

There is a similar silence and obscuring of effects in Palestine. Like the voices of US prisoners and discussion of the prison industrial complex seen in *Public Secrets*, we rarely receive discussion in mainstream Western

Figure 2.7 The splash screen for *Points of View*, courtesy of Zohar Kfir (www.points-of-view.net).

media about the Israeli occupation of Palestine and its stultifying effects on the lives of everyday Palestinians. In fact, public support of the Palestinian cause can result in firings, widespread public shaming, and accusations of anti-Semitism, as seen in the recent cases of scholars like Steven Salaita and Marc Lamont Hill. Further, the widely used mapping service Google Maps has omitted many Palestinian villages, roads, and other areas within navigation systems, erasing Palestinian history and borders into an amnesiac digital oblivion.[103] Kfir's *Points of View*, a title that speaks to both a diversity of opinion and various points on a map that the viewer/user is able to figuratively zoom in to view, intervenes and rectifies this erasure of Palestinians from public discourse and maps.

Points of View is an ongoing interactive project that maps Palestinian video footage created through B'Tselem's Camera Distribution Project, which seeks to document human rights abuses in Israeli-occupied territories in the West Bank and the Gaza Strip; educate the Israeli public about previously unseen abuses; and work to end the occupation through legal, governmental, and broader media channels. B'Tselem engages in a multifaceted strategy focused on accountability. In early 2007, B'Tselem added a video advocacy component to their work, initially dubbed "Shooting Back" but is now known under the name "The Camera Project." To date, the project has distributed cameras to over two hundred Palestinian families, with a particular focus on areas in the Gaza Strip and the West Bank, which B'Tselem has identified as most prone to violations. This works to counter the fact that, as Davis describes, "the Palestinian struggle for freedom and determination is often minimized and rendered invisible."[104] The thousands of hours of footage the project has acquired is stored in a vast video archive, and *Points of View* grew out of Kfir's exploration of this footage.

In a recent interview with i-docs.org, Kfir contends that this archive is "comprised of highly complex snapshots, some with violent content and others with testimonies that can be difficult to watch . . . it was the type of material that is often stripped of subtlety and dimension when it is inserted into media accounts."[105] She is able to reinscribe subtlety and dimension through her choice of interface, which is an interactive map of the Israeli-Palestinian territories. Kfir also reinscribes affect and empathy through her choice of videos and their contextualization through caption and placement on a virtual map that features the ever-shifting encroachment of borders of Israel into Palestine. The use of the map quickly allows viewers/users to gain an overview of the contested region, identify various boundaries, and situate the video "nodes," which convey both typicality and pervasiveness. Videos and stories are grouped through "tags," which are a common keyword function used by blogs and other media sites as way to both organize thematically similar elements and filter out unrelated material. The tags employed by Kfir, which are color coded for easy navigation, are organized by place (Gaza, East Jerusalem, Hebron, Tel Aviv) and theme (settlers, violence, IDF, youth, women). The initial places, themes, and corresponding videos that comprise the map were also chosen through a direct collaboration between Kfir and the archivists in B'Tselem's video department.

The interface allows the viewer/user to click on multiple filters at once to refine their engagement with the site while spatially locating the chosen places and themes on the map. Viewers/users also have the option to click nodes around the site to follow various video trails connected by a given tag. Whether the viewer/user engages with just the tags of interest or follows the predetermined trails, the experience is decidedly nonlinear and speculative. Kfir provides the literal and figurative map that structures the videos and their various contexts. But it is the viewers/users who both create a narrative through their interaction with various threads of experience and make meaning from those threads in a way that is open-ended and only partially guided. Kfir sought to create an interactive project "that both situates the footage in its location and time of origin and creates new narrative threads of meaning from the stories that emerge over time."[106] Her hope is that in the future "an ever growing database of unique testimonies" provided in *Points of View* will help to "cross reference events and locations in various points of time," a mode of engagement also furthered by Forensic Architecture and their recent collaborations with B'Tselem.[107]

Points of View is open-ended in terms of its technological architecture. Kfir planned the project as ongoing and not a fixed media object. She argues, in the aforementioned interview with i-docs.org, that "the platform was designed to sustain hundreds of videos," and she hopes that it will grow to function as a "curated archive" of much of B'Tselem's acquired footage while becoming both an "interactive web documentary as well as a platform for research and teaching."[108] To these ends, Kfir designed the project with an open source model, a form of production and development that promotes access via a free license to the "back end" of a site's design.[109] In other words, Kfir continues to partner with B'Tselem and other groups and individuals by providing access that enables users to upload their own content within the interactive map structure. This structure strategically deploys the B'Tselem footage while providing viewers/users with contextualized, locative snapshots of the Palestinian experience in a way far more enriching and affectively impactful than simply watching one video or one traditional documentary. In addition, the use of the overhead map allows viewers/users to locate and see the contours of systemic state violence. As Kfir contends, "My wish was to expand the linear, fixed approach of traditional documentary filmmaking and create an ongoing interactive documentary that situates the footage in its location and time of origin and creates new narrative threads of meaning from the stories that emerge over time."[110]

The affective radicality of the project for the viewer/user is located in two main components: the accumulation of evidence that speaks to the pervasiveness of the occupation, which elicits empathy and the accumulation of practices of militant resistance that then elicits hope and solidarity. The Gaza section of the map ("Gaza-An Inside Look"), for example, contains a video trail comprised of five separate videos. Kfir organizes this section by the tags "Gaza," to denote where the videos were shot, and "youth," to designate that the videos were made mostly by students. The Gaza video selected grows out of the aftermath of the Gaza War also known as Operation Cast Lead, an armed conflict between Israel and Palestinians residing in the Gaza Strip. The conflict began December 27, 2008, and lasted until January 18, 2009. According to the official Israeli line, Operation Cast Lead was an effort to stop rocket attacks originating in the Palestinian sections of Gaza. During the conflict, Israeli Defense Forces (IDF) unleashed a multifront assault, bombing Palestinian homes and assets from the air and seas as well as launching a comprehensive ground invasion and blockade of the entire Gaza Strip. The conflict resulted in the widespread destruction of property and the deaths of thousands of Palestinian citizens. Shortly after the hostilities ceased, B'Tselem provided cameras to fifteen university students who were beginning their studies in fields such as communication and journalism and asked them to film their everyday lives in the wake of the destruction.

When the viewer/user scrolls over one of the five nodes placed on the map where the videos were made, an information pane drops down from the left-hand side of the screen and informs them of the title of the film, the name of the videographer (if known), the tags attributed to the video, and a brief summary of the context in which the videos were shot. In the case of the Gaza section, Kfir provides a brief description of B'Tselem's efforts in the wake of Operation Cast Lead. When one clicks on a given node, the video appears on a separate screen, accompanied by production information, the aforementioned tags, and a brief description of the video. The Gaza section includes the videos *Tunnel Youth* (Unspecified Director, 2009), *Summer Games* (dir. Fadi al-Ghorra, 2009), *War Games* (dir. Muhammad al-Aloul, 2009), *Hip Hop Lessons* (dir. Muhammad al-Majdlawi, 2009), and *Making Sand out of Ruins* (Unspecified Director, 2010).

The short video *Tunnel Youth* transports the viewer/user inside a dark and dank-looking tunnel (one of many) under the Gazan town of Rafah, which is being reinforced and maintained by a group of Palestinian boys that appear fourteen to sixteen years old. In her description of the video, Kfir notes that the boys spend many long hours each day working in these tunnels, having left school for this work in order to support their families. The tunnel serves as conduit for food, medicine, and weapons to be transferred among Palestinians in Gaza away from the view of IDF soldiers and outside the ever-shifting legal constraints of the Israeli embargo policy. The opening shots of the video reveal the boys wearing headlamps, operating a winch, smoking, and laughing with one another. The popular Palestinian song "Heroes of the Tunnels" plays with a muffled, tinny sound through one of the boys' cellphones, serving as a makeshift, diegetic soundtrack for the entirety of the video.

Following the initial sequences, the cameraman interviews the boys, engaging them on how and why they decided on this dangerous, claustrophobic job. One boy, filmed closely to emphasize the small space of the tunnel, succinctly states, "There's no work elsewhere, so we have to work here," which underscores the profound lack of economic opportunity in an area walled in, cutoff, and facing possible destruction at a moment's notice. Another reinforces this idea contending that "all the crossings are closed; we have to work here." He is referencing the plethora of checkpoints (arteries into Israel where the economy is healthy) that had been blockaded in the aftermath of Operation Cast Lead. Yet another boy sums up the precarious situation: "Our lives here . . . we pray before we go down (into the tunnel)."

The boys face the threat of the tunnel closing in on them and are only able to receive liquid sustenance (water and milk) through a pipe that leads outside the tunnel. Their only contact with the outside is through the use of walkie-talkies. The boys depicted, with their faces blurred to protect their identities, are covered in dirt and emaciated. The baseness of their existence is shocking and underscores the Palestinian plight in Gaza.

In other sections of the map, East Jerusalem and Hebron for example, follow a similar structure to the Gaza section, albeit with different themes. The Hebron section, comprised of four videos, follows a trail of clashes between Palestinian residents of Hebron, IDF forces, and Israeli settlers between 2010 and 2012. A particularly disturbing video, *Officer Head-butts Palestinian, Youth* (dir. Zidan Sharabati, 2012), is shot surreptitiously from an apartment above an IDF checkpoint near the Beit Hadassah settlement in Hebron City Center. The video depicts the harassment, brutal beating, and eventual arrest suffered by seventeen-year-old Thair Ghanam at the hands of an IDF soldier. Whereas the Gaza section provided a glimpse into aspects of everyday life involving work, play, and culture, the Hebron section focuses on facets of everyday life that involve unremitting violence, checkpoints, and the encroachment of Israeli settlers, as well as the unyielding, often nonviolent, practices of resistance on the part of the Palestinians protecting their land. This set of videos, shot as part of the broader Camera Distribution Project, fits squarely into the evidentiary mode and exemplifies the types of videos deployed by B'Tselem in legal proceedings. Deployed by Kfir, they work as affective evidence targeted at the viewer/user. In the East Jerusalem section, Kfir presents a selection of short films from the "Six Voices" project, a component of the larger Camera Distribution Project, began in 2010. B'Tselem gave cameras to six Palestinians and Israelis living in occupied East Jerusalem and asked them to create video diaries of their lives and the chaos and volatility wrought upon them by the occupation. Thaer Qirresh's contribution, for example, chronicles the tribulations of his family life in a residential building they have lived in since the 1930s. In July 2010, settlers took over every other apartment in the building. Qirresh chronicles the routine harassment they face in the building they have occupied for nearly ninety years. Israelis Sara Benninga chronicles her international activist work to end the occupation while Yonathan Mizrahi documents his alternative cultural tours of the City of David, a popular tourist attraction run by a settler organization.

Kfir's project recasts these videos as a part of a broader effort to visualize and open the view of the occupation while rooting it in a variety of specific affective appeals. "Affect," Kathleen Stewart argues, "is the promise, or threat, that something is happening—something new, emergent, capable of impact."[111] The invocation of two seemingly opposite ideas, that of a promise and of threat, the former of which implies trust and reciprocity and the latter a wielding of a form of power, is particularly apt in regard to *Points of View*. The promise Stewart mentions exists between Kfir and the subjects represented, an implied assurance to represent their thoughts, actions, and feelings accurately while the threat emerges from the collection and critical mass of these witnesses and testimonies and their inherent challenge to power. As examined above, depending on the specific context, these appeals vary from intense empathy for the boys stuck in the tunnel, to disgust and outrage over the treatment of everyday Palestinian people at the hands of the IDF—and toward solidarity with practices of resistance. This diversity of appeals works to affect the viewers/users on many levels of engagement while orienting them to the larger, militant critique of the occupation. *Points of View*, much like *Public Secrets*, offers the viewer/user a different form of knowing, one that is endowed with affectivity to buttress and amplify the mass of effective evidence presented. The impact, force, and affective radicality of Kfir's project will only increase as more videos and points on the map are added in the coming years.

Affective Radicality

Public Secrets and *Points of View* intervene in political and social struggles by accumulating, contextualizing, and deploying affective militant evidence through the interactive documentary forms. They use these forms and the power of the curated militant evidence to engender the potentially transformative forces of affective radicality. In doing so, they render visible usually hidden, or "unseen," subjects and carceral structures while providing a platform for the representation of marginalized and disenfranchised groups. The projects also rely heavily on concepts of witness, testimony, and the cultivation of affective identification with both digital active witnesses and systemic, seemingly intractable injustices. The use of new media technology, as deployed in these projects, enhances the political power of the documentary form by providing an interface and design architecture for the dissemination of vast archives of information, media, images, and perspectives that more traditional forms are unable to accommodate. It also opens the space and spectatorship of documentary practices, situating them within global networks and intersectional activist causes, moving viewers/users to participate, learn, and interact—a fluid and networked hub capable of reaching, engaging, and activating the collaboration of a global cadre of viewers/users. Finally, *Public Secrets* and *Points of View* are deeply indebted to partnerships with larger organizations involved in social and political justice struggles. These projects effectively augment their transmedia and other advocacy efforts, serving as one of many means of potential political engagement.

Thinking back for a moment to Gregg and Seigworth's idea of an affective encounter as a "momentary or sometimes more sustained state of relation," shows how these projects operate on both an affective and political level. During their engagement with either *Public Secrets* or *Points of View* viewers/users are immersed within a momentary affective relationship with the archive of subjects and digital active witnesses presented as well as the larger systemic critique. It is left up to viewers whether or not they are sufficiently moved to click and explore beyond the project, to turn their engagement outward and sustain their relation to the encounter—from personal movement to mass movement. Whereas these projects certainly expand the form, distribution, and reception of documentary, no single interactive project is a panacea or will single handedly change the world. Rather, they should be seen as politically engaged, documentary-based art forms that are beginning to reflect an emerging and growing global solidarity in concert with the increased documentation and mass of evidence of abuse against systematic forms of oppression. Thus, the force of affective radicality functions within the logic of amassing: opening to myriad encounters that beget empathy, information, evidence, imbrication within existing networks of militant activists, and ideally, the beginning of sustained mass movements.

This chapter and the last have theorized two potential forces of radical documentary practices in the digital age, effective and affective radicality. While the two concepts have been separated in order to fully explore them, it is not meant to suggest they operate in isolation or are mutually exclusive. Rather, militant evidence fundamentally relies on context and audience and thus often moves and operates fluidly between both forms of radicality. The next chapter examines the role context and archives play in considerations of radicality through an examination of amateur made documentaries produced in Iraq during the recent war and US occupation. These videos foreground the experiences of ordinary Iraqi citizens living under occupation, a point of view lacking in Western media accounts. Like the work discussed in this chapter, these amateur documentaries rely heavily on militant evidence consisting of digital active witnesses, testimonies, and an appeal to everydayness to create counterarchives and new, more open spaces for recognition, empathy, and dialogue within Iraq and globally.

Notes

1. For an excellent discussion of the many ecologies documentary circulates within in the digital age, see Kate Nash, Craig Hight, and Catherine Summerhayes, eds., *New Documentary Ecologies: Emerging Platforms, Practices and Discourses* (New York: Palgrave Macmillan, 2014).
2. Jane Gaines, "Documentary Radicality," *Canadian Journal of Film Studies* 16, no. 1 (Spring 2007): 13.
3. Jane Gaines, "Political Mimesis," in *Collecting Visible Evidence*, ed. Jane Gaines and Michael Renov (Minneapolis: University of Minnesota Press), 92.
4. Adrian Miles, "Interactive Documentary and Affective Ecologies," in *New Documentary Ecologies: Emerging Platforms, Practices and Discourses*, ed. Kate Nash, Craig Hight, and Catherine Summerhayes (New York: Palgrave Macmillan, 2014), 80.
5. Ibid.
6. For *Public Secrets*, see http://www.sharondaniel.net/ for the artist's site and www.publicsecret.net for the project's site; for *Points of View*, see http://zzee.net/wordpress/ for the artist's site and http://points-of-view.net/ for the project's site.
7. Angela Y. Davis, *Freedom Is a Constant Struggle: Ferguson, Palestine, and the Foundations of a Movement* (Chicago: Haymarket Books, 2016), 21.
8. Ibid., 57.
9. Ibid., 59.
10. See http://prisonvalley.arte.tv/?lang=en.
11. See http://acallfromherman.nfb.ca/#/intro and https://www.theguardian.com/world/ng-interactive/2016/apr/27/6x9-a-virtual-experience-of-solitary-confinement.
12. Gil Hochberg, *Visual Occupations: Violence and Visibility in a Conflict Zone* (Durham, NC: Duke University Press, 2015), 1.
13. Ibid., 11.
14. Ibid., 166.
15. See http://theinvisiblewalls.btselem.org/he.
16. See https://interactive.aljazeera.com/aje/palestineremix/films_main.html.
17. Ellen Mara De Wachter, "'I'd rather lose prizes and win cases': an interview with Eyal Weizman of Turner Prize-nominated Forensic Architecture," *Frieze*, May 2, 2018, https://frieze.com/article/id-rather-lose-prizes-and-win-cases-interview-eyal-weizman-turner-prize-nominated-forensic.
18. Ibid.
19. Ibid.
20. See https://visualizingpalestine.org/.
21. Melissa Gregg and Gregory Seigworth, eds., *The Affect Theory Reader* (Durham, NC: Duke University Press, 2010), 1.
22. Ibid., 2.
23. Brian Massumi, "The Thinking-Feeling of What Happens," *Inflexions* 1, no. 1 (2008): 35.
24. Kathleen Stewart, *Ordinary Affects* (Durham, NC: Duke University Press, 2007), 2.
25. Brian Massumi, *Politics of Affect* (Cambridge, UK: Polity, 2015), 79.
26. Ibid., 82.
27. Siegfried Kracauer, "Jean Vigo," *Hollywood Quarterly* 2, no. 3 (1947): 261.
28. Jean Vigo, "Toward a Social Cinema" in *French Film Theory and Criticism Vol. 2: 1929–1939*, ed. Richard Abel (Princeton, NJ: Princeton University Press, 1988), 61.
29. Ibid., 60–61.

30. Ibid., 61.
31. Ibid.
32. Steven Ungar, "Jean Vigo, *L'Atalante*, and the Promise of Social Cinema," *Historical Reflections* 35 (2009): 66.
33. Dudley Andrew, "*L'âge d'or* and the Eroticism of the Spirit," in *Masterpieces of Modernist Cinema*, ed. Ted Perry (Bloomington: Indiana University Press, 2006): 133.
34. Ungar, "Jean Vigo, *L'Atalante*, and the Promise of Social Cinema," 64.
35. Vigo passed away at age twenty-nine on October 5, 1934, from a combination of septicemia and tuberculosis.
36. James Chapman, *Cinemas of the World: Film and Society from 1895 to the Present* (London: Reaktion, 2003), 209.
37. Bill Nichols, "Documentary Film and the Modernist Avant-Garde," *Critical Inquiry* 27 (2001): 591.
38. Beyond these more abstract influences, Dulac's tutelage had more concrete effects as well. In 1930, Dulac, along with Guy Ferrand, had become coheads of production at the recently established Gaumont-Franco-Film-Aubert (GFFA), whose sports-documentary arm, *Le Journal Vivant*, had been asked to make a film portrait of French swimming hero Jean Taris. Dulac commissioned Vigo to make this film, which eventually became the motion study *Taris ou la Natation* (1931). See Michael Temple, *Jean Vigo* (Manchester, UK: Manchester University Press, 2005).
39. Steven Ungar, "Jean Vigo, *L'Atalante*, and the Promise of Social Cinema," 71.
40. Joris Ivens, "Repeated and Organized Scenes in Documentary Film (1953)" in *Joris Ivens and the Documentary Context*, ed. Kees Bakker (Amsterdam: Amsterdam University Press, 1999), 268–269.
41. Nichols, "Documentary Film and the Modernist Avant-Garde," 606.
42. Joris Ivens, "Notes on the Avant-Garde Documentary," in *Joris Ivens and the Documentary Context*, ed. Kees Bakker (Amsterdam: Amsterdam University Press, 1999), 224. Originally published as "Quelques réflexions sur les documentaries d'avant garde," *La Revue des Vivants* no. 10 (1931): 518–520.
43. Ellis and McLane, *A New History of Documentary Film*, 47.
44. Bakker, ed., *Joris Ivens in the Documentary Context*, 251.
45. Nichols, *Introduction to Documentary*, 149.
46. Joris Ivens, *The Camera and I* (Berlin: Seven Seas, 1969), 149–150.
47. Ibid., 151.
48. Ibid.
49. Ibid., 120.
50. See Thomas Waugh, *The Conscience of Cinema: The Works of Joris Ivens 1912–1989* (Amsterdam: Amsterdam University Press, 2016).
51. Ivens, *The Camera and I*, 137.
52. Ibid., 273.
53. Ibid., 228.
54. Ibid., 228, 231.
55. William Alexander, *Film on the Left: American Documentary from 1931 to 1942* (Princeton, NJ: Princeton University Press, 1981), 296.
56. Julianne Burton, "The Camera as "Gun": Two Decades of Culture and Resistance in Latin America," *Latin American Perspectives* 5, no. 1 (1978): 59.
57. Ibid., 60.
58. Bill Nichols, "Newsreel, 1967–1972: Film and Revolution," in *Show Us Life: Toward a History and Aesthetics of the Committed Documentary*, ed. Thomas Waugh (Metuchen, NJ: Scarecrow, 1984), 135.

59. Michael Renov, *The Subject of Documentary* (Minneapolis: University of Minnesota Press, 2004), 8.
60. Nichols, "Newsreel, 1967–1972: Film and Revolution," 137.
61. Renov, *The Subject of Documentary*, 138.
62. Ibid.
63. See Martha Rosler, "In, Around, and Afterthoughts (On Documentary Photography)," in Marth Rosler, *Martha Rosler: 3 Works* (Halifax, Canada: Press of the Nova Scotia College of Art and Design, 1981), and Allan Sekula, "Dismantling Modernism, Reinventing Documentary," *The Massachusetts Review* 19, no. 4 (Winter 1978): 859–883.
64. Martha Rosler, "A Case for Torture Redux," *Jump Cut* no. 51 (Spring 2009), https://www.ejumpcut.org/archive/jc51.2009/Rosler/text.html.
65. Chuck Kleinhans, "Forms, Politics, Makers and Contexts: Basic Issues for a Theory of Radical Political Documentary," in *Show Us Life: Toward a History and Aesthetics of the Committed Documentary*, ed. Thomas Waugh (Metuchen, NJ: Scarecrow, 1984), 320.
66. Chuck Kleinhans, "Forms, Politics, Makers and Contexts: Basic Issues for a Theory of Radical Political Documentary," 320–21.
67. Ibid., 323.
68. Nichols, *Introduction to Documentary*, 101.
69. Helen de Michiel and Patricia Zimmermann, "Documentary as Open Space," in *The Documentary Film Book*, ed. Brian Winston (London: British Film Institute, 2013), 358.
70. It has variously been dubbed "database documentary," "participatory documentary," "web documentary," "interactive documentary," "i-docs," "cross-media documentaries," and "docuwebs."
71. Stefano Odorico, "Documentary on the web between realism and interaction; A case study: *From Zero—People Rebuilding Life after the Emergency* (2009)," *Studies in Documentary Film* 5 (2011): 236.
72. Ibid., 241.
73. Hart Cohen, "Database Documentary: From *Authorship* to *Authoring* in Remediated/Remixed Documentary," *Culture Unbound* 4 (2012): 328.
74. Massumi, "The Thinking-Feeling of What Happens," 2.
75. Ibid., 13.
76. Ibid., 14.
77. Lev Manovich, *The Language of New Media* (Cambridge, MA: MIT Press), 35.
78. See Bhaskar Sarkar and Janet Walker's recently edited collection, *Documentary Testimonies: Global Archive of Suffering*.
79. Kate Nash, "What Is Interactivity For? The Social Dimension of Web-Documentary Participation," *Continuum: Journal of Media and Cultural Studies* 28, no. 3 (2014): 383–395.
80. Jessica Clark and Pat Aufderheide, "Public Media 2.0: Dynamic, Engaged Publics," *Washington: Center for Social Media* (February 2009): 6–7. http://cmsimpact.org/sites/default/files/documents/pages/publicmedia2.0.pdf.
81. Daniel Marcus, "Documentary and Video Activism," in *Contemporary Documentary*, ed. Daniel Marcus and Selmin Kara (New York: Routledge, 2016), 191.
82. Mandy Rose, "Not Media About, But Media With," in *iDocs: The Evolving Practices of Interactive Documentary*, ed. Judith Aston, Sandra Gaudenzi, and Mandy Rose (New York: Wallflower), 52.
83. Ibid., 63.
84. Ryan Watson, "Interview with Sharon Daniel," *Studies in Documentary Film* 13, no. 3 (2009): 283.
85. Ibid.

86. See http://vectors.usc.edu/issues/6/bloodsugar/.
87. See http://www.jnow.org/. California has seen the largest expansion of prisons and mass incarceration in the United States in the past seventy years.
88. Sharon Daniel, "On Politics and Aesthetics: A Case Study of *Public Secrets* and *Blood Sugar*," Studies in Documentary Film 6, no. 2 (2012): 218.
89. "American prisons are hell. For women, they're even worse," PBS News Hour, November 28, 2018, https://www.pbs.org/newshour/show/american-prisons-are-hell-for-women-they re-even-worse.
90. Ibid.
91. Because she partnered with Justice Now, Daniel was able to have the group designate her as such an advocate and allowed her access, though she still had to abide by what she terms "Kafkaesque regulations" and invasive search procedures and surveillance of her conversations.
92. Sharon Daniel, "New Media Documentary: Technology and Social Inclusion," YouTube, accessed December 2, 2020, https://www.youtube.com/watch?v=JiHBxCDleus.
93. Sharon Daniel, "Public Secrets: Authors Statement," *Vectors: Journal of Culture and Technology in a Dynamic Vernacular*, 2 no.2 (2007), http://vectors.usc.edu/projects/index.php?project=57&thread=AuthorsStatement. Daniel appropriates the term "public secrets" from Michael Taussig. See Michael Taussig's *Defacement: Public Secrecy and the Labor of the Negative* (Stanford, CA: Stanford University Press, 1999).
94. Ruth Wilson Gilmore, "Abolition Geography and the Problem of Innocence," in *Futures of Black Radicalism*, ed. Theresa Gaye Johnson and Alex Lubin (New York: Verso, 2017), 237. See also Ruth Wilson Gilmore, *Golden Gulag: Prisons, Surplus, Crisis, and Opposition in Globalizing California* (Berkeley: University of California Press, 2007) for a wider account of the violence of the prison industrial complex.
95. Daniel, "Public Secrets: Authors Statement."
96. Sharon Daniel, "The Public Secret: Information and Social Knowledge," *Intelligent Agent*, 6 no. 2, http://www.intelligentagent.com/archive/Vol6_No2_community_domain_daniel.htm.
97. See Fredric Jameson, "Politics of Utopia," *New Left Review* 25 (2004): 35–54 and Angela Y. Davis, *Are Prisons Obsolete?* (New York: Seven Stories, 2003).
98. Daniel, "On Politics and Aesthetics: A Case Study of *Public Secrets* and *Blood Sugar*," 215.
99. Daniel, "The Public Secret: Information and Social Knowledge."
100. Daniel prefers the term *database documentary* to describe her work.
101. See Jacques Rancière, *Dissensus: On Politics and Aesthetics*, trans. Steven Corcoran (London: Continuum, 2010).
102. Daniel, "On Politics and Aesthetics: A Case Study of *Public Secrets* and *Blood Sugar*," 216.
103. See http://www.7amleh.org/ms/.
104. Davis, *Freedom Is a Constant Struggle: Ferguson, Palestine, and the Foundations of a Movement*, 8.
105. Jess Linington, "Points of View: Putting Occupied Territories on the (Interactive) Map," *i-Docs.org*, September 10, 2014, http://i-docs.org/points-of-view-putting-occupied-territories-on-the-interactive-map/.
106. Sarah Stein Kerr, "Interactive Documentary 'Points of View' Showcases Citizen Video in Gaza and the West Bank," *Witness.org* (blog), February 2015, http://blog.witness.org/2015/02/interactive-documentary-points-view-showcases-citizen-video-gaza-west-bank/.
107. Ibid. See also Robert Mackey, "Israel Tampered with Video Strike That Killed Two Palestinian Boys, Investigators Say," *Intercept*, December 18, 2019, https://theintercept.com/2018

/12/19/israel-airstrike-gaza-two-boys/. Forensic Architecture recently released a video that proves Israel manipulated video evidence of an airstrike that killed the two teen boys in Gaza.

108. Sarah Stein Kerr, "Interactive Documentary 'Points of View' Showcases Citizen Video in Gaza and the West Bank."

109. The project uses custom-coded versions of the applications Python, HTML 5, and WebGL.

110. See http://i-docs.org/points-of-view-putting-occupied-territories-on-the-interactive-map/.

111. Kathleen Stewart, "Arresting Images," in *Aesthetic Subjects*, ed. Pamela R. Matthews and David McWhirter (Minneapolis: University of Minnesota Press), 431.

3. Amateur Counterarchives in Iraq

As THE FIRST heavily documented and mediated international conflict after 9/11, the most recent Iraq War and the plethora of documentaries produced about it was the focus of sustained critical attention, particularly in the five years after the initial invasion in 2003. In the field of documentary studies, much of this attention focused on the political functions of such images and the novel ability to hear from Iraqi citizens about the effects of war and occupation on their lives, as it occurred, in opposition to US and Western global media fictions. Film scholars Charles Musser and Malcolm Turvey, for example, in special issues of the journals *Framework* in 2007 and *October* in 2008—both devoted to artistic, media, and film responses to the war—delineated similar lists of the various phases of these initial documentaries, which include a period of "representing the Iraqi" films directed almost solely by Western filmmakers.[1] These films, including *My Country, My Country* (dir. Laura Poitras, 2005), *The Blood of My Brother* (dir. Andrew Bernard, 2005), and *Iraq in Fragments* (dir. James Longley, 2006), are bold, earnest, and mostly successful attempts to represent the lives of Iraqis under occupation and in the midst of war. But they are rendered and filtered through the perspective of white professional filmmakers. However, these films, Turvey argues, are highly unique in that they allow the viewer access to what Iraqis actually "think and feel" about the war, "*while it is happening*, something that is unprecedented in both the history of cinema and warfare."[2] What is more remarkable and important but went much less noticed was the emergence of independent documentary filmmaking done by Iraqi citizens through the Baghdad-based Independent Film and Television College (IFTC) between 2004 and 2012. These short, amateur documentaries, many resembling home movies, were distributed throughout Iraq and globally in festivals, galleries, universities, on the internet; some were even attached to one of the early DVD releases of Longley's Academy Award–nominated *Iraq in Fragments*.[3]

This chapter analyzes the work of the IFTC and three short amateur documentaries made in conjunction with it: *Hiwar* (dir. Kifaya Saleh, 2005), *Let the Show Begin* (dir. Dhafir Taleb, 2005), and *A Candle for the Shabandar Café* (dir. Emad Ali, 2017). All three films, a form of "art under occupation," were made during and deal directly with the vagaries of the war and occupation as it occurred. Second, through the deployment of militant evidence by digital active witnesses, each engages with the necessity of artistic, documentary, and counterarchival practices as a means of healing a society in peril. The films considered in this chapter were shot during the end of 2004 through 2007. This period coincided with the first democratic elections in Iraq (January 2005), a referendum on the new constitution (October 2005), a US troop surge (January 2007), and escalating sectarian, insurgent, and terrorist violence. All three films were widely screened in festivals and other venues throughout the world and have been released internationally on DVD.[4] They express a mixture of tension, hope, and skepticism of the Iraqi citizen and Iraqi culture in the construction of a "new" Iraq. The IFTC training and their student filmmakers' uses of documentary coupled with widespread transmedia efforts in the wake of war and occupation also serve as models for groups like Abounaddara and Bidayyat, explored in the next chapter, and many other ordinary citizens, collectives, and media-training initiatives that seek to document and intervene in the wars and occupations that have intensified and spread in the region since the beginning of the US "war on terror" declared after 9/11.

Jane Gaines argued in 2007 in the aforementioned issue of *Framework* about the burgeoning group of Iraq war documentaries and the reclaiming of the importance of "the real" for documentary, particularly in antiwar and media activist efforts, saying, "These documentary works have been made against the backdrop of the fiction to end all fictions, that is, the fiction of the existence of weapons of mass destruction, the trumped-up excuse for U.S. mobilization to the Gulf, the most contradictory of situations in which an enemy is fabricated and evidence falsified as justification for making a region safe for the expansion of capital. An average of one hundred Iraqis now die every day. Documentary works to change any understanding of the Iraqi people as 'casualties of war.'"[5]

Documentary practices reassert the truth, subjectivity, and vital agency of the Iraqi citizen against the fictions, narratives of terror, and humanity-erasing military speak (i.e., "casualties of war") fed to US and global publics. When war, in one sense, is fought on the plane of images and narrative, antiwar media activist and documentary efforts, to function radically, must amass counterinformation, often reliant on digital active witnesses testifying to or documenting the realties they face. They do so to lay bare the material conditions of existence that are hidden from public discourse and historical records. Further, when they come directly from amateurs on the ground, the militant evidence produced gains currency and potency. The films and videos analyzed in this chapter would not normally be characterized as radical. They are fairly mundane in their content and form, comprised of depictions of everyday life by amateur filmmakers. This does not, however, deradicalize the gesture contained in the context of their production, which creates a visual testimonial counterarchive in the form of sounds, images, and stories of ordinary Iraqi's living under active US occupation.

IFTC courses were open to men and women from all walks of life. Yet, there is a certain privilege assumed when one has the time and means for filmmaking within such a perilous situation. Many of the films depict writers, artists, and intellectuals; additionally, some of the student filmmakers were part of or had access to these circles before they began making documentaries. While this does not render their point of view less valid than any other Iraqi, there is a feeling that for all the pioneering work the school has accomplished, the larger world gained a somewhat limited perspective on Iraqi life. The evocation of everyday life and banality in the idea of the "radically banal" in this chapter is not meant to convey a sense of universality of experience. Rather, it analyzes the work of emerging artists with the power (for the first time in their lives) to express themselves through filmmaking and distribute those representations to a global audience. This chapter thus explores a limited case of documentary representation and context in which banality functions as a radical response to extreme duress.

The IFTC films function as militant evidence in four ways, which have intertwined affectively and effectively radical functions. First they work to form what Paula Amad has called "counter-archives," which, in this context, create a record of a microperspective view of history and memory that both account for Iraq's past, document its present, and help to shape its emerging future.[6] In the wake of war and amid occupation, artists and filmmakers look to reorient the history that was derailed during Saddam's reign between 1979 and 2003 and during the initial phases of the war when massive official document, art, film, government, and media archives were destroyed. These counterarchives are also a challenge to the reconstruction of the official state archive, which is detailed in the first part of the chapter. As Ghaith Abdul-Ahad argues, "Artists are emerging from the atrophied, censorious Saddam years, from the distortions of taste provoked by state patronage and control and the horizons foreshortened by sanctions and are beginning to document what is around them."[7] Second, they foster new "public domains," spaces of recognition, empathy, and communication both globally and in Iraq through transmedia efforts of promotion, distribution, exhibition, and education.[8] Third, they serve a radical function in the specific time and context of their making and circulation, the "radically banal," an assertion of humanity amid the ruins of war. And finally, these radically banal films laid the groundwork for future and continued media development, protests, and the emergence of an independent Iraqi film culture. While Iraq under the rule of Saddam Hussein had a thriving film industry, the state commissioned and sanctioned all the films. There was no independent filmmaking culture, or easy access to cameras, celluloid, the internet, or digital video. This particular cultural context is necessary to understand the reception of the amateur documentary practices of the IFTC and the films made there by student filmmakers.

In Iraq, the idea of the radically banal is a reaction against the exploitative function of what filmmaker Jill Godmilow has termed "the pornography of the real" and serves an affirmative function.[9] Through the representation of the everyday in the midst of the constraints of violence and occupation made by filmmakers just awakening to the power of cinema, banality is a radical response hinging on the twin contexts of inchoate filmmaking culture and the aftershocks of war. With the spectacular, catastrophic visuality of Operation Shock and Awe, it is easy to forget the individual human lives so adversely and irreversibly affected by the destructive rationality and spectacle inherent to modern warfare.[10] As Paul Virilio reminds us, "War is a symptom of delirium operating in the half-light of trance . . . it can never break free from the magical spectacle because it's very purpose is to produce that spectacle."[11] Within this spectacle of Iraq in 2003, tightly managed by the mainstream global press, the self-representation of the everyday citizen in the form of amateur made documentary films had added resonance on two further registers: as microhistorical and political acts against both US occupation and the former status quo in Iraq, which had suffered oppressive censorship under Saddam. There is an entire generation of Iraqis occupied by the ideology, customs, and authoritarianism of Saddam Hussein and his ruling Baath party. Thus, the idea of art under occupation used to describe the IFTC films mentioned above has a dual function. It is a response against US military–inflicted devastation and occupation and the Baath-ified cult of personality around Saddam, which resulted in deeply propagandistic media and harsh penalties for speaking out against the regime and represents an occupies a prominent place Iraqi consciousness and historical memory.

To frame the arguments outlined above, this chapter first examines the history and activities of the IFTC, the destruction of the Iraq National Library and Archive (INLA) in 2003, and the media and political culture that has arisen since the dissolution of the IFTC in 2014. Next, it explores the concept of what Alisa Lebow calls the "first person political," which is especially potent in the case of Iraq—which became a more open space for expression after the fall of the regime—and relies on its amateur status, everydayness, and use of digital active witnesses and testimony for its currency.[12] In addition is a brief examination of Abbas Fahdel's five-hour-and-thirty-four-minute documentary, *Homeland: Iraq Year Zero* (2015), a masterful use of first person politics and politicization of the everyday in Iraq, while John Greyson's *14.3 Seconds* (2009) is read as illuminating both the contradictions of Iraq's fragmented cultural archives and the importance of archival images to the narration of history. Later in the chapter, theoretical and philosophical considerations of the archive, witnesses, and testimony as well as historiography are used to analyze the contribution of the IFTC films to post-Saddam Iraq and the global community.

First Person Political: Amateurs, Microhistories, and the Archive

The IFTC was cofounded when London-based, expatriate, independent filmmakers Kasim Abid and Maysoon Pachachi returned to their native Iraq among the remnant shards and detritus of the US Operation Shock and Awe bombings, which inaugurated the Iraq war. "Art under occupation is a matter of survival," argues Pachachi. "The world is being fragmented and unmade, and you need a way to think about what is going on, using the camera as a means of discovery. You then put the images together to construct something from the shards of experience."[13] Art, in this case, is neither a luxury, a leisure-time pursuit, nor a reaction to complex philosophical or art-historical questions that have little to do with lived reality. In a world that has become fragmented and violent, art functions as a means of survival. Both Abid and Pachachi had extensive experience holding filmmaking courses in a situation of occupation and daily violence, having taught in Palestine between 1994 and 2003.[14] The impetus for the IFTC emerged from both a lack of representation of ordinary Iraqi citizens in Western media and a bursting forth of creative energy repressed under Saddam Hussein. "I was very struck during the first Gulf War," Pachachi says, "when I was watching hours and hours of media coverage. You never saw one ordinary Iraqi person expressing an opinion. And there are so many stories in Iraq, and so many years of being silenced."[15] The story of war is often told in statist narratives, erasing the material effects on everyday people. The IFTC successfully trained film and media makers to counter that erasure in a period of destruction years before the globalized, networked digital age had fully emerged.

The IFTC was a free-of-charge, nonprofit film school for burgeoning Iraqi independent filmmakers. Its funding came exclusively through donations from individuals, private charities, such as the Heinrich Böll Foundation and the Open Society Institute, and trade unions, such as the Actors Equity Union in the United Kingdom. "We set ourselves up as a UK nonprofit company," Pachachi says. "We decided not to rely on any institution or state money. We want to try to remain independent and the Iraqi state is not one that we have been particularly keen to be involved with."[16] Initial seed money came in the form of a $22,000 grant from the California-based NGO Internews, which has been active for nearly thirty years supporting independent media projects throughout the world.[17] More consistent funding for the IFTC was harder to come by, and each set of courses and other projects were funded on a per case basis. Each course ran between one and three months and covered everything from the basic technical aspects of filmmaking to more advanced work in documentary and fiction production. Given the circumstances in which the courses were being held, under active US military occupation and fighting, simply attending them held extreme peril for many students. In early 2006, for example, a series of explosions blew out all the windows of the school. On another occasion a student was kidnapped from inside the building.[18]

A series of mortar attacks near the school later that year and ever-increasing numbers of street closures, curfews, and roadblocks made it virtually impossible for students to attend classes. Pachachi and Abid were forced to relocate the school to Damascus, Syria in early 2007, eventually reopening in Baghdad in early 2009.[19] Though the physical school was in peril for nearly two years, the work of international distribution and transmedia advocacy and attention for both the school and the films increased. In March and April of 2008, Abid and Pachachi traveled to the United States for a variety of screenings and panel discussions, including the Montalvo Arts Center in Saratoga, California, as part of the IRAQ: REFRAME program, which sought to reconfigure the dialogue regarding the war, and Iraq as a whole, through programs presenting various artistic practices and life stories of Iraqis living under occupation.[20] In addition, extensive discussion and screening sessions were held in New York City at Columbia University, the Open Society Institute, the Pomegranate Gallery, and, most notably, New York University's Tisch School of the Arts cinema department, which loaned the school books and video equipment and created a partnership for Iraqi students to enroll in intensive summer filmmaking courses.[21] Enrollment continued into 2012, and the website for the school was active until 2014, but the IFTC has since been closed.

Beyond chronicling an extreme situation of war and occupation, what importance does the amateur or home movie status endow on the IFTC films? The scholarly attention the amateur or home movie has received in recent years encompasses three threads of engagement that are germane to considering amateur documentaries in Iraq: the status of such films as historically important forms of microhistory; the supposed authenticity and truthfulness of such films; and their ability to function politically as a form of visual history. As Liz Czach argues, "Amateur moving images are an important part of a country's visual heritage . . . and take on a particularly strong resonance in countries where more mainstream forms of filmmaking . . . have been found wanting or absent."[22] In Iraq, strict censorship and wide propagandistic use of the media and films during the Saddam years left a gaping cultural void and a lack of personal self-representations of everyday life.

As home movies and amateur films, these types of self-representations are the most "suitable filmic document to study 'history from below,' as proposed by microhistorical approaches," argues Efrén Cuevas, which privilege the scale of subjective and material effects of historical circumstances rather than grand narratives.[23] Further, Zimmermann has argued that amateur filmmaking can be "an active, constantly changing historiographic practice that creates . . . collaborations and convergences across borders of nations, identities, genders, ethnicities, races, sexualities, and politics" and "acts of mourning for those who have passed, markers of loss and trauma."[24] This is reflected in films such as *Hiwar*, which memorialize the loss of life and archival destruction of the war in the openness of the IFTC to all genders regardless of ethnic group (Sunni, Shia, Kurdish) or class and in the IFTC's transmedia practices that brought students and their films across Iraq and the globe to museums, universities, and film festivals. Finally, these films offer a radically banal and microhistorical view of the war and occupation that was absent from contemporaneous media accounts and official narratives.

Aditionally, the amateur IFTC films work as forms of what Alisa Lebow calls the "first person political," which has emerged across the Arabic-speaking world in recent years in the wake of wars, conflicts, uprisings, and occupations that have engulfed these regions in the post-9/11 era. In these overmediated spaces of global crises, Lebow argues that within the first person political is "an embodied and integrated politics, where the filmic strategy itself—of placing the filmmaker at the center of the revolutionary metaphor . . . through the filmmaker's personal/political incursions . . . is a way of enacting the political."[25] In Iraq, amateur filmmakers act as digital active witnesses to politically intervene in their world. Moreover, Lebow emphasizes the idiosyncratic "conditions of political engagement" filmmakers face in a given context, which shape the production and reception of such films.[26] The idea of conditions of political engagement guides this chapter, particularly in regard to the idea of the radically banal, a context-specific response to Operation Shock and Awe and occupation. These conditions shift over time in Iraq due to a renewed commitment to independent media and filmmaking. In the years following the initial invasion and occupation, the use of social media becomes a conduit for global communication, information consumption, and recently the basis for political protest, broadening both the conditions and possibilities of political engagement. These are discussed later in the chapter after analyzing the IFTC films. But first, an analysis of Fahdel's *Homeland: Iraq Year Zero* as a recent and illuminating first person political use of home movies from Iraq. This is followed by Greyson's *14.3 Seconds* to foreground the fraught and open nature of archives and narratives in Iraq after the war.

Abbas Fahdel's *Homeland: Iraq Year Zero* (2015) is an epic version of the first person political—a two-part documentary that spans more than five-and-a-half hours. Fahdel, who was living in France in 2002 as the rumbles of war against Iraq began in earnest in the United States, decided to fly home to Iraq to document the life of his middle-class extended family residing in a residential area of Baghdad. Fahdel filmed more than one hundred and twenty hours of footage on a small, consumer-grade camera in 2002 and 2003. The film functions as both a personal home movie that documents Fahdel's family before and after war and occupation and a first person political account and searing critique of that war and occupation. We witness a radically banal depiction of life amid ruins with all its surreal disorientation and gripping anxiety of possible violence lurking around every corner. In the final minutes of its staggering runtime, and just as the viewer may be getting ready for a sense of closure with the narrative and family, an unknown, unseen gunman kills Fahdel's twelve-year-old nephew, Haidar, a vivacious presence throughout the film. Two of his cousins were later killed in the same manner. Haidar's death is the reason Fahdel abandoned the footage for ten years; he did not return to edit it into a film until 2013. The full shock of the moment takes some time to register with the audience, as the death is so unexpected. Yet, it provides a macabre though potent representation of the senseless violence that enveloped Iraqi citizens during the occupation and the profound effects of that violence.

Part one of the film, shot in February 2002, begins with warm and familial scenes of a typical Baghdad family relaxing in their home. As the children watch cartoons on television and music videos on their computers, the adults take in soccer matches and pro-Saddam news propaganda. In street scenes, the markets are full of food and customers. Fahdel's family also visits the bustling al-Muttanabi Street, where merchants line the sidewalks with books, many photocopied. The street is a locus for intellectuals, journalists, and writers. Part one portrays a thriving if not mundane middle-class life, but Fahdel also inserts some political content that foreshadows the tragedies to come. Near the end of part one, Fahdel's family visits the commemoration site for the February 13, 1991, US bombing of the al-Amiriyah shelter during the first Gulf War, which killed more than four hundred civilians. The blown-out roof and some of the structure have been preserved and turned into part of a museum. Photos of charred corpses, including children, line the walls. This is a trauma seared into the memory of Iraqi citizens, many still suffering the effects of the embargo imposed after the first Gulf War, which was little mentioned in Western news media at the time. Haidar narrates his shock as he views the images, relaying that the bodies were torn apart by the explosives, unaware he will soon be the victim of war himself. Part one ends on March 20, 2003, the day the United States began bombing Baghdad and inaugurating the second Iraq War.

Part two, "After the Battle," resumes in April 2003, two weeks after the initial bombing and invasion by US and allied troops. Helicopters whir overhead, convoys of US Army trucks patrol the highways, and many of the main Baghdad streets have been blocked off by military police, creating a maze of checkpoints. Fahdel films a series of tracking shots from inside his uncle's car that depict the rampant destruction of buildings, many reduced to rubble. Haidar describes the situation of seeing US soldiers all around the city: "They are free to do what they want. They are occupiers and we cannot oppose them . . . our country has become like Palestine." Many of life's rhythms continue, such as going to school and running errands, but it is done amid a constant troop presence. Fahdel's brother-in-law worked at a local radio station for thirty years, and it was bombed to ruins. We also meet a man whose family's house (as well as that of his neighbors) was bombed, leaving them homeless and with no authority to appeal to for aid or shelter.

While these specific bombings are not at the magnitude of the al-Amiriyah massacre of the previous war, their representation by Fahdel makes an effective political statement that what is glibly written off as "collateral damage" has profound effects on the lives of innocent people. Back at the family house, there have been changes as well. The Fahdels, like many other families, have set up satellite dishes, which were banned under Saddam, and now stream news and entertainment from Arab and European providers. All of a sudden, the television brims with sex, violence, advertisements, and English-language programming. In the realm of news, there used to be three main newspapers, now Iraqis choose from over fifty from around the world. At school, the children have begun removing images of Saddam from their textbooks. One of Haidar's sisters relays the contradiction they face: "The United States liberated us from Saddam, but now they occupy our country." One authoritarian ruler has been replaced by another. To underscore the point, later in part one, as the family watches the World Trade Center towers fall on 9/11 during an al-Jazeera documentary, Fahdel's uncle sums up how it has affected the globe: "It's those two towers whose collapse caused the disintegration of many universal values." The massive ripples are still being felt throughout the Middle East today.

While the media culture of the country was renewed and expanded, Iraqi cinema and its film archives were in ruins. Toward the middle of part two, Fahdel travels to the Ministry of Information building, where the Office of Cinema and Theater was located. The building was heavily bombed and destroyed by fire. Iraqi actor Sami Abdul Hameed joins Fahdel at the Ministry and later at the Baghdad Cinema Studios and Film Archive, which had also been destroyed. There, Hameed pokes amid the rubble of half burned celluloid cannisters, old props, and costumes. At one point, Hameed finds a hat that he wore in the film *The Great Question / Al mas'ab al-kubra* (dir. Mohamed Shukri Jameel, 1983), in which he played Sulayman, a Nationalist Leader who kills Colonel Leachman (played by Oliver Reed), a colonial governor in the British occupation of Iraq in 1920. As he holds the celluloid remains of an unnamed film, Hameed asks, "Is this Iraqi cinema? Is this our heritage?" Hameed asserts that this destruction of the archive both prevents future generations from experiencing historical films and representations of censorship and repression of the Saddam years as well as the destruction of possible evidence of crimes left in documentary footage. It also speaks to the question of who gets to tell the narrative of history. The archive is conceived of as a way to accumulate and store facts that undergird the truths of these narratives. Yet, when it is exploded and ruined, made up of traces and fragments, the archive is up for grabs; anyone can stake a claim to its meaning or use the shards to construct new meanings and new histories.

The fragmentary oblivion left of Iraq's archives is the main concern of Canadian video artist John Greyson's short, experimental documentary/fiction hybrid *14.3 Seconds* (2009). Greyson's film, which originated as an installation piece, centers on eight scraps of film celluloid totaling 14.3 seconds. Greyson procured the footage from a journalist friend who had been covering the invasion of Iraq and had occasion to visit the ruins of the same studios and archive seen in *Homeland: Iraq Year Zero*.[27] While there, the unnamed journalist grabbed some scraps of celluloid and brought them home to Canada. Eventually, the scraps were identified as having come from two films: the aforementioned *The Great Question* and *al-Qadisiyya* (dir. Salah Abu Seif, 1982). All of these aspects of the film are factual. It is what Greyson does with the clips when the fictions begin to take shape. After watching the clips of the films in their entirety, the viewer is informed that they are part of a larger "Iraq Coalition Archive Restoration Project" (ICARP), which is headed by the fictional Lieutenant Ron Brocha of Wichita, Kansas, and Salah al-Shami from Tikrit, who serves as the main translator. We are told that they and their team have been able to complete some initial restorations on three (actual) films: *Cairo-Baghdad / al-Qahira-Baghdad* (1945), *al-Qadisiyya,* and *The Long Days / al-Ayyam al-Tawila* (1980).

Yet, when the supposedly restored portions of these films are presented, they are just the aforementioned 14.3 seconds of footage, played on a loop and adorned with new titles, directorial credits, and plot descriptions. As the footage plays, captions describe the action we are supposedly seeing accompanied by a unique musical score. Further, Greyson often presents portions of the text that he displays as redacted (blacked out) while also purposefully mistranslating words, titles, names, and descriptions. Peter Limbrick argues that through these strategies, "*14.3 Seconds* engages the history of secrecy around the practices of Iraqi occupation by evoking the archive's capacity to stymie transparency and to generate instead multiple readings."[28] It also, he contends, speaks to Greyson's own queer and outsider status to these film fragments. Beyond these compelling interpretations, the film also speaks to the desire of having the archive signify something of historical or cultural significance. When held by governments and powerful interests, archives reflect sanctioned narratives and historiography. In the hands of those outside those interests, the archive can signify new and emergent ways. This is shown in Saleh's *Hiwar* and Taleb's *Let the Show Begin*, where a combination of witnesses, testimonies, and uses of the archive allow artists and filmmakers to dislocate historiography.

Witness, Testimony, and Dislocated Historiography

Saleh's twelve-minute documentary, *Hiwar*, focuses on the Hiwar Center in Baghdad and its founder, artist Kasim Sebti. The film literalizes tensions between history, archive, and memory by combining interviews, archival photographs, and direct cinema-style shots of the center to portray the complexity and necessity of art under occupation. The Hiwar Center was founded in 1992 as a meeting place for artists and intellectuals and as a makeshift gallery for the artists to display their works. As Dr. Hamoody Jasim, a patron of the center, asserts, "In the 1990s the Hiwar Center was a lung through which intellectuals could breathe. Writers and painters met there, and it was the first gallery to encourage Iraqi art." Besides being a gallery, the center serves as an informal archival storehouse for a range of Iraqi artworks. In an early sequence, we watch Sebti moving through a series of small rooms containing row upon row of artworks in different mediums. In voice-over, Sebti informs us that the center has "a storehouse of sculptures, paintings, and other works—the work of professional artists and work by younger artists which deserves attention, so we hold an exhibition almost every month." All in all, the center holds about four hundred works in various mediums, from the pioneers of Iraqi art to the works of the newer and younger artists. In the most striking sequence of the short video, Sebti sits among a pile of scraps of paper and refuse while he measures a piece of cardboard. In voice-over, Sebti comments that Iraqis thought the Iraq-Iran war would last for only two years, but it went on for eight. "So," he says, "I began to see my role as a social one." After a cut to a close-up of his face, he asserts, "I was a witness." The role invoked by Sebti as a witness giving testimony rearticulates his place as a subject able to speak for those who cannot.

The archive, as well as the role of witnesses and testimonies, has been a concern to philosophers and theorists since the horrors of World War II. As Giorgio Agamben contends in regard to Michel Foucault's archival logic, "The archive's constitution presupposed the bracketing of the subject ... and was founded on the subject's disappearance into the anonymous murmur of statements. In testimony ... the empty place of the subject becomes the decisive question."[29] This testimony occurs in a new space "outside the archive and the *corpus* of what has already been said."[30] "Bearing witness" argues Jacques Derrida, "is always to render public."[31] Bearing witness in this manner necessarily makes testimony a public act, yet the ability to testify also has its roots in a singular, personal experience that involves the instant. "I can only testify," Derrida contends, "in the strict sense of the word, from the instant when no one can, in my place, to what I do."[32] The thing that one is able to testify to, for Derrida, is a permanent secret. This secret is premised on the experience of subjectivity, what was felt and seen within an instance and is stored permanently. Because they cannot be verified empirically, the secret and the instant are bound together. The dialectic between secret/instant and public utterance thus moves testimony and bearing witness from acts of

Figure 3.1 Still from *Hiwar*.

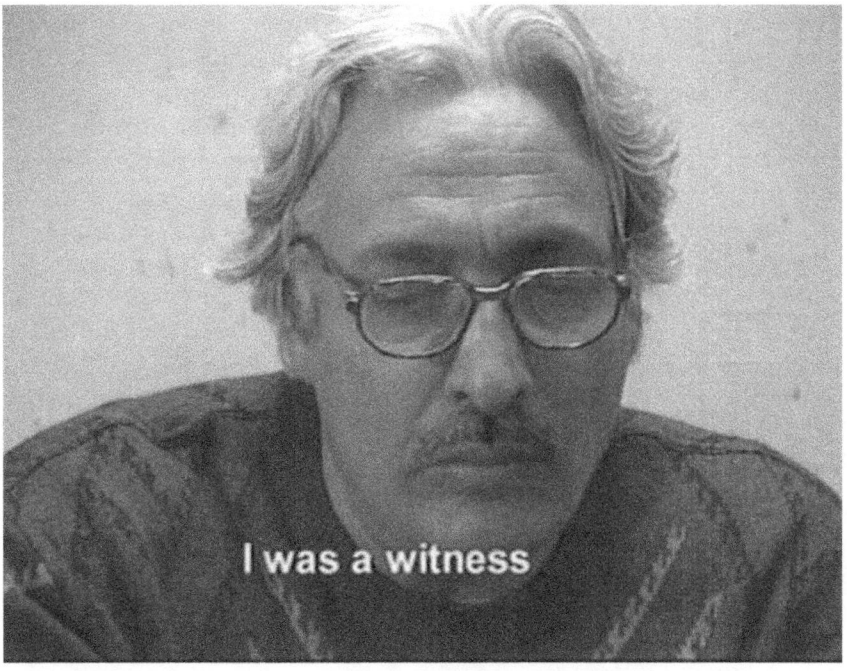

Figure 3.2 Still from *Hiwar*.

juridical importance to something more personal and never fully realized. To testify would be to inform someone of something. Yet, because it involves a secret, the knowledge conveyed to those who did not experience the exact same thing in the exact same way can only be incomplete. Witnesses can only testify on the condition that they survive. The testimony thus becomes irreplaceable—only survivors are able to relate their singular experiences.

In *Remnants of Auschwitz: The Witness and the Archive*, Agamben picks up on and extends many of the trains of thought that Derrida invoked. He chooses to use the term *vocation* to describe the duty of the survivor: "the survivor's vocation is to remember."[33] The idea of bearing witness to something missing "alters the value of testimony" significantly, forcing us to "look for its meaning in an unexpected way."[34] For these proxy witnesses, there exists a contradiction between what is said and what cannot be said fully—the impossibility of bearing witness to something for which one does not have language, for which one cannot articulate through language. Agamben begins to explore this contradiction through the figure of the archive and the enunciation of testimony. "In opposition to the archive," he writes, "which designates the system of relations between the unsaid and the said, we give the name *testimony* to the system of relations between the inside and the outside of *language*, between the sayable and unsayable . . . between a possibility and impossibility of speech."[35] Agamben reconciles this distinction by asserting that the relation between archive and language "demands subjectivity."[36] This subjectivity "appears as witness," allowing it to speak for those who cannot.

After a series of quick cuts to Sebti's hands as they manipulate the pages and scraps around him, we are confronted with a medium shot of Sebti sitting behind the larger pile. As the narrative moves into the present situation, Sebti invokes the burning of the libraries and archives in Baghdad, which provoked his current project: "My most recent work came out of my seeing the library of the Fine Arts Institute burning in front of my eyes." As the camera pans in close to reveal the piles of book covers, text, and scraps that litter the small room, Sebti describes his most recent project: "I started thinking about it all. These books, which had been shredded could be used to make art . . . I used the covers of old books which had been trodden underfoot or burned—the result was an unusual artwork." The next cut is to a medium shot of two pieces hanging on the wall in the gallery. One piece is a human-looking creature and the other is a relief collage in a frame. Both artworks are made from an amalgam of brown cardboard—ripped, glued, and expropriated. Sebti calls this project "The Mask of the Text." He suggests that the "book jackets, which used to cover these texts, are a kind of

Figure 3.3 Still from *Hiwar*.

mask concealing a great deal . . . the cover became the end product while the text remained under my feet, because I don't believe in a text, which cannot protect itself. The cover speaks of our bitter experience. It is a witness to the intentional burning of our libraries and cultural centers."

Sebti enunciates his testimony outside the archive and the corpus of what has been said while literally using the material of the archive to create new works of art and discarding the "what has been said" in the form of the pages of text as valueless—a transformative and productive reappropriation of the archival form and logic. The film concludes with shots of people reconstructing the Hiwar Center, which was bombed in 2004. An intertitle states that the Center received a grant from International Relief and Development to rebuild. Final shots show brick being laid, walls being knocked down, and beams being restored—a hope faintly revived in renewal and creation.

Walter Benjamin maintained a keen interest in the "hollowed-out" (*ausgehöhlt*) commodity form, especially the monuments to industrial capitalism, like the nineteenth century Arcades of Paris. His interest lay chiefly in the afterlife of these disused buildings and commodities. This chapter extends Benjamin's theory of memory and work on film to the IFTC documentaries produced in Iraq. In this context the topography is one of hollowed out buildings and disused spaces in which those who inhabit the land are hollowed out in the sense that sanctions, war, dictatorship, and the perpetual backdrop of daily extreme violence render the experience of the ordinary person moot. The extremity of the situation fragments the world of the everyday Iraqi to the point where experiences become atomized and meaningless. Shards of lives lived end up on heaps to be discarded, as if the person did not truly exist. Devoid of sentimentality, the documenting of lives across Iraq are a locus for constructing sites of shared experience and affect. It also constructs a new space for exchange and thought outside official state (Iraqi/US) narratives and sanctioned forms of televised media. The documentary film becomes an object made up of fragmented lives preserved for reflection and as an archive of memory and experience within a certain time and place: under occupation. Benjamin's theory of memory encompasses this detritus of material scraps and fragments of memory collected into a whole entity.

In Convolute N of *The Arcades Project*, Benjamin reconsiders the historiographical project by arguing for (and demonstrating in his writing technique) a montage approach to history.[37] This historical materialist approach provides for new angles of vision to counter rational, linear, positivist progression—an approach consistent with an emerging, irruptive, and transformative view of historical reality.[38] In film history, the concept of montage in documentary emerges in conjunction with Soviet radical film editing and filmmaking. Among its main tenets, and intimately tied to the intervention of the camera into everyday life, is Dziga Vertov's conception of the "kino-eye" elucidated in chapter 1. Here a notion of truth is achieved via the cinematic apparatus through its conquest and collapse of space and time and its visual linkage between bodies. The singularity of the kino-eye endows the individual filmmaker with an extraordinary power to both represent and erupt the present moment. "The movie camera," Vertov contends, "was invented in order to penetrate deeper into the visible world, to explore and record visual phenomenon, so that we do not forget what happens and what the future must take into account."[39] When filmmakers or digital active witnesses represent themselves and their reactions to a singular event, they add to a plethora of images, subjectivities, bodies, and approaches.

This visual linkage between bodies in a collision of images radically alters the linearity of history by creating a montage of multivalent perspectives patched together within different moments in time and across various spaces. In stark contrast to the reports of much of the Western media and governments, this approach offers a space for the pain and suffering of the event to come to life within a foregrounding of the present. The montage approach decenters the myth of linear progress and historical concepts of temporality. This concept of history allows for the stories and lives of the vanquished to be illuminated and heard. In this new historiographical form, history is constructed from the ruins and stray fragments left in the wake of destruction, not simply watched from afar in the reconstructive space of the state archive. Applied to film and video, the historical narrative is dislocated, actualized, and polyvalent. The patchwork of culture is sewn together to create a new counterarchive, a structuring and forming of historical disruptions. *Hiwar* explored the expropriation of archival material in the service of art, while the next IFTC film analyzed, *Let the Show Begin*, deals directly with the place of filmmaking as space of renewal, communication, and an archive of the present.

Let the Show Begin, a fifteen-minute documentary, portrays the behind-the-scenes preparations for the first ever Iraq Short Film Festival, which took place on September 28, 2005, inside the Magic Lantern children's theater in Baghdad. The idea for the festival grew out of discussions among the loose collection of 250 artists who comprise the Contemporary Visual Arts Society (CVAS) in Baghdad. The president of the society, Nizar al-Rawi, a graphic designer and art critic, spearheaded the festival. The film opens with tracking shots (filmed through the dirty window of a car) of street scenes marked by smoldering piles of refuse. As we confront these images, the setting for the festival is explained in voice-over: "We're putting on this festival in the middle of a war. Baghdad is like the trenches; barbed wire everywhere and curfews—or an explosion and everyone crouches behind sandbags." These scenes of war and its unpredictability, violence, and constraints on the lives of those living in its midst are sharply contrasted by the next shot of a car pulling into a gated building, the site of the upcoming festival.

Contrary to the destruction and disorder witnessed on the street, the secure building offers a site for creation and construction. In the next sequence, the electricity powered by a diesel generator begins to flow, as evidenced by the sudden illumination of a fluorescent light. Following this, we meet a series of unnamed workers who are responsible for design, photo restoration, and translation. All are shown performing the jobs they describe in voice-over, with emphasis on the materiality of their occupations. The photo restorer is seen at his computer digitally retouching a series of photographs

Figure 3.4 Still from *Let the Show Begin*.

documenting the cinema of Iraq from the 1940s through the 1970s, followed by a close-up of a restored production still. The poster and leaflet designers are shown printing, cutting, and producing in a workshop. In the next sequence, a man affixes a row of the aforementioned posters to a brick wall in Baghdad. In voice-over, one of the artists notes the objections to the festival: "People say, 'What are you doing at a time like this? Iraq's in political crisis with no security, this isn't the time for culture.'" As the voice-over continues, a shot of two men working to erect the main screen in the auditorium at the Magic Lantern is intercut into the sequence. The voice-over continues: "We do not agree—if you have something to offer, this is precisely the right time to do it, this moment of such political upheaval." The intercutting of the shot of the screen being erected amid this rebuttal to critics is particularly apt. It connotes both a screening out of the trauma of living in the midst of a war zone while also providing a material object for creativity, hope, and culture to be projected upon. The screen offers the promise of temporary relief and the possibility of cultural renewal amid upheaval—an inscription of a new form of history and a locus for the community to gather.

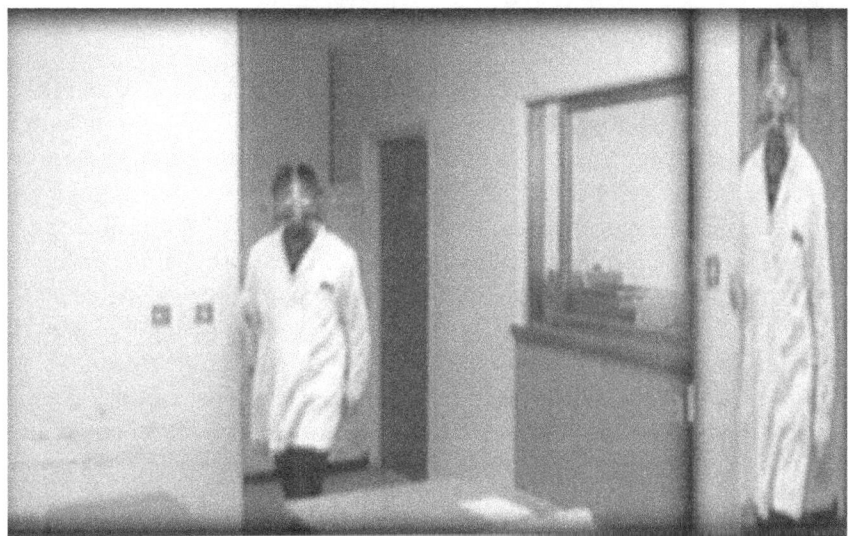

Figure 3.5 Still from *Let the Show Begin*.

The five days of the festival are portrayed through a series of shots of audience members filing into the auditorium and mingling among the restored photos of Iraq's cinematic history. These shots are intercut by two montages of brief moments from many of the fifty-eight films screened at the festival. The images shown in the montages run the gamut from explosions, people in the street, helicopters overhead, and children playing in ruined buildings to men fishing, an animated sequence of a boy with a ball, and a doctor wearing a gas mask. An elderly Iraqi artist comments, "We spent all our lives dreaming, not really hoping. We used to dream that we would realize something, be able to do something." Though a common trope, the montage sequence takes on more profound significance when contextualized within the current turmoil in Iraq as an act of archiving the new images of the present. It also gestures toward a new form of historiography, one culled from the multiple visual fragments of a society in transition. Premised on irruptions and fragments, this mode of historiography reorients vision and possibility, engendering a new and unbounded logic of possibility and agency—the promise that we "can do something" instead of simply dreaming. As Pachaci contends, "I think that for all of us Iraqis who are trying to make things—films, books, theater, whatever—what we do is perhaps an unconscious form of resistance against the destruction and fragmentation all around us."[40]

Counterarchives, Public Domains, and the Political

Much like the aforementioned destruction of the film archives on April 10 and 12, 2003, the Iraq National Library and Archive (INLA) was severely looted and burned, erasing thousands of years of cultural history. Saad Eskander, the current director of the INLA, estimates that 60 percent or more of the collections were stolen, burned, or otherwise destroyed: "Within the space of three days, the Iraq National Library and Archive lost a large portion of Iraq's historical memory. Hundreds of thousands of archival documents, historical records, and rare books were lost forever."[41] During the reign of Saddam Hussein, the INLA was reduced to a means of legitimizing the totalitarian state. As Eskander states, "The Ba'ath regime was backward and anti-modernist in its political, social, and cultural orientations. It opposed and abhorred multiculturalism, multi-ethnicity, peaceful coexistence, and solidarity among the nations. Culture and education were subjected to ideological needs."[42] Members of the Ba'ath party routinely monitored the activities of students and scholars who accessed the collections, which, unsurprisingly, deterred many people from studying them. In addition, the regime let the archival collections fall into disrepair long before 2003. The regime had no interest in maintaining a historical memory before their time in power began in 1979. Books, documents, photographs, and other archival materials became inert objects that were essentially cut off from the society at large and laid to rest in the tombs on the INLA. In fact, the Ba'ath regime's Minister of Culture, Hamid Yousif Hammadi, "publicly named the INLA the cemetery of books."[43]

Eskander has worked to reverse the totalitarian modes of thinking and reawaken a long abandoned historical memory as the reconstruction of the nation is imagined. He contends that "in the life of a new nation, like that of Iraq, national libraries and national archives can (and should) play a key role in the formation of national identity, true citizenship, and civil society. Such institutions can also play a constructive role in the dissemination of democratic, liberal, and humanistic values."[44] Eskander believes the fall of the Saddam regime left a large cultural vacuum, one in which the INLA has a major role to play in modernizing the country politically and religiously. Eskander hopes to engender a plural, liberal, and secular society that is progressive in its thinking and cultural values. "The new culture will help to put an end to the remnant of the totalitarian values and concepts that still dominate the minds, spirits, and behavior of a large number of Iraqis, including the educated, university students, and scholars."[45] He asserts that chief among the duties of the INLA in this period of rebuilding and modernization is the right of access for anyone to information, one of the chief aims of the de-Ba'athification of the archives. Eskander contends that "to build a new Iraq, you have to have access to the right information. Iraq cannot be built if you distort history or write history according to ideology. We must shed new light on our history and reconsider our past."[46] He is allowing all previously censored books and documents to be collected and is maintaining one or two copies of Ba'ath party documents for scholarly use.

The access to information is a hallmark of a well-functioning liberal society, and Eskander's efforts to modernize and democratize the INLA are certainly admirable. There is, however, a strain of show and tell that renders the everyday Iraqi citizen a passive spectator, occluded from the process of history making. "This war," he argues, "opened a new opportunity to *show* people a new society in a new state."[47] The status of the archive in Iraq is of one constantly being reconstructed to both reflect on past injustice and foment support for emerging values. History is being written and concretized in a self-conscious and new direction based on the status of the INLA as an official site of historical memory in the mode of Western nations. The "official" state archive is being reconstructed in an effort to both provide an account of Iraq's past history and engender support for emerging values.

As touched on earlier, the status of the archive as a site of historical memory, official repository, and material practice to legitimize the state within a metaphorical site of power has come under scrutiny by various critics. For Foucault, the archive is not a metadiscourse, nor is it the institution itself or the collection of documents attesting to narratives of state power and national values. It is, rather, polyvalent and specific, comprising the law of what can be said. He stresses the importance of the incomplete fragments and traces of history, an idea that decenters the locus of the archive. This decentering of the archive begets a decentered subjectivity. In this unstable position, one stands within the ever-emerging dynamic archive in a place of difference, rather than in a stable position before a linear and continuous mode of history.[48] For Derrida, the compulsion to collect and store in the face of an ever-receding memory and ultimately death (the death drive in Freud) is a pathology he names "archive fever" (*le mal d'archive*). The compulsion is not merely a will to compile and store as an accumulation of the past, but, Derrida contends, it encompasses a desire or promise for a future based on the aforementioned accumulation. Where Foucault's account of the archive is a consideration of the "law" and the limits set forth by regulatory mechanisms, Derrida posits the failure of regulations by rearticulating the ethical dimension of hermeneutics and rewriting history within a disjointed concept of the archive. In this anarchic scene of impressions and ever-receding memory, "the archive takes place at the place of originary and structural breakdown of the said memory."[49] As in Foucault, power manifests itself in control, in this case of the archive. As Derrida concludes, "There is no political power without control of the archive, if not of memory."[50]

When various artistic practices that are not part of the officially sanctioned historical memory proliferate, they engender new archives that are anomic or imaginary. These archives rearticulate memory and political power in a new modality that accounts for excised images and narratives in a new, unregulated system of legitimation. "These imaginary archives," explains Tess Takahashi, "often envision unrecorded pasts, produce other means of legitimizing information, make old systems signify differently, and imagine as yet undetermined futures through the evocation of everyday personal experiences of suffering, displacement, and loss."[51] The emphasis on personal experiences relies on a mode of self-archivization, a recording of one's experiences that relays the visceral within a specific space and temporality. The production of individual stories revolving around specific lives or local events represents the subject within a transmissible, visual mode—an archival trace of history that elicits the response of others.

What do the visual counterarchives provide that the largely document-based, official archive cannot? The archive is certainly a major concept, practice, and resource in twentieth-century art. There is an obsession, especially in the West, with thinking, practicing, and using the archive. This practice chiefly revolves around installation art in which the object itself becomes thematic. There is a heavy emphasis in these pieces on the interaction between the spectator and the work. Art reformulates the nature of viewing by reordering the notion of memory through a mode of questioning that destabilizes memory as written or recorded. Artists bring this destabilization of memory forth by employing the visual as a mnemonic device. This effect is especially realized through the redeployment of everyday objects—or in the case of film, images of everyday people. This visual mode produces counterarchives. This archive is dynamic yet unstable because moral and social codes have been eroded or abandoned and because the archive is produced by those who feel both alienated from society and disorientated by the perceived absence of a social or moral framework. It arises from a desire for the mnemonic in a time of duress, such as totalitarian rule, sanctions, war, or occupation in which human subjectivity has been destroyed. "Mnemonic desire," argues Benjamin Buchloh, "is activated especially in those moments of extreme duress in which the traditional material bonds among subjects, between subjects and objects, and between objects and their representation appear to be on the verge of displacement, if not outright disappearance."[52]

For Hal Foster, this mnemonic desire is appended by a grounding in materiality; the "archival artists seek to make historical information, often lost or displaced, physically present."[53] The creation of these types of archives runs counter to the official archive in that it reimagines the archive from the perspective of the disenfranchised subject who is able to speak only because the dominant social and moral codes have become dismantled and whose disorientation is a radical perspective that actively works to remake society from the fragments, shards, and detritus lying around them.

In terms of documentary filmmaking, the archive has recently come under consideration from a variety of critics. In her discussion of independent documentary films that engage explicitly with the archive and the experience of making sense out of traces and fragments of material, Jaimie Baron contends that they are responding to an "historiographic crisis," whereby "they inhabit and thematize the desire for coherent history confronted by the unruly vestiges of its passage."[54] The historiographic crisis is certainly evident in the current historical moment in Iraq. However, the drive to coherence must be explained within a mode of polyvalent, yet subjective, production marking a disruptive, decentered historiography. "The subject of documentary," Malin Wahlberg argues, "is not reduced to the implied therapeutic aspect of self-representation and introspection but offers a historical perspective on ways in which the representation of the self, matters to others."[55] In this way, the production of individual stories revolving around specific lives or local events represents the subject within a transmissible, visual mode—an archival trace of history that elicits the response of others. In intercultural films and videos especially, "the trace is not necessarily operating on the level of images and physical objects but in fragmentary signs of faces, sounds and reconstructed views, which are simultaneously linked to and separated from the past."[56]

Fragmented lives and bodies are sewn together within an eruption of the past into the present moment, forming an alternative telling of history that invokes an "ethos of narration that is related . . . to the possibility of poetic narration to give voice to historical experience, to impinge a microperspective on the linear axis of official history."[57] This microperspectival reinvention of history brought forth by filmmakers' and video artists' approach to historical experience reflects "the testimonial function and historical value of the moving picture as archive memory."[58] As Zimmermann asserts, "The materiality of the archive—texts, artifacts, documents—drives film and media history . . . its political urgency . . . can be mapped in these gaps and fissures: the structuring of the marginal and the inchoate, the chaotic and the untamable—practices which refuse the rules and therefore reveal the most about the disruptions of historical processes."⁵⁹ These disruptions revolve chiefly around the emergence of microhistories, militant evidence of ordinary, everyday people and places of Iraq that have experienced the direct effects of war and occupation.

Emad Ali's twenty-five-minute documentary, *A Candle for the Shabandar Café*, exemplifies a microhistorical view as it interweaves the destruction of the personal and the historical, illustrating Wahlberg's dictum of self-representation as important to others. It does this by chronicling the destruction of the Shabandar Café, founded in 1917, on the aforementioned al-Muttanabi Street in Baghdad, a center for bookstores and intellectual life. Ali's story encompasses his experience of the destruction of his home by mortar attack in December 2006, which killed his father and wife and burned much of his body. Ali had already shot preliminary material for his short documentary but had to take months off from filming. During this time in March 2007, a suicide bomb was detonated outside the café, destroying his filmic subject. When he went back to film after months of recovery from the mortar attack, he was ambushed and shot by two men and left to die on the side of the road.⁶⁰

Ali's film is composed of five distinct segments, differentiated by shifts in color and/or intertitles. The prelude opens with a rooftop view of al-Muttanabbi Street, confronting the viewer with a line of razed building façades and rubble.⁶¹ After the title screen, Ali switches to color for a series of shots of men reading, smoking, conversing, and drinking tea amid the bustling café. One patron, Shamsaldin al-Zahawi, posits the café as a kind of intellectual refuge, describing it as a place that "all kinds of intellectuals and older Baghdadis come. There are writers, poets, and composers of music. It's different from other cafés, there's no dominoes, backgammon, shouting or loud TV." Ali focuses his camera on faded, sepia-tinged photographs of old Baghdad, which are followed by a series of shots of al-Muttanabbi Street, jammed with book stalls, vendors, and people deeply engaged in reading and conversation. The prelude ends with an eruption of the present into the past. The viewer sees a medium close-up of the intact façade of the café. As the camera slowly pans left, the image dissolves into a black-and-white image of the destroyed building seen earlier. As counterhistorical, archival memories, these films function on a political register, especially in their depictions of the everyday lives, events, and places inhabited by Iraqi citizens. Wahlberg asserts that "a common trope in political documentary" is "the shaky street scene representing a *true* image of the past, the trace turning into a revolutionary sign."⁶² The revolutionary sign and potentiality lie not in the image itself but rather in what they represent and transmit to the viewer and the filmmaker. This reciprocity of witnessing and testimony is premised on the realism engendered by the "shaky street scene" and other images that invoke the ordinary, the "real."

Part One opens with black-and-white images of reconstruction paired with shots of former patrons praying outside the remains of the café. Yet, the mood quickly changes—and the images go back to color again. The viewer watches scenes of everyday life within the café: writers typing, staff washing glasses and preparing tea. Mohammad al-Ikhshali, owner of Shabandar, places the café in context, both geographically and politically. Historically the location of the café on al-Muttanabbi Street placed it steps from the center of government through the reign of the Ottomans, King Faisal, and Prime Minister Nuri al-Said, from the early to midtwentieth century. Al-Ikhshali informs us that the café, in those times, was a locus for union organizing in 1933 and for the radical political demonstration known the al-Wathbah uprising, or "Uprising of the Bridge," in 1948. The uprising was initially a response to the secret renewal of the 1930 Anglo-Iraqi Treaty, which tied Iraq's monarch and its land and economy to British interests. It eventually morphed into a demonstration against the stark inequality and lack of viable economic opportunity for the majority of Iraqi citizens.[63] According to al-Ikhshali students gathered in the café while being surrounded by Baghdad police. The interview is intercut with black-and-white images of destruction: a worker sweeping debris from the second floor of the destroyed building followed by a medium close-up of single lit candle affixed to the crumbling wall. Ali cuts to an interview with another patron, Fadhil al-Khayat, who continues the line of political engagement into the present day by criticizing US occupation: "Here I am," he says, "in the Shabandar café, telling the story of American 'democracy' and that of those they brought with them." The section ends with a long shot of two men talking at a café table in the lower frame, which is dominated by a large wall of archival photos and objects above them.

Part Two concludes the films' primary focus on the café. A first intertitle informs us of the suicide car bombing on March 4, 2007, which killed twenty-six and wounded fifty-four people while destroying the café and much of the street. A second intertitle informs us that the owner of Shabandar, Mohammed Al-Ikhshali, lost a son and four grandchildren in the bombing. The intertitle is followed by somber shots of a number of patrons and al-Ikhshali himself gathering outside the café for a makeshift memorial service. One patron, Abdul Satar, contends that "this place is the stream which feeds Iraqi culture . . . it is redolent of history. It's an illusion to think that people can be completely defeated . . . there is hope despite all the destruction."

Part Three shifts away from a focus on the café's destruction to the physical and emotional destruction present in the life of the filmmaker involved in the filmmaking process. Part Three opens with the simple intertitle: "The director of this film, Emad Ali, began shooting in the summer of 2006. In December a mortar bomb struck his house." For the rest of this section, we are confronted by Ali giving direct testimony of the events of December 2 intercut with images of his burnt, ruined home. Matter-of-factly, Ali tells us that "in the third hit, my father and wife were killed. I had burns all over my body." He invokes the occupation itself as barrier to immediate medical care: "there was a curfew that night—8pm—it was hard to get to the hospital, the one near us was surrounded by armed groups." Ali is left with only memories. "Nothing was left," he asserts, "it was all burned." His testimony is accompanied by a close up of two tattered, burnt pictures of his wife and father, the only remains from his home.

The epilogue brings us back to the explosion at the café and its function as a conduit for Ali to return to his film. Once again, an intertitle contextualizes the proceeding images by informing us that Ali picked up a camera for the first time in months to film the destruction of Shabandar. The first image is a medium close-up of Ali lying down on a bed—rather than being seated as in the previous section. The shot reveals that he is lying with his leg elevated, wrapped in a bandage, and held together by thick metal rods. He testifies that he was ambushed and shot in the leg, chest, and foot before being left "in the gutter for fifteen, twenty minutes" before anyone helped him. Two doctors tend to him by opening the wound's dressing to reveal a significant open gash in his leg. The film ends in black and white with a tracking shot of al-Muttanabbi Street before the suicide attack, full of books and people. Ali leaves us with a final image of the old, intact façade in black and white. All of these depictions implicate the viewer, enabling a perspective and experience that would otherwise be denied to them. This alterity allows for reflection, engagement, and the formation of human connection. This reciprocity of witnessing is premised on the realism brought forth by the representation of the everyday and other images that invoke the banal, the ordinary, "the real." As Bill Nichols posits, "Realism aids and abets empathy" and is "a form of visual historiography."[64] Realism works two ways in the political dimension: first, the portrayal of real bodies, mimetically reproduced before us, is an act of production and representation that allows for the affective engagement and involvement of the viewer. This experiential form is reinforced through a presentation of typicality. As Nichols argues, "Typicality . . . the affective engagement of the viewer with social tensions and pleasures, conflicts and values—move the viewer away from the status of observer toward that of participant. Something is at stake. Namely our very subjectivity within the social arena. The move beyond observation to experience . . . opens up a space for contestation."[65]

This space of contestation, a subjectivity engendered by participation is premised on a political type of phenomenology that, for Nichols, begets "a recognition of the priority of experience as the social ground for foundation for actual praxis. Central to this question is our experience of the body. Documentary film insists on the presence of the body."[66] It also lends vitality and individuation to the visual historiography, which defines the second dimension of the effect of realism in this political dimension. "The text locates on the person of its subjects," Nichols contends, "the tensions, conflicts, contradictions, and paradoxes of a historical moment, making them real, as though for the first time, because they are rendered with a specificity they never had before."[67] The complexity of the historical moment in and among the subjects (bodies) of documentaries grounds the paradoxes of historiography and competing claims. It projects them on the body and allows for an experience of the real premised on the experience of affect. This reciprocity of witnessing implicates the viewer in the experience of the event presented and begets an intersubjectivity as political provocation and archival assertion. Further, Lebow argues, drawing on a Jean Luc Nancy's notion of intersubjectivity melded with Jacques Ranciere's concept of dissensus, that "subjectivity is always intersubjective" and allows the first person political to "intervene in the distribution of the sensible" through new forms of engaging and perceiving the everyday as a form of disruptive political action.[68]

Imagined and deployed in the way Nichols and Lebow allude to, the urgent importance of digital active witnesses capturing militant evidence must be asserted as vitally important to the current historical moment. The very nature of the documentary—its subjects, its images, and its power—relies on a radical tradition not found in other forms of filmmaking or artistic practice. Documentary, as Jane Gaines contends, "uses the world to transform the world."[69] Documentary filmmakers and media activists occupy a unique and strategic position within the on-the-ground realities of the present historical moment: "Documentary makers are positioned is such a way that they see, with their attention to everyday life, things coming unraveled . . . where the probe of the contradiction then may be performed by ordinary people."[70] This new collection of militant evidence, composed of banal images, stories, and lives, can form counterarchives and new spaces of resistance premised on the recapturing of the political potential of the first person film.

Zimmermann names these emerging spaces of resistance, catalyzed by first person and collective media making, "public domains," relocating the term from one of juridical or proprietary connotations to one that is "more plural and beyond an exclusive focus on the fixity of the image and the artifact."[71] Public domain, in this pirated mode, revolves chiefly around the concept and practice of an inclusive and collaborative heterogeneity that "activates new ways of thinking, acting and connecting with others"—in other words, a space that allows for the creation of new publics.[72] In this context, the liminal space of the ordinary person is reimagined and recuperated. Especially with regard to Iraq, the restorative aspect of public domain rests in the idea of a place where "ideas and exploring new vectors and relationships replace panic, amnesia and anesthesia"—symptoms directly induced by the spectacle of Operation Shock and Awe.[73] As Pachachi asserts, "I think it's important for films like this to be made because this extraordinary time in Iraqi history needs to be documented in terms of people's understanding of what happens as a result of policies in various parts of the world."[74] In these ways, first person, amateur filmmaking in Iraq served as a creative and generative outlet for personal healing amid unimaginable trauma and as a form of urgent microhistory.

By the end of April 2011, the situation in Iraq had stabilized to the point that the IFTC was able to launch a traveling film festival throughout the country in the cities of Baghdad, Basra, and Ebril. By this point, the school had trained over one hundred filmmakers and had sixteen different student films to exhibit in each city. While the student films had already gained increased international attention, they had only rarely been shown to audiences in Iraq. Much like the conception of Third Cinema put forth by Getino and Solanas, Abid and Pachachi considered the screenings a conduit to a national dialogue forged through the possibilities of cinema: "We hope that these screenings will open a serious, honest dialogue about different aspects of Iraqi life and will encourage young Iraqis, men and women, to use the possibilities of cinema to express their personal thoughts, stories and feelings. At a time like this it is perhaps particularly important for all of us to tell our stories and to describe the world as we see it. And maybe this is a kind of resistance against the destruction that surrounds us."[75]

This resistance to destruction encompasses not only the physical remains of bombings and crumbling infrastructure. There was and continues to be a deterioration of human rights, particularly in regard to freedom of assembly and press and the rights of women. While the last US ground troops departed Iraq on December 18, 2011, the newly elected US-backed government of Nuri al-Maliki quickly filled the power void, sparking charges of corruption and police state tactics as his government violently dispersed protests, killed and imprisoned journalists, and set up secret prisons.

Emad Ali's second film, *Speak Your Mind* (2011), examines the detainment and kidnapping of three Iraqi journalists, directly engaging with this contemporary climate in Iraq. By January 2012, Human Rights Watch Mideast director Sarah Leah Whitson asserted that "Iraq is quickly slipping back into authoritarianism as its security forces abuse protesters, harass journalists, and torture detainees, despite U.S. government assurances that it helped create a stable democracy, the reality is that it left behind a budding police state."[76] While freedom of expression and intercountry dialogue were spurred on by the practice of documentary and its distribution, Abid and Pachachi felt that they could go a step further in using these same modes to insert ideas about contemporary human rights discourse into Iraq in light of this renewed space of political contestation.

Between February 25 and 28, 2012, the IFTC and the Iraqi Cultural Association partnered to launch Baghdad Eye Human Rights Film Festival, bringing together an array of international and Iraqi films dealing with key themes of women's rights, the rights of children and youth, and the right to freedom of expression and opinion.[77] The festival was first held at Baghdad University and showcased a variety of fiction and documentary films, including five documentaries specifically about Iraq. The success of the first iteration of screenings led organizers to hold the festival at universities in Basra, Najir, and Fallujah between February 29 and March 12. Abid viewed the festival through a didactic lens when he argued that "Baghdad Eye is the first ever attempt . . . in Iraq using the art of cinema to raise awareness to help people understand the concept of human rights which has been published in the (UN) Universal Declaration (of Human Rights) and to spread these themes of the declaration."[78] The festival thus kept the Iraqi citizenry informed of the effects of the deteriorating situation referenced above. It did this by inserting Iraqi human rights concerns and corresponding militant evidence into a prominent place in the global conversation while asserting the unique and invaluable place of documentary practice under extreme duress as a means of engaging an international audience. The discourse of human rights and the use of documentary as more explicitly political tools have emerged in Iraq. Unfortunately, the IFTC ceased operations in 2014, but Iraqi media, film culture, and activism have all become both more vital and more contested as they have adopted digital and social media.

Beyond the IFTC

In terms of film culture, the Iraqi Independent Film Center (IIFC) has taken up where the IFTC left off. First founded by filmmaker Mohamed al-Daradji in 2003, the IIFC has been operational since 2009. The center has offered a series of filmmaking classes and "its members describe it as an unrestricted space for critical thinking and filmmaking, with a focus on education, film production, and the promotion of Iraqi culture as its central pillars."[79] In the past ten years, the IIFC has produced more than fifteen short films and five features, which have been played at festivals throughout the world. In addition, while filming his feature *Son of Babylon* (2009) al-Daradji created a "Mobile Cinema Festival," which toured around Iraq showing IIFC productions. Finally, al-Daradji's recent film *Journey* was the first Iraqi made feature to play in a Baghdad theater since the reign of Saddam Hussein. Recently, film theatres have made a comeback in Baghdad, showing mostly Hollywood and Egyptian films. It is al-Daradji's and the IIFC's hope that this will be the first of many Iraqi made films within an emerging local film industry.

After the war and occupation in 2003, the media environment in Iraq quickly went from five tightly controlled propaganda sources to a wide-open market of more than two-hundred Iraqi owned outlets, including newspapers, television, and radio stations.[80] Benjamin Isakhan argues that the former experience with propaganda is a form of media literacy, and "this media literacy, coupled with the many independent Iraqi papers publishing freely across the nation ... is crucial in re-establishing a participatory and engaged public sphere."[81] Yet, this engaged public sphere is constantly bombarded by US-owned media outlets. Isakhan argues that United States "malevolence extends to active suppression and manipulation of the Iraqi media, including forced closures of outlets that contradict or challenge its position, and its undisclosed placement of intentionally biased articles in reputable and independent Iraqi newspapers."[82] Though, to their credit, Iraqis have stridently refused to consume US-backed news outlets, preferring independent Iraqi or pan-Arab sources.[83] In recent years, news outlets have increasingly been split along the varied ethnic and religious factions in Iraq, fostering sectarian conflicts and protests. Further, as the digital age opened the media environment, social media has been overtaken by a range of groups looking to wield power and/or shape public consciousness, particularly activists and terrorist groups, such as ISIS, whose sophisticated use of social media spurred a wave of extremist violence in 2014.

Social media has become so powerful that Iraqi authorities have blocked access as a way to quell protests, the mass demonstrations and protests against high unemployment and water shortages in Basra in the southern Iraq in July 2018, for example. When police forces decided to break the protests by firing tear gas and beating participants, they made sure to block access to the internet. That way, protestors could not share images of the assaults by police, nor could they communicate or organize countermeasures. Further, public activism on social media, particularly for women, can prove deadly. Iraqi activist Soad al-Ali, one of the organizers of the aforementioned protests in Basra and founder of the NGO al-Wedd al-Alaimi for Human Rights, was found shot to death. Tara Feres, another outspoken Iraqi woman in Baghdad, had a huge social media following. She was shot and killed in broad daylight in her car. While certainly more open than during Saddam's rule, Iraqi traditional and social media have become sites of struggle over sectarian political, ethnic, and religious lines.

During the war in Iraq, documentary film and video emerged in a new mode—self-representations of the effects of war on the occupied while it happened. The radically banal images of witnesses and testimonies represented in the documentary films and videos produced by Iraqi citizens helped to create counterarchives. The archives reimagined the process of historiography from the ground up. In addition, the distribution and exhibition of these films engendered new public domains. Through the deployment of militant evidence through the first person political, the IFTC became a conduit for creative expression and a means for Iraqis to have their voices heard during the war and occupation. In 2019, the novelty of releasing images from locals in Iraq to the larger world while living amid war, bombings, and other routine forms of violence seems quaint. Today, we receive media coming from spaces of war and occupation regularly. From the Arab Spring, when protestors organized and documented large-scale uprising via cell phones and social media sites in Egypt, Tunisia, and other countries, to routine police killings and violence in the United States, and culminating with the overmediation of the war in Syria since 2011. There is now an expectation of content from spaces of war and occupation from the people themselves. The next chapter examines the limits of militant evidence within a larger assertion of a "right to the image" by everyday Syrians, who want to have power over their own images, girding against dehumanization and victimization preferred by global social and traditional media ecologies of images and news.

Notes

1. Charles Musser, "War, Documentary and Iraq Dossier: Film Truth in the Age of George W. Bush," *Framework* 48, no. 2 (Fall 2007): 9–35 and Malcolm Turvey, "Iraqis under Occupation: A Survey of Documentaries," *October* 123 (Winter 2008): 234–241.

2. Turvey, "Iraqis under Occupation," 235. Contrary to Turvey, I would argue that these are not unique in the history of cinema or warfare.

3. These international festivals include: the UN Association Film Festival, London; Augsburg Film Festival, Germany; Women's Film Festival, Seoul, South Korea; Iraqi Film Festival, Den Haag, Netherlands; International Festival of Human Rights, Geneva, Switzerland; Oxdox Documentary International Film Festival, Oxford, United Kingdom, and the Arab Film Festival, San Francisco, California.

4. *Hiwar* and *Let the Show Begin* were both initially distributed as supplements to James Longley's *Iraq in Fragments* (2006). *A Candle for the Shabandar Café* was first released as part of the DVD compilation "Baghdad Shorts Collection, Vol. 2" (Arab Film Distribution). The other two films were also included in the first volume.

5. Jane Gaines, "The Production of Outrage: The Iraq War and the Radical Tradition," *Framework* 48, no. 2 (Fall 2007): 47.

6. Paula Amad, *Counter-Archive: Film, the Everyday, and Albert Kahn's Archives de la Planète* (New York: Columbia University Press, 2010). I am using the term in a much different context from Amad, who was discussing film and photography archives in France in the late 1800s and early 1900s.

7. Ghaith Abdul-Ahad, "Art under Fire," *Guardian*, November 21, 2004, http://www.guardian.co.uk/artanddesign/2004/nov/22/art-iraq.

8. A term used by Patricia Zimmermann. See Patricia R. Zimmermann, "Public Domains: Engaging Iraq Through Experimental Digitalities," *Framework* 48, no. 2 (Fall 2007).

9. Jill Godmilow, dir., *What Farocki Taught* (1998, Video Data Bank, DVD). This is a phrase Godmilow uses in her explanation of why she feels Harun Farocki's *Inextinguishable Fire* (1969) is such an important antiwar film and why she chose to remake it. Sometimes the most radical gesture is not to simply engage in the spectacle of destroyed bodies. As Farocki's film opens: "When we show you pictures of napalm victims, you'll shut your eyes. You'll close your eyes to the pictures. Then you'll close them to the memory. And then you'll close your eyes to the facts."

10. I am adapting this term from Akira Mizuta Lippit and his notion of "catastrophic light." See Akira Mizuta Lippit, *Atomic Light: Shadow Optics* (Minneapolis: University of Minnesota Press, 2005).

11. Paul Virilio, *War and Cinema: The Logics of Perception* (London: Verso, 1999), 7–8.

12. Alisa Lebow, "First Person Political," in *The Documentary Film Book*, ed. Brian Winston (London: British Film Institute, 2013), 257–265.

13. Anne Ashford, "Iraq: Filmmaking under Occupation" (Interview with Maysoon Pachachi)," *Socialist Review*, July/August 2006, http://socialistreview.org.uk/308/iraq-filmmaking-under-occupation.

14. Jim Quilty, "Bearing Witness to Life in Occupied Baghdad," *Daily Star*, June 13, 2009, http://www.dailystar.com.lb/Culture/Arts/Jun/13/Bearing-witness-to-life-in-occupied-Baghdad.ashx#axzz2QwuBn5aI.

15. Ashford, "Iraq: Filmmaking Under Occupation (Interview with Maysoon Pachachi)."

16. Quilty, "Bearing Witness to Life in Occupied Baghdad."

17. See http://www.internews.org/. See also Anwar Faruqi, "Emad Ali's Film about Iconic Café Screened at Baghdad Festival," *The Daily Star*, May 6, 2011, http://www.dailystar.com.lb/ArticlePrint.aspx?id=137991&mode=print.

18. Ashford, "Iraq: Filmmaking Under Occupation (Interview with Maysoon Pachachi)."

19. https://web.archive.org/web/20090402214143/http://www.iftvc.org/;https://web.archive.org/web/20090403193833/http://www.iftvc.org/films.htm.

20. See http://montalvoarts.org/programs/iraq_reframe/.

21. "Student Films," https://web.archive.org/web/20090403193833/http://www.iftvc.org/films.htm.

22. Liz Czach, "Home Movies and Amateur Film as National Cinema," in *Amateur Filmmaking: The Home Movie, the Archive, and the Web*, ed. Laura Rascaroli and Gwendolyn Young, with Barry Monahan (New York: Bloomsbury, 2014), 27.

23. Efrén Cuevas, "Change of Scale: Home Movies as Microhistory in Documentary Films," in *Amateur Filmmaking: The Home Movie, the Archive, and the Web*, ed. Laura Rascaroli and Gwendolyn Young, with Barry Monahan (New York: Bloomsbury, 2014), 140.

24. Patricia R. Zimmermann, "Introduction. The Home Movie Movement: Excavations, Artifacts, Minings," in *Mining the Home Movie: Excavations in Histories and Memories*, ed. Karen L. Ishikuza and Patricia R. Zimmermann (Berkeley: University of California Press, 2008), 24.

25. Lebow, "First Person Political," 261.

26. Ibid.

27. Peter Limbrick, "*14.3 Seconds*: Politics, Art and the Archival Imagination," *Visual Anthropology* 29 (2016): 212.

28. Ibid., 215.

29. Giorgio Agamben, *Remnants of Auschwitz: The Witness and the Archive*, trans. Daniel Heller-Roazen (New York: Zone Books, 1999), 145.

30. Ibid., 171.

31. Derrida, *Demeure: Fiction and Testimony*, trans. Elizabeth Rottenberg (Stanford, CA: Stanford University Press, 2000), 30.

32. Ibid.

33. Agamben, *Remnants of Auschwitz*, 26.

34. Ibid.

35. Ibid., 145.

36. Ibid., 146.

37. As Benjamin argues regarding montage: "I needn't *say* anything. Merely show. I shall purloin no valuables, appropriate no ingenious formulations. But the rags, the refuse—these I will not inventory, but allow, in the only way possible, to come into their own: by making use of them." Much in the same way, Vertov and the Iraqi filmmakers don't necessarily offer extraneous commentary, but rather they allow the images constructed of various fragments and rags of the everyday to come into their own and thus allow the viewer, in seeing the montage, to peer deeper into the visible world and construct and think a new material form of history. See Walter Benjamin, "Convolute N [On the Theory of Knowledge, Theory of Progress]," in *The Arcades Project*, trans. Howard Eiland and Kevin McLaughlin (Cambridge, MA: Harvard University Press, 1999), 460.

38. Benjamin, "Convolute N [On the Theory of Knowledge, Theory of Progress]," 460.

39. Dziga Vertov, "Kino-Eye," in *Kino Eye: The Writings of Dziga Vertov*, ed. Annette Michelson, trans. Kevin O'Brien (Berkeley: University of California Press, 1984), 67.

40. Faruqi, "Emad Ali's Film about Iconic Café Screened at Baghdad Festival."

41. Saad Eskander, "The Story of the Cemetery of Books," keynote speech at the Internet Librarian International Conference, London, October 10–12, 2004, https://www.infotoday.com/it/dec04/eskander.shtml.

42. Ibid.

43. Ibid.

44. Ibid.

45. Ibid.

46. Rory McCarthy, "Iraq's Library Struggle to Rise from the Ashes," *The Guardian*, December 21, 2004, https://www.theguardian.com/world/2004/dec/21/education.books.

47. Ibid. Emphasis mine.

48. Michel Foucault, *The Archaeology of Knowledge*, trans. Alan Sheridan (New York: Pantheon, 1972).

49. Jacques Derrida, *Archive Fever*, trans. Eric Prenowitz (Chicago: University of Chicago Press, 1996), 11.

50. Ibid., 4.

51. Tess Takahashi, "The Imaginary Archive: Current Practice," *Camera Obscura*, 22 no. 3 (66) (2007): 180.

52. Benjamin Buchloh, "Gerhard Richter's 'Atlas': The Anomic Archive," *October* 88 (Spring 1999): 137.

53. Hal Foster, "An Archival Impulse," *October* 110 (Fall 2004): 4.

54. Jaimie Baron, "Contemporary Documentary Film and 'Archive Fever': History, the Fragment, the Joke," *Velvet Light Trap* 60 (Fall 2007): 14.

55. Malin Wahlberg, *Documentary Time: Film and Phenomenology* (Minneapolis: University of Minnesota Press, 2008), 9. Wahlberg is drawing on Michael Renov's work on the subject within documentary films. See also Michael Renov, *The Subject of Documentary* (Minneapolis: University of Minnesota Press, 2004).

56. Ibid., 58.

57. Ibid., 39.

58. Ibid., xiv.

59. Patricia R. Zimmermann, "Public Domains: Engaging Iraq through Experimental Digitalities," *Framework* 48, no. 2 (Fall 2007): 76.

60. As Pachachi describes: "He decided he needed to do this epilogue to the film, and so he went and picked up a camera for the first time in months, and he shot some wonderful material, which is also, which is cut into the film. As he was walking away from shooting one day, two men grabbed him, and he ran away, but they shot him in the leg, and he fell on the pavement and bled. So that is what happened to him, and he survived." Susan Stamberg, "College Trains Young Iraqi Film Makers," interview by Maysoon Pachachi, *Weekend Edition Saturday*, NPR, April 8, 2008, http://www.npr.org/templates/story/story.php?storyId=89408895.

61. Ali does not divide his film this way overtly. In the interest of a more lucid analysis, I have taken the liberty to categorize the five sections as: Prelude, Part One, Part Two, Part Three, and Epilogue.

62. Wahlberg, *Documentary Time*, 132.

63. Students, union leaders, workers, and leftist political organizations went on strike and demonstrated for the majority of January 1948, eventually losing over three hundred demonstrators in a violent confrontation with police on the Ma'mun Bridge in Baghdad on January 27. See Ilario Salucci, *A People's History of Iraq: The Iraqi Communist Party, Worker's Movements, and the Left 1924–2004* (Chicago: Haymarket Books, 2005).

64. Nichols, *Representing Reality*, 172, 177.

65. Ibid., 194.

66. Ibid., 232.

67. Ibid., 236.

68. Lebow, "First Person Political," 261.

69. Gaines, "The Production of Outrage," 46.

70. Ibid., 47.

71. Zimmermann, "Public Domains," 66.

72. Ibid., 67.

73. Ibid., 72.

74. Stamberg, "College Trains Young Iraqi Film Makers."

75. Ibid.

76. "Iraq: Intensifying Crackdown on Free Speech, Protests," *Human Rights Watch*, January 22, 2012, http://www.hrw.org/news/2012/01/22/iraq-intensifying-crackdown-free-speech-protests.

77. Support also came from the Czech NGO People in Need, United Nations Development Programme (UNDP), United Nations Educational, Scientific and Cultural Organization (UNESCO), and the United Nations High Commisioner on Refugees (UNHCR).

78. "Iraq Film Festival Aims to Promote Human Rights," *Ahram Online*, February 28, 2012, http://english.ahram.org.eg/News/35603.aspx. Full text of the Universal Declaration of Human Rights can be found at https://www.un.org/en/universal-declaration-human-rights/index.html.

79. Nazli Tarzi, "The Rebirth of Iraqi Cinema," *openDemocracy*, June 18, 2015, https://www.opendemocracy.net/en/north-africa-west-asia/rebirth-of-iraqi-cinema/.

80. Benjamin Isakhan, "The Post-Saddam Iraqi Media: Reporting the Democratic Developments of 2005," *Global Media Journal* 7, no. 13 (Fall 2008): 11.

81. Ibid.

82. Ibid., 19.

83. Ibid., 20.

4. Syria and Abounaddara

RADICAL DOCUMENTARY AND GLOBAL CRISES began with the invocation of an image of a black screen in Abounaddara's short documentary *REC* (2012) with words in red: *Hama 1982*. The black screen represents a lack of digital active witnesses—ordinary people armed with cameras that could have captured the event.[1] The blackness in reference to Hama 1982 also has another deeper meaning for Syrians—it functions as a mark of the erasure of dissent. As Donatella Della Ratta asserts in her book about visual media in Syria since the start of the war, the massacre against the members of the Muslim Brotherhood and other protestors in the city of Hama in 1982 (referred to in Syria simply as "The Events") "is the most infamous symbol of a joint erasure of dissent from both the physical and the immaterial space of Syria's collective imagination," where between ten thousand and forty thousand people were executed "in the complete absence of any recorded evidence or visual documentation."[2] As Robin Yassin-Kassab and Leila al-Shami contend, this led to a widely internalized repression "in the post-Hama years, as Syria became a kingdom of silence, a realm of fear."[3] While not visible in the literal sense, the trauma of Hama in 1982 resided for decades in the collective imaginations of Syrians as a ruthless warning about the limits of protest and free expression. Now, events such as Hama in 2012 are recorded by thousands of people armed with cell phones, distributing the images through digital networks in Syria and around the world.

Since 2011, Syria has been a site of profound overmediation as many Syrians transformed from ordinary citizens to digital active witnesses, wielding smart phones and digital cameras that have produced networked images to further their own Arab Spring revolution after decades (much like in Iraq) of strongman dictatorship. As Della Ratta notes, "Image making in Syria had finally found an opportunity to flourish in the realm of politics in the guise of a collective life activity accessible on a mass scale."[4] This collaborative and vocational image-making culture extends from a host of groups, including the anonymous film collective Abounaddara, which engages with the Syrian conflict through effective and affective radicalities at the limits of militant evidence. In Abounaddara's case, through a mass of short films, they present an affectively radical version of Syria to challenge both mainstream representations and the power of Assad regime. In the face of atrocity, they present satire and critique. Among an erasure of human lives, they foreground simple testimonies. Amid images of ruins, they provide images of community. In the rubble and destruction, they offer human connection and a space for rebelliously productive creativity.

Beyond affective radicality, individual digital active witnesses and human rights organizations within Syria have also sought to capture militant evidence of the crimes, oppression, and brutality they have faced since 2011 in an effort to engender effective radicality and the potential jurisgenerative and sociogenerative effects of wielding such militant evidence. But, as the violence intensified, month by month, the mass of images the digital active witnesses produced were commodified and decontextualized by the global media, who were largely barred from entering Syria and experiencing it and capturing images firsthand. They chose instead the most violent and dehumanizing images produced by others, and those unsurprisingly dominated the narrative. While revolutionary organizations, creative work, and vast human rights documentation flourished in Syria, the global discourse demanded brutal images of warfare and apocalyptic destruction. In addition, due to changes in YouTube's terms of service and mass takedown requests, thousands of hours of militant evidence were removed from public circulation. Syria has been shot to death, represented by a plethora of networked images that comprise a macabre, digital archive of genocide.

Moreover, despite the vast quantities of militant evidence documenting all manner of crimes against humanity, the international community has largely turned a blind eye to Syria, or has used it as space for proxy wars. As Jay Weisberg argues in his review of the documentary *Silvered Water, Syria Self-Portrait* (dir. Ossama Mohammed, 2014), which consists primarily of amateur cell phone footage, "If only film could make a difference, then 'Silvered Water' would possibly spark action, but not even Mohammed can believe in such idealism in a world all too used to standing aside."[5] In one sense, the overmediation of Syria has produced a flood of affective and effective militant evidence, so much so that it has practically rendered images

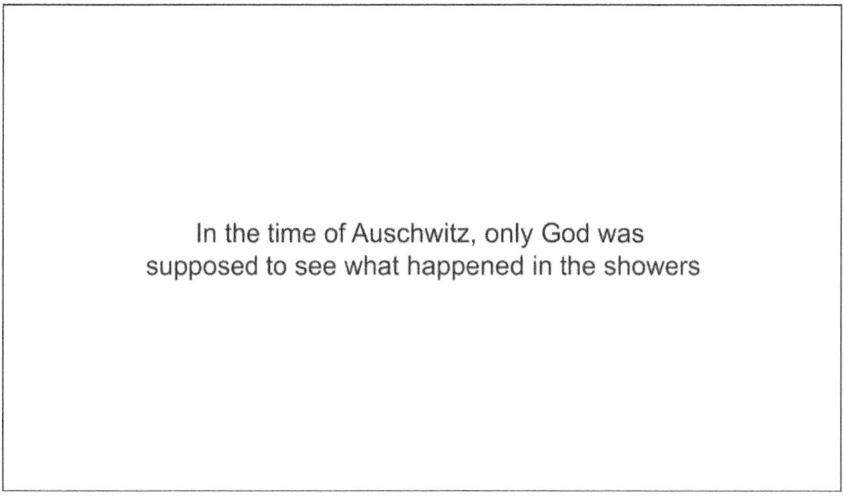

> In the time of Auschwitz, only God was
> supposed to see what happened in the showers

Figure 4.1 Still from *Aleppo*.

of atrocity banal—there is just so much death and destruction that is hard to comprehend. Further images then only work to anesthetize rather than activate. In their simple, yet jarring short film *Aleppo* (2016), Abounaddara presents two white screens with text, one after another. The first reads, "In the time of Auschwitz, only God was supposed to see what happened in the showers. Today the final solution is broadcast live on the world's screens."[6] The world clearly saw and understood what was happening in Syria but did very little to stop it. This tension is the crux of the investigation in *Radical Documentary and Global Crises*: Can images made by amateurs and activists on the ground exert any force in a world saturated by and indifferent to them? Why make them at all?

Part of the problem, as Wendy Kozol suggests, echoing Jacques Ranciere's contentions in his 2010 book, *Dissensus*, is that there is "no direct path from images of violence to political activism."[7] Further, "new communications technologies and multiple media platforms have resulted in the rapid increase of available imagery from conflict zones. But visibility, even displays of intense grief and suffering, has not necessarily brought with it the political or social recognition" and "has not provoked sustained moral outrage, much less effective political opposition."[8] In Kozol's argument, political or social recognition is still certainly possible but involves different questions of engagement, critically "the question of what it means to 'matter.'"[9] The idea of mattering in the context of *Radical Documentary and Global Crises* returns

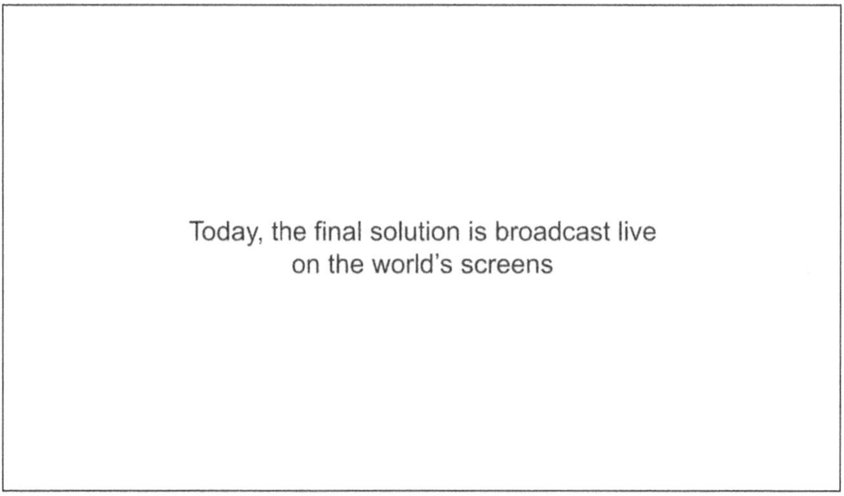

> Today, the final solution is broadcast live on the world's screens

Figure 4.2 Still from *Aleppo*.

us to a fundamental question: In the face of so much violence and violent images, how can everyday people assert their values, voices, and agencies?

For Abounaddara, the answers to all of these questions form an integral component of the work of the anonymous, digital active witnesses who compose the group. Their short documentary-based films act as a corrective to lazy media depictions of everyday Syrians as victims or terrorists while also girding against the use of violent or dehumanizing imagery. As Chad Elias notes, they are "focused not on violence but on quotidian representations that express the normative ideals of the revolution itself."[10] This use of the quotidian or every day follows the same sort of deployment of amateur images in Iraq explored in the previous chapter. Further, much like the participants in those Independent Film and Television College (IFTC) courses in Iraq, "Abounaddara uses the medium as a tool of survival: death is incessantly evoked in words but not shown."[11] This is not a tactic of avoidance; rather it is a purposeful strategy on the part of Abounaddara to survive conditions in Syria while also curtailing the spread of stereotypical images portraying Syrians as dehumanized savages.

In an interview in the *Nation* before the 2015 Human Rights Watch Film Festival, Charif Kiwan, the official spokesperson for (and only non-anonymous member of) Abounaddara, evoked the Lumière Brothers and the beginning of film history when asked what he wants the groups' films to do. "Did you know," he asks, "that the first time a Syrian character was represented on film, he was represented as a fanatic?" Kiwan is referring to the 1897 re-enactment scene in *Assassinat de Kléber* (dir. Lumière Brothers), which depicts the 1800 assassination of French General Jean Baptiste- Kléber by Suleiman al-Halabi in Cairo during the postrevolutionary days of French colonial expansion under Napoleon. Kiwan argues that "the Lumière Brothers completely misrepresented al-Halabi, giving him a beard when he had none," and later the French "searched for scientific proof of fanaticism . . . exhibiting al-Halabi's skull at the Musèe de l'Homme with the word 'fanatic' inscribed on it. We need to be done with such representations."[12] It may seem like an odd thing to ask in the midst of a war—to demand the urgency of addressing issues of representation when faced with dire life-and-death situations. Yet, for Abounaddara it is of critical importance.

Syrians have been living amid war crimes, bombings, civil war, and a capricious revolutionary situation. As amateur filmmakers, this situation endows the members of the collective with a number of acute ethical responsibilities in regard to representation: first, to the people who they film, who could potentially face danger for having appeared; second, to let those same people speak as unmediated by outside forces as possible; and third, to facilitate a representation of Syria for the international community that challenges preconceived notions of victims, dignity, and agency. These ethical responsibilities also revolve around a concern for the uses of images in such situations. Susan Sontag delineates this tension in her book *On Photography*, arguing that in an age where one knows the world through and is surrounded by images constantly, "photographic seeing" must be "constantly renewed with new shocks, whether subject matter or technique, so as to produce the impression of violating ordinary vision"[13] This inclination toward needing novel shocks in order to renew one's perception is a trend Abounaddara actively works against. In other words, they are vigilant at preserving the dignity of victims in the face of a flood of images of mangled bodies, dead children, and unidentified citizens fighting in the bombed-out streets; images craved by an insatiable global media that is unable to produce its own images of the conflict. Yet, this is balanced by the other possible vocation of documentary images, as Sontag notes that "photographs are often invoked as an aid to understanding and tolerance. In humanist jargon, the highest vocation of photography is to explain man to man."[14] Further, Abounaddara engages in a "model of cinema founded on a fundamental human right to make and consume images."[15] Moreover, in her review of the recent Syrian documentary *For Sama*, Teo Bugbee argues that the film, like many other documentaries from Syria consisting primarily of amateur and cell phone footage, "provides a coherent account of a humanitarian crisis from the perspective of the wounded and displaced."[16] And beyond the displaced, for those who have perished fighting or filming the revolution, "the use of the cell phone as a tool of witnessing raises new possibilities for a kind of posthumous address to the living."[17] In everything they do, Abounaddara works to counter the usual received, decontextualized, and dehumanized images of Syrians as extremists, victims, or rebellious protestors while creating a living archive of the effects of war and revolution from below. They aim to empower individuals to create their own images and produce an emerging civil society outside of existing power systems.

This chapter analyzes the documentary practices (an "emergency cinema") and some of the short films produced clandestinely by Abounaddara in Syria since 2011. Abounaddara was founded in Damascus in 2010, one year before the revolution began, and the collective has been documenting the Syrian uprising and war since April 2011. They attempt to intervene in the conflict by deploying militant evidence on a number of levels: first, to reinscribe humanity and personhood to the images of war-ravished landscapes strewn with ruins; second, to assert a "right to the image" within a holistic interpretation of international human rights law; and third, to actively resist the brutal oppression and media censorship under the regime of Bashar al-Assad by strategically deploying their films as "sniper shots" in ongoing revolution. The films, which range from witness accounts, photomontages, newsreel/film-tracts, mock advertisements, and recontextualized historical images are shared widely on social media and video-sharing sites, such as Vimeo and YouTube, forming an intimate, living archive of life in Syria. Each video is subtitled in multiple languages to garner the broadest possible audience. The work of Abounaddara extends the discussion began in the previous chapter, which examined student filmmaking in Iraq that dealt with common humanity, everydayness, and countermedia narratives, but they add the elements of anonymity, wide networked digital dissemination, and the wish to provoke and sustain revolutionary fervor in Syria in the midst of a protracted and violent struggle. As Christy Lange argues, "Abounaddara's approach, above all, is to amplify the multiple and disparate voices of the Syrian people," where amplification emerges from accumulation, polyvocality, heterogeneity, and the creation of spaces for anonymous deployments of militant evidence from an alternative sphere of media and communication.[18] "These are films that are absorbed slowly," Lange argues, "their power accumulates through aggregation."[19]

In Syria, the deployment of militant evidence functions as a reclaiming of the meaning and potency of the image and of the commitments to radicality from the evacuations of meaning rendered by networked circulation. Abounaddara's commitment to self-determination, collaboration, and independent media is a corrective for commodification and the dimensions of global narratives, rendering the microhistorical and the everyday as the most-valuable perspective. Abounaddara repurposes ubiquitous technologies, networks, and social media in affirmative, archival, alternative, and world-making ways. They assert the importance of the human in a world of images and data. Abounaddara engages the terrain of transmedia advocacy with the mission of transforming the conditions for image making and the images of Syrians. They deploy militant evidence through all the means at their disposal: social networks like Facebook and Twitter, video-sharing sites like Vimeo, museums, academic institutions, and many other venues. Why? Because representations have material effects on real people, and everyone should be able to control and claim their own images. Abounaddara asks viewers to think globally about image production and circulation and the right to claim one's own image in an age where its dissemination relies on a networked digital vortex of contexts that allow easy appropriation. Here, images can be instrumentalized or altered by anyone, rendering the original image maker disposable.

This chapter explores how Abounaddara advocates for an "emergency cinema" as both an analogy and an act of production that privileges spaces of collectivization—rather than the sectarian ones—freedom of expression, and urgency, all of which pushes the boundaries of radical documentary practice in the digital age while returning the militant use of documentary to its revolutionary roots. The chapter looks at Abounaddara's work in Syria and its link to radical filmmaking in Cuba in the 1960s, particularly the work of Santiago Álvarez and Julio García Espinosa's notion of "imperfect cinema," arguing that Abounaddara's practices constitute a "digital imperfect cinema." The chapter also explores linkages between Cuban filmmakers and Joris Ivens, who worked closely with them, and Chris Marker, who returned to France with a renewed revolutionary commitment prior to May 1968. Then, there is a brief analysis of the image-making practices that have arisen in Syria since 2011 and the aforementioned removal of militant evidence from YouTube. And finally, the bulk of the chapter is devoted to an extended analysis of Abounaddara's practice of emergency cinema through their manifestos and a number of their films produced since 2011.

Rooting Militant Evidence: Cuba and Imperfect Cinema

The Cuban revolution in 1959 and the use of cinema in building the Cuban nation and sustaining the revolution is an important flashpoint in the history of the radical documentary and offers a historical model for some of

Abounaddara's documentary practices and deployment of militant evidence. In the 1960s, there was a confluence of interaction and education between filmmakers in Europe and North America who traveled to Cuba to experience the revolution firsthand and share their filmmaking expertise with Cuban filmmakers while the Cuban filmmakers shared with them their revolutionary practices and ideologies. Filmmakers in Europe, North America, and the Soviet Union had been producing and exchanging varied forms of documentary, avant-garde, and other noncommercial films for decades with Latin American filmmakers through cine-clubs. At the same time, workers' groups and other alternative spaces of exhibition in Latin American countries were almost completely shut out of the cycle of production and exchange. As Julianne Burton argues,

> In Latin America, with the exception of Brazil . . . the film society movement did not emerge until two decades later—its inception ranging from the early 1940s in Uruguay and Argentina to the 1950s in countries like Chile, Bolivia and Cuba, and the mid-sixties in Peru and elsewhere. This temporal lag meant that Soviet cinema of the 1920s, early surrealist works and other examples of the European avant-garde, as well as subsequent landmark documentaries by Robert Flaherty, Joris Ivens, and the disciples of John Grierson in England, Canada, and elsewhere could not be seen with any frequency in Spanish speaking Latin American countries until the 1950s and after.[20]

While lacking the myriad filmic influences and rapid evolution of documentary form and content, Latin American countries in the post–World War II period were fertile ground for a distinctive, regional practice of documentary. A number of factors contributed to the evolving place of documentary as a means of personal and political expression. By the late 1950s, vibrant film societies, filmmaking courses, and international film festivals, as well as the proliferation of 8 mm and 16 mm equipment, allowed individual, amateur, independent budding filmmakers a quick route to self-expression.[21] Burton argues that this "urge to self-expression was almost invariably circumscribed by inescapable social, economic, and political realities." So much so that even when films were "not explicitly political in origin or orientation . . . they would soon acquire a political dimension."[22] The political dimension that Burton alludes to is galvanized by three main factors: first, the reconsideration of the hegemonic power of the United States in Latin America, "giving rise to renewed political nationalism and developmentalist ideologies;"[23] second, the role of cultural production, especially film, as a way to express nationalistic sympathies and self-determination; and third, the collaboration of European filmmakers, conduits of the aforementioned radical filmmaking traditions, such as Ivens and Chris Marker.[24]

Ivens first visited Cuba in September 1960 after an invitation from the Castro government arranged by the French writer Georges Sadoul and Alfredo Guevara, founder of the Cuban Institute of Film Art and Industry (the *Instituto Cubano del Arte e Industria Cinematograficos*) or ICAIC. By this point in his career, "Ivens represented the engaged documentarist par excellence, a man whose career itinerary recapitulated the chronology of national liberation movements around the world."[25] While Ivens was known throughout the world, many Cuban filmmakers had never seen his films.[26] During his initial visit to Cuba, Ivens engaged the three-hundred-person staff of the ICAIC in lectures, screenings, extensive dialogues, and working sessions on the theory and practice of documentary. He also set to work on two short, silent documentaries, *Travel Notebook* (1961) and *A People in Arms* (1961), filming the majority of the material for both during his initial six-week stay. This filmmaking tour comprised a crew of young ICAIC filmmakers, including noted cinematographers Jorge Herrera and Ramon Suarez, who shot many of Tomas Gutierrez Alea's films, including the fictional masterpiece *Memories of Underdevelopment* (1968). *Travel Notebook* aligns with the travelogue form and documents Ivens's tour of Cuba while providing a subjective evaluation and representation of various sites of everyday life and revolutionary institutions. *A People in Arms*, which follows a single brigade of the "People's Militia" over the course of a few weeks, details the grassroots preparations by Cubans to mobilize and fully commit to defending the revolution. It also shows a host of anti-American demonstrations in Havana and elsewhere in Cuba.

Ivens's activism in Cuba extended beyond mere engagement with Cuban filmmakers and the lending of his expertise. Ivens also secretly worked with the Cuban army. "After the Bay of Pigs Invasion," writes Hans Schoots, "the Cubans seriously expected another military attempt to overthrow the revolution and planned to film the following confrontation."[27] Spending his time outside of Havana at the Frank Paìz School, "Ivens was in charge of training between forty and sixty military camera operators . . . as Castro had explained that he wanted 'practical people who work fast. Soldiers, not artists.'"[28] The idea of "soldiers not artists" is one that Ivens took to heart. As Susan Martin-Márquez elucidates, this model extends beyond Cuba as Ivens became involved in a much larger project to promote revolutionary filmmaking in a number of countries in Latin America.[29] The previous "official" account of this activity claimed that it had emerged from an initiative conceived at the 1960 Leipzig Film Festival, which offered scholarships to third world filmmakers to study at the East German film school *Deutsche Film-Aktiengesellschaft* (DEFA). In reality, the initiative, led by Ivens and variously known as the "Joris Ivens Brigade," "the brigade," and "the organization," was clandestinely based in Havana without any formal legal existence.[30] Here, Ivens met with officials from various Latin American countries, provided equipment and other resources, and arranged for training at courses conducted either at DEFA or ICAIC.[31] This arrangement was beneficial for both parties. Emerging militant filmmakers in Latin America received training from an eminent radical filmmaker with vast technical expertise attuned to the development of socially conscious documentary, and Ivens provided a model for an active, revolutionary engagement for European and North American filmmakers intent on becoming participants in what was seen at the time as the beginning of worldwide revolution.

Shortly after Ivens's engagement with the ICAIC, Marker visited the island and filmed the material for *Cuba Si!* in and around many of the same sites seen in *Travel Notebook*: the highlights were, in Waugh's estimation, of the "revolutionary grand tour" given to the cadre of committed filmmakers who visited from abroad. Like Ivens's films, *Cuba Si!* was censored by the French government and not screened publicly in Europe until 1963. Marker returned to Cuba again some years later to film *Le Bataille des Dix Millions / Battle of the Ten Million* (1970), employing Álvarez as his cinematographer to document a failed ten-million-pound sugar crop harvest. Yet, as Waugh contends, "Despite Marker's close interaction with Cuban filmmakers, there was never the sense as with Ivens that he had come to put himself completely at the disposal of Cuban filmmakers and that the filming of his own work was secondary to this aim."[32] This discussion is not meant to imply that Ivens and Marker and had any sort of extraordinary influence on the development of Cuban cinema. Instead, it demonstrates they were part of an internationalist milieu and intrepid conduits for ideological and cinematic exchanges between Europe and revolutionary struggle in both Latin America and globally. Marker's drive to provide counterinformation through his films reveals a journalistic impulse that would also be deployed by his Cuban contemporary, Álvarez. This journalistic impulse and drive toward counterinformation is updated again by Abounaddara. In Abounaddara's case, they control their images and their rights to them and craft their own representations to be shared globally. Though they are quite cognizant of and make frequent reference to political cinema and film history, Abounaddara are forging a unique radical documentary practice for the digital age. They also have much more in common with Álvarez and his decolonized, revolutionary practices than they do with Ivens and Marker, though they are all working within the same tradition of radical documentary.

Álvarez was born in Cuba in 1919 to Spanish parents. He made his way to the United States in the late 1930s and worked as both a coal miner and a dishwasher before enrolling as a student at Columbia University. In the 1940s, he returned to Cuba, where he studied philosophy at the University of Havana, joined the Partido Socialist Popular (Cuban Communist Party), and cofounded the organization Nuestro Tiempo (Our Time), a "leftist cultural society that combined film viewing with political education."[33] While working as a television music archivist in the mid-1950s, he was active in the underground struggle against the Fulgencio Batista regime. After the revolution he was appointed as vice president at ICAIC, taking over the newsreel division in 1960. Cuban revolutionary leaders had a particular affinity for the potential of filmic practice for the development of ideology. In a speech to intellectuals and other Cuban cultural figures in 1961, Fidel Castro articulated the cultural policy of the revolution, emphasizing the centrality of film. He argued that "some intellectual or artistic creations are more important than others as far as the ideological development of the people is concerned." In this regard, "the most fundamental and highly important media is the cinema, as well as television."[34]

Michael Chanan contends that, as in Soviet Russia, where Lenin had extolled the virtues and utility of cinematic practice to the revolution, Cuban cinema after the revolution "became a living analogue of the development of cinema within the Revolution, because here the audience has become, together with the filmmakers, participant observant participators in the same process . . . cinema in Cuba became, in a word, highly animated."[35] Similarly, Joshua Malitsky asserts that, like Vertov, Álvarez's journalistic impulse sought to "shape the attitude of the collective and did so avowedly" by harnessing the power of cinema to hasten the ideological development of both the Cuban people and sympathetic, engaged cineastes abroad.[36] His cinematic practice likewise worked to form what Chanan calls a "surrogate public sphere," an encounter with social reality within the Communist Party–controlled press and broadcasting, whereby filmmakers' privileged position placed them "a little to the left of what anyone else was allowed to say."[37] In Abounaddara's case, their work also functions as a surrogate public sphere but not in the service of the state—rather in militant opposition to it. In Syria, media and news is tightly controlled by the Assad regime. While that control remains during the war, the fighting has made a space for alternative forms of media to circulate with much less resistance.

Between 1965 and 1970, Álvarez produced a number of groundbreaking works. These include *Now* (1965), *Hasta la Victoria Siempre / Always till Victory* (1967), *L. B. J.* (1968), and *79 Primaveras /79 Springtimes of Ho Chi Minh* (1969).

Now, which won the Palm d'Or at the 1965 at the International Festival of Documentary and Short Film in Leipzig, is a five-minute pamphlet-style film that connects the problem of racism in the United States to broader struggles for Third World liberation. Álvarez uses of a series of still images culled from the pages of *Life* magazine and other available archival sources, frequently employing a quick zoom to underscore the point he is making, such as the pain on the face of an African American woman as police detain her. He also uses the technique to reveal new information, as when he zooms down to reveal a seemingly banal image of a well-dressed young woman whose hands are bound with handcuffs. The technique also heightens the engagement and identification of the viewer with the subjects portrayed by repeatedly offering close-ups of their eyes and faces. This approach is buttressed by well-chosen filmic sequences of demonstrations, protests, and mass arrests. Throughout the film, Álvarez deploys a forceful and somewhat ironically positive song by Lena Horne, also titled "Now," which was set to the music and rhythm of the traditional Jewish folk song "Hava Nagila" ("Let Us Rejoice").

Álvarez masterfully juxtaposes a rapid-fire montage and the use of still images. A notable sequence of still photograph editing occurs toward the end of the film. He begins with a medium shot photograph of two hooded Ku Klux Klan members before zooming in to provide a close-up. This is followed by a graphically matched, close-up image of a young, scared looking African American child ostensibly looking up at them in horror. The next image depicts a large burning cross that Álvarez zooms out from to reveal a group of Klansmen outfitted in their robes and carrying rudimentary torches. This is followed by an image of an African American man in obvious physical pain and distress surrounded and being detained by white police officers. Álvarez completes the sequence with a repeat of an image of the aforementioned young boy, a young African American woman clutching her purse, and slaves' bound hands. The implicit sense of the sequence is conveyed in just thirteen seconds through the use of seven images and some simple zooming; namely that America's ongoing problems with racism and discrimination follow a direct line of development from the days of slavery and the Ku Klux Klan to contemporary practices of police and other figures of white supremacy—all of that with some pilfered magazine photos. In a similar way, Abounaddara makes the most of available materials—in their case, the individual, anonymous production of militant evidence created by members of their collective. Like Álvarez, they favor short, powerful films with a straightforward and often militant message.

One of the finest examples of Álvarez's work in this regard is *79 Springtimes*, an elegiac film that combines footage of Ho Chi Minh's life and state funeral with American bombing raids and mass demonstrations against the Vietnam War in the United States. Álvarez was invited by the Communist government of North Vietnam to film the funeral, accompanied by his longtime cameraman, Ivan Napoles, who had traveled with him to Vietnam on a prior occasion for the filming of *Hanoi, Tuesday the 13th* in 1967. Coupled with the song "Section 43" by Country Joe and the Fish, the soundtrack by Aldeberto Galvez underscores the visual dynamic, as does the inclusion of poems by Ho Chi Minh and Jose Martí. Álvarez opens the film with an ironic juxtaposition of images: flowers blooming intercut with slow-motion footage of bombs falling from US planes. The flowers, emerging naturally from the ground in an organic fashion, represents both the natural connection of the Vietnamese people to their land and their collective "ground-up" response to fighting against US oppression. In contrast, the top-down nature of the falling bombs connotes unfeeling military might with little regard for the people living below.

Throughout the film, Álvarez intercuts images of Vietnamese suffering that were not in wide circulation in the West at the time. In the film's final sequence, introduced by the intertitle "Let not socialist division cast a shadow on the future," Álvarez pushes the concept of representation to its extreme by employing a montage of ripped, torn, scratched footage, images of film strips, and sprocket holes that intercut images of fighters on both the American and North Vietnamese side. This is coupled with a jarring, discordant soundtrack comprised of overlapping sounds of bombs dropping, bombs exploding, and rapid gunfire. This deployment of avant-garde techniques of battle footage results in a powerful evocation of the war for the viewer. It also conveys how the horror and overwhelming trauma of the war exceed representational means. Citing the "ferocity of the visual onslaught" and the "absolute freedom of its narrative organization," filmmaker Travis Wilkerson declares that *79 Springtimes* "was the single most revolutionary document of the cinematographers' most revolutionary period."[38] Álvarez's use of compilation in his films is not just an aesthetic choice but rather one of doing the most with limited resources coupled with an emerging sense of a distinctive, ideologically informed, "imperfect" revolutionary cinematic practice, which will be updated by Abounaddara's digital imperfect cinema. The original notion of "imperfect cinema" is articulated by Espinosa in "For an Imperfect Cinema" in 1969, a concept that also informs Hito Steyerl's use of the poor image, a characteristic of militant evidence in the digital age.

In "For an Imperfect Cinema," Espinosa puts forth his theories on the place of art and artists within the revolutionary Cuban context.[39] But, his writings are also highly relevant and linked to the emergence of image making in Syria, particularly in the case of Abounaddara. In his essay, Espinosa asserts his conception for a new poetics of an "imperfect cinema" (revolutionary) opposed to a "perfect cinema," which is "technically and artistically masterful" (reactionary). Part of the impetus for his writing was a certain level of anxiety at the fact Cuban cinema had received the accolades and "approval of the European intelligentsia."[40] The definition of imperfect cinema encompasses two main factors: the participation of spectators as both makers of meaning, in the sense of both engagement and authorship, and the movement of art from the realm of an elite, autonomous category to the people. This move returns cinema to the masses free from critics and other intermediaries who judge quality and meaning in ways that do not register the works' utility to the people or the revolution. In regard to the latter, Espinosa states,

> Imperfect cinema is no longer interested in quality or technique. It can be created equally well with a Mitchell or with an 8mm camera, in a studio or in a guerrilla camp in the middle of the jungle. Imperfect cinema is no longer interested in predetermined taste, and much less in "good taste." It is not quality which it seeks in an artist's work. The only thing it is interested in is how an artist responds to the following question: What are you doing in order to overcome the barrier of the "cultured" elite audience which up to now has conditioned the form of your work?[41]

Espinosa's assertion that makers of imperfect cinema are no longer interested in quality or technique may seem like a punting of the question of aesthetics. The matter is a bit more complicated. Espinosa is not arguing that aesthetics have no place in a revolutionary cinema; rather, he highlights the need for an overcoming of elite and colonized standards of taste. The revolution demands its own new forms, or what Espinosa describes as a "new poetics for the cinema," which "will, above all, be a 'partisan' and 'committed' poetics, a 'committed' art, a consciously and resolutely 'committed' cinema."[42] Espinosa's conception is similar in spirit to Waugh's use of the term described in the introduction, but its deployment in this instance is specific to the Cuban revolution. As Espinosa contends, "The filmmaker who subscribes to this new poetics should not have personal self-realization as his object. From now on he should also have another activity. He should place his role as revolutionary or aspiring revolutionary above all else."[43]

An imperfect cinema is a people's cinema where everyone is encouraged to participate. With digital technologies, people need not remain spectators but instead can become an author, capturing and disseminating images of everyday life and the events surrounding them. In the context of Syria, Della Ratta directly links this vocational, everyday aspect of filmmaking to the Cuban approach to revolutionary filmmaking. She asserts that "much as in Cuba in the 1970s, in Syria in the 2010s filming seems to have become an ordinary, ongoing life activity."[44] She contends that since 2011, the act of filming "has been appropriated by a wide spectrum of the country's citizenry ... every day, everyone films and is filmed in Syria, a country where the visual form has been turned into a device to perform violence, and the quintessential tool to resist it."[45] Further, while shorter in duration than Àlvarez's, Abounaddara's films exhibit a similar level of militancy, use of sound and music, and blend of genres to create satires and critiques. In addition, the quality and types of images produced work as a counterforce to the slick and stable images proffered by the Assad regime within dominant media ecologies. As Elias notes, "The technically flawed digital image," analogous to conceptions of imperfect cinema and the poor image, "functions as a counter to the professional images of the Syrian state media apparatus."[46] Elias draws on the conditions of image production in each case "between the regime's use of tripods to construct the illusion of a stable, unshakable political order" to "the heavily pixelated, trembling images that are captured in amateur cell phone videos" to argue that the aesthetics presented as a direct result of the context of image production endows the images of amateurs with the force of critique and counterforce through the degraded quality of the image.[47] In Syria, a contemporary, digital imperfect cinema has arisen to counter the flawless, slick images produced by state-controlled television stations and periodicals since gaining power in 2000 and to document the real conditions of life in Syria for everyday people.

When Bashar al-Assad took power in 2000, despite the fact he was Hafez's son, there was hope he would modernize Syria and move to a more democratic form of rule. Early in his reign, the regime seemed to be moving in that direction. As Yassin-Kassab and Al-Shami argue, by "checking all the boxes of liberal democratic discourse, Assad spoke of greater transparency and accountability, of shaking up the bureaucracy and fighting against corruption."[48] He even offered a decree soon after taking office "that prohibited the public display of his image."[49] This offered a refreshing break from the authoritarian rule of his father, whose image was a common sight in Syria. Political detainees were released, independent publications were allowed to flourish, and independent civil organizations were permitted to form and advocate openly. For example, the human rights group Committees for the Defense of Democratic Freedoms and Human Rights in Syria (CDF) was re-established followed by the Syrian Center for Media and Freedom of Expression in 2004.[50] Yet, all of these advancements were short-lived. By late 2001, Assad was deploying the *Mukhabarat* (secret police) to break up opposition group meetings and had passed Decree No. 50, which severely tightened media censorship and led to the closure of independent media outlets. In addition, Assad has always maintained a very close relationship with the Syrian television industry, employing dramas, news stations, and other programming to project a stable, all-powerful, seemingly liberal and democratic image immune from dissent. Abounaddara and other independent film and video organizations in Syria directly challenge this repressive, weaponized-image regime by capturing and broadcasting the realities of life in Syria, militant evidence, to counter the regime's carefully constructed media image. Abounaddara represents the previously unrepresentable while offering a polyvocal space of critique.

Shooting Syria and Disappearing Video Evidence

Like Hama in 1982, the current conflict emerged after ruthless government suppression of a local protest movement. In early March 2011 in the city of Daraa, protestors gathered to demand the release of a group of fifteen teenage boys who had been arrested and tortured for antiregime graffiti. They had sprayed various revolutionary slogans they had seen on social media during the Arab Spring uprising in Egypt and Tunisia. Assad's security forces opened fire on the demonstrators, killing several. Later in March, after weeks of growing protests around the Omari Mosque in Daraa, security forces again opened fire on the crowds, killing more civilians. But the protests continued. In the next weeks, "hundreds were rounded up from their homes, the city's mobile phone coverage was cut, and military and police checkpoints were set up in the streets."[51] This absurd repression was quickly shared via social media and led to further protests in Damascus, Homs, and many other cities throughout Syria. State media responded by offering conspiracy theories about outside infiltrators and images of highly manufactured pro-regime rallies in Damascus, complete with Bashar T-shirts and participants overcome with emotion and support for their leader, similar to a Donald Trump rally in the United States. Yet, it was the "grainy images taken on mobile phones and shared on social media—of unarmed Syrians being beaten and shot—that told an entirely different story."[52] As Elias notes, soon after they realized the potential catalyzing power of amateur cell phone images, the Assad regime "immediately made it a crime to possess a camera in public space, and they brutally targeted anyone found taking images on a cell phone . . . implicit in this legal action is the regime's recognition that images themselves are agents of political power rather than second-order representations of it."[53]

While amateur-produced cell phone images do indeed have great potential power, as has been argued throughout the book, Syria became a site of overmediation that has spawned all manner of violence. Unlike the Iraq War, which was also overmediated but from a Western perspective, images from Syria are digitally networked. As Della Ratta argues, "Syria is in fact the first conflict of our networked age" that "brings to light the participatory dimension of violence in the networked age."[54] Here, the "networked image opens up a new visual political economy in which multiple makers and keeps emerge and clash."[55] Further, as Josepha Wessels contends, the mass of Syrians using their cellphones and cameras to document the war engendered "a kind of 'grassroots televising' of war unique in the history of war and conflict . . . making the Syrian conflict the first 'You Tubed' revolution."[56] In a study of YouTube videos from Syria posted between 2014 and 2015, Wessels identified eight different categories:

1. Humor and creative nonviolent resistance
2. Protest videos from the first phase of the uprising
3. Torture and war crime videos
4. Direct frontline battle footage
5. Citizen experiences of war
6. Pro-Assad videos
7. Anti-Assad videos
8. Pro-jihadi videos[57]

Wessels's taxonomy reveals some of the major groups clashing in a battle of images. On the one hand, you have positive developments, like creative expression and nonviolent resistance on the part of citizens and amateurs armed with cell phones and those working with groups like Abounaddara. Then there are the Daesh (a.k.a. ISIS/ISIL) videos, which fall into the category of jihadi propaganda, battle footage, and war crimes. Daesh and jihadism were able to enter into the vacuum of power created by the Assad regime, which rather than listening to their citizen protestors or accommodating dissent, pursued a scorched-earth strategy of total destruction. "Hundreds of barrel bombs dismantled Aleppo—more than any city since World War II—and Deir, al-Zor, Homs, Daraa, and suburban Damascus," leading to the greatest refugee crisis since World War II.[58] In the face of barrel bombs, the camera is a poor weapon. However, despite the vast overmediation of Syria, the camera is a crucial producer of militant evidence and that evidence has been steadily disappearing from video-sharing sites like YouTube.[59] Organizations such as Syrian Observatory for Human Rights, the Violations Documentation Center, Sham News Agency, and Aleppo Media Center, in addition to thousands of individual citizens, had uploaded videos to YouTube and other video-sharing sites at a high rate. Even in 2019, as the broader conflict had waned, fifty videos from Syria on average were uploaded daily. However, in 2017, a machine learning program deployed by YouTube flagged and terminated many Syrian videos and channels for violating their terms of service, which prohibits certain graphic content.[60] The aforementioned Violations Documentations Center, a partner with WITNESS, lost more than thirty-two thousand videos of human rights violations when their channel was taken down. Videos have also been removed through cyberattacks and mass, coordinated "flagging" of videos and because individual users will remove their own footage out of fear for their safety.[61] Fortunately, with the help of the human rights activist group Syrian Archive, they were able to recover most of the lost footage.[62]

Syrian Archive was formed by Syrians in partnership with a host of human rights, legal, and archival organizations, including WITNESS, to archive and protect the militant evidence produced in Syria.[63] Syrian Archive curates militant evidence that documents and represents human rights violations and other war crimes and crimes against humanity "by all sides during the conflict in Syria with the goal of creating an evidence-based tool for reporting, advocacy and accountability purposes."[64] Much like the work of WITNESS, B'Tselem, and Forensic Architecture discussed in previous chapters, the work of Syrian Archive is collaborative and global and deploys militant evidence within defined transmedia investigations and advocacy projects. Further, they provide a powerful framework of legibility and understanding for seemingly disparate or unconnected captured militant evidence. They aggregate, curate, and verify individual instances of such evidence, using transparent open-source formats, into meaningful actions and powerful digital archives, working to bring forth effective radicality. For example, in 2017, Syrian Archive marshalled a variety of militant evidence to prove that the United States had illegally bombed a mosque on March 16, 2017, in al-Jinah, a small village on the outskirts of western Aleppo.[65] Using on-the-ground witness video and Twitter posts, cross-referenced with satellite imagery and photos of bomb remnants, Syrian Archive was able to prove the illegal targeting of the mosque, which was populated by praying civilians at the time of the bombing.

While Syrian Archive and other on-the-ground human rights groups work to engender an effective radicality, employing the vast digital archive produced in Syria since 2011, in Abounaddara's case, they work more firmly to generate affective radicality, providing affective snapshots that cohere into a new form of representation that emphasizes the humanity, creativity, and agency of the Syrian people. As Della Ratta notes, "The revolution has been *shot* yet the *shooting* in not over, as history will write the final scene. Snapshots are antidotes to oblivion and violence because, ultimately, 'forgetting extermination is part of extermination."[66] Abounaddara provides this antidote to oblivion and violence through their practices of the generative shooting and production of images they call emergency cinema, a practice against extermination and for revolution.

Abounaddara: Emergency Cinema and a Right to the Image for All

Abounaddara was founded in Damascus in 2010, one year before the revolution began, and the collective has been documenting the Syrian uprising and war since April 2011. The name of the group translates from Arabic to "the man with glasses," and as Abounaddara references on their website, this name functions on a number of levels. First, it refers to the association, in Arabic culture, of nicknames for people based on their professions. Second, it alludes to Vertov's concept of the "kino-eye." And third it alludes to Godard's later Dziga Vertov Group, which sought to meld art and militant activism. In addition, beyond their active uploading of videos to sites like Vimeo, the work has been featured in a range of other contexts, including the Human Rights Watch and Sundance Film Festivals, the latter of which they won a Short Film Grand Jury Prize (2014) for their film *Of Gods and Dogs*. They have also been featured in a variety of museums, universities, and other exhibitions, including the 2015 Venice Biennale, which they withdrew from over censorship, in addition to winning the Vera List Prize for Art and Politics presented by the New School in 2014. Though the group is very clear that they appreciate this mainstream recognition, they are adamant that their participation in these events is merely to confront those in positions to receive these images within contexts and parameters set by Abounaddara with a more complex, and in their view accurate, portrayal. This includes attention to the intricacies of the current situation that resist facile narratives, not act as a spectacle of victimization, and work as conduit toward revolution within Syria. They argue that "this is our home and our people. We try to blur the boundaries between journalism, art, and cinema, and highlight propaganda. . . . We are not obliged, like journalists or reporters, to give you facts. We are not addressing the viewer as a judge. We want just them to be punched, touched, and linger in their imagination. To invite them to reconsider the way they see Syrian society or the Middle East in general."

Beyond elucidating openness to a variety of forms of media within a larger expectation that as a collective that deals in the currency of primarily documentary images, there may be an implied expectation that facts should be objective or unbiased. But this is not Abounaddara's mission. They are not producing militant evidence to be deployed in the same spaces as B'Tselem or WITNESS, which tend toward more official settings. Rather, the collective finds purpose in its advocacy for a renewed and forceful conception of representation for Syria and the whole of the Middle East, which has suffered from years of being cast as terrorists or dehumanized victims of violence. To address their approach and further elucidate their theories on the place of the documentary image in the globalized digital age, this section will later analyze Abounaddara's two manifestoes, released three years apart, which put forth their theories on the "right to the image" and a "politics of the image" in the face of dehumanization.

The urgency, extremity, and danger of the situation even exceeds those of the amateur filmmaking done in Iraq, and as such, the collective must add anonymity to their practice (in many cases) for even though they deal with witnesses relaying testimony, the revealing of their identities is done with the utmost caution. In addition, as they argue, this is also a tactic: "We want you, the regime—we want everyone to think that the filmmaker is everywhere. We want to empower our society to produce its own images independently of its all-power systems . . . our films are not products of the market. Our films are addressed to humanity."[67] Here, the filmmakers can lie in wait, like snipers, for their opportunities to intervene. For, as Kiwan posits, "anonymity is really a great space to invent a new world."[68] Abounaddara names the type of documentary practices they engage in an "emergency cinema," a practice that draws on a radical tradition in Syrian cinema as well as radical documentary history more broadly.

When the regime of Bashar al-Assad's father, Hafez al-Assad, took power in 1971, "they killed cinema."[69] "Our parents," asserts Kiwan, "used to go to the cinema every Friday. But the Assad regime instituted a state monopoly on cinema and ended private production, leaving only a handful of theaters in the country, mainly in Damascus."[70] At the same time, the regime created a tightly state-controlled television network system to manufacture propaganda and consent among citizens. In the current climate, regime propaganda competes for airtime with well-produced Daesh videos recruiting martyrs. Syria has had a long tradition of oppositional filmmaking, but it was always up against the image-making power of the state. Under Hafez al-Assad, Syria has descended into one-party, authoritarian rule. "Assad's Syria . . . was fascist in the most correct sense of the word . . . it sought to replace class conflict with devotion to the absolute state."[71] Yet, prior to Hafez al-Assad's clampdown on cinema, Syria certainly had filmmakers whose work evinced radical ideologies. For example, Omar Amiralay, a self-taught filmmaker who began making documentary films in Syria in 1969, played a catalyzing role in the Damascus Spring events of 2000. His films, which evince a quiet, yet militant opposition to Ba'athist ideology, blend a thematic and aesthetic focus on the ordinary, everyday people and places in work such as *The Chickens* (1978) and *Everyday Life in a Syrian Village* (1978), which is still banned in Syria, to experiments with modernist avant-garde practices like in *Film Essay on the Euphrates Dam* (1969). Amiralay was exiled to France in the 1980s before returning shortly before the new millennium and passed away at sixty-six in February 2011, shortly before demonstrations began. He is an important source of inspiration for the group, particularly his film *Everyday Life in a Syrian Village* because it "documents reality as well as blurs the boundaries between art and militancy."[72]

The group bases their notion of emergency on Walter Benjamin's idea that "the tradition of the oppressed teaches us that that the 'emergency situation' in which we live is the rule," where the concept of emergency is based on disturbing and inventing: "disturbing the machine that maintains the rules of the emergency situation, especially the rules of the film and media industries, and inventing new rules of representation."[73] For example, in their film *I Will Cross Tomorrow* (2012), the group employs a set of rushes filmed by a fellow documentarian and teacher of cinema named Bassel Shehadeh, who had returned to his hometown of Homs to train citizen journalists to film and participate in the ongoing revolution.[74] Though he was not a member of the collective, Abounaddara presented it as "his" film, one of the few in their creative output that is not anonymous. The film is marked by claustrophobic framings, running diegetic commentary, and a series of shots "on the run," whereby the subjects of the film, hoping to avoid the snipers firing all around them, say their prayers and then sprint in the direction they need to go, all while holding their phones and recording.

If, for instance, one decoupled many of the images from the diegetic sounds accompanying them, and had no knowledge of the context of their making, it would appear to be, in many moments, an experimental film. This is due to the fact the unintentional avant-garde techniques of abstraction flow directly from the function of the camera as a human appendage for documentation in a state of war. Thus, the physicality of the footage is rendered both highly affective and potent while also formally abstract on another visual register. Urgency and aesthetics collide under a state of emergency. Surprisingly, Abounaddara dedicated the film to the sniper—they refer to him as "Brother Sniper". On their Facebook page, when the film was uploaded, they wrote: "I will cross tomorrow. You can kill me, but your children will see my image. With love, Bassel Shehadeh."[75] Beyond the fearless, militant declaration is a larger statement by Abounaddara, namely that the regime can kill individuals but not defeat the resistance.

In sum, the task for Abounaddara is enormous. "We don't feel we are dealing with a war. We are dealing with a revolution" and are "working to represent this explosion of energy" by creating bullet films, not to kill the spectator but to affectively awaken them in a militant direction, faced with a plethora of militant evidence. Thus, as filmmakers, they avoid "the "capture of tragedy or the confrontation or the current news as it unfolds;" instead, they seek to "construct a new image with the tools of cinema" that dislocates the spectator away from a mainstream, global flow of approved media images by constructing a documentary practice in a new temporality.[76] The idea is thus:

> always to collapse things, to let the image tell more than you are seeing. We like the idea of a dialectical image, as expressed by Walter Benjamin, an image that makes possible an encounter between past and present while opening new perspectives. There are two ways to represent reality: One is to say that the image is evidence. I show you the soldier with his weapon shooting and I tell you, as a filmmaker, he's committing a crime; see the evidence, see the proof. The other way is not to use the image to give proof or evidence, but to suggest to and address the viewer not like a judge but like a universal human being who has to ask himself some questions about the present and the past.[77]

Abounaddara wants to destabilize the viewer and the idea of documentary evidence. In this way, they recast militant evidence from exposure, shock, and proof to one of openness, memory, and unfolding. Merely showing mutilated, anonymous corpses overwhelms the memory with those images, obfuscating the scale of the tragedy. Yet, as Kiwan argues, if "I give you a testimony—if you see the tragedy through the eyes of a child—for example, we filmed children telling stories about massacres—I have a duty to give you space for imagination"[78]—and not just imagination but a radical openness, on the level of a fundamental and unyielding assertion of humanity, to consider the plight of distant others not as victims but as digital active witnesses, potential allies and comrades, wielding militant evidence as one of many emerging and affirmative radical documentary practices in the networked digital age.

Abounaddara's initial manifesto, "A Right to the Image for All (2012)," opens with a recognition of the "hyper speed" at which images are captured, edited, disseminated, and consumed and the paramount role that images have in constructing our "political, ethical, and intimate" lives and realities.[79]

When such hypermediation collides with the current climate of endless wars, occupations, mass incarceration, and human rights abuses as well as the need to document, expose, and adjudicate injustice, it often "creates typical images of victims," which robs the individuals and groups enmeshed in these horrible situations of their humanity. The images, they argue, comprise the "human debris of human madness," where emaciated and mutilated bodies are depicted among bombed-out, dystopian landscapes, ruins, and/or refugee camps.[80] Such images traffic not in the representation of people (their lives, friends, relatives, social networks, etc.) but of bodies that simply stand for human suffering, not dignity, life, or peace. These representations of human suffering arise in the context of political and ethical choices made within legal and institutional frameworks that govern things like privacy and control of one's image. Celebrities, Abounaddara argues, have a legal system in place so that they can "own" and protect their images and have a platform to "speak" by "virtue of social conventions, economic power or political circumstances" that empower such speech.[81] But importantly they ask: "What about those who cannot speak? The persons whose humanity is suppressed in images from wars, mass violations of human rights and other similar situations are not allowed to speak. Their humanity stops at the rights of bystanders to freedom of expression. You can have the dignity of a person or be a victim, but you are not allowed to be both; and, most importantly, you are not legally allowed to choose what you want to be. Your wounds can speak, but you cannot."[82]

The violence, gruesomely evidenced on people's bodies, is the real currency of wars, occupations, mass incarceration, and human rights violations as its legibility is both universal and exceptional. But the representation of humanity and dignity is a casualty of mediation and the demand for constant representations of novel, spectacular, and shocking images. Given this perilous situation, Abounaddara identifies a paramount concern in the globalized digital age: a universal right to one's own image for "persons and groups reduced to 'bare life' in wars, human rights abuses, and other similar situations" based on a holistic reading of existing international law that emerges from a "bundle" of already guaranteed rights. Abounaddara argues that "this bundle is what we get when we seek the concrete meaning of the fundamental human rights included in the Universal Declaration of Human Rights (UDHR), the International Covenant of Civil and Political Rights (ICPR), and the Covenant of Economic, Social, and Cultural Rights (ICESCR) as they relate to images of individuals and groups."[83] Yet, beyond the official considerations, how does the group consider the concept of the right to the image? "It's dignity," asserts Kiwan. He continues,

Since the beginning of the revolution, the first word of the demonstrators was *karameh*—dignity. And as filmmakers we have to translate what *karameh* means in formal and aesthetic terms. We believe that people should be required to represent powerless individuals with dignity. Sensational media corrupt our revolution. . . . But our project is to use the existing rules—the rights to privacy, self-determination, and dignity—to arrive at principles globally respected regarding the right to one's image. We demand that the principle of dignity in representation be respected by the media. There are many abuses around the world, where images of dead bodies are cynically used to gain more viewers. This trivializes evil to the point where the media is playing the same game of the horrific spectacle as ISIS.[84]

Thus, Abounaddara's appeal for dignity is firmly rooted in an account-codified by international human rights law as a way to craft an ethical argument for privacy, dignity, and self-determination within a pervasive media environment obsessed with spectacle and dehumanization.

In a follow-up manifesto titled "Montrons l'horreur en Syrie pour sortir de l'ignominie" (2015), published widely in translation as an editorial in international newspapers, the collective revisited their earlier manifesto, refining their call and focusing on the history of the ethics of representation since the images of the liberation of Nazi concentration camps in the wake of World War II. These images, they argue, were used by filmmakers "in the service of human rights, and their films were shown in courts, schools, and cinemas."[85] Yet, the rest of the world watches "unflinchingly the spectacle of a crime against humanity broadcast practically live from Syria." Images of mangled corpses (a "spectacle of abasement") accumulate daily; there is no lack of evidence or awareness of what is going on. But, as Abounaddara contends, it is " not enough simply to display corpses to make the world open its eyes. Images must also be produced and distributed within an appropriate framework."[86] As it stands, the group argues that global media companies who have been denied access to cover Syria from the inside, traffic in and appropriate a decontextualized, dehumanizing flow of images that render death and abasement routine. This lax attitude towards visual representation directly benefits Daesh, the Assad regime, and global news advertisers. The group bases its appeal to the international community on both the "dignity" and "personhood" enshrined in the UNDHR after the Holocaust within the larger ethical responsibility of on-the-ground image makers in the midst of both a nascent revolution and an ongoing crime against humanity. They advocate for individual Syrians speaking directly to the international community through their short videos, rather than what Robyn Creswell has called "mute collectives of the dead."[87] Yet, there is no overarching ideology or political commitment other than a fierce desire to challenge representations of Syria and prevent easy conclusions about the revolution—a mission to lift Syrians from the status of victims to active and anonymous participants in a fluid and fragile revolutionary situation.

Abounaddara attempts to clear and protect an immaterial space for this situation to maintain itself. As Kiwan argues, "We try to show context, but without any Marxist or theoretical or intellectual perspective. We just allow our work to be open-ended, to suggest that there are many aspects of reality, because the danger is to stereotype and reduce this general and popular uprising to stereotypical characters, places, and events."[88] To make films in Syria, according to Kiwan, involves "either collaborating with a unique narrative system that is sanctioned by unrelenting censorship, or else resisting. We chose to resist. However, unlike our older colleague Omar Amiralay, who was the first to do so, we had no public, or any material with which to interest distributors."[89] As noted above, Abounaddara views filmmaking in Syria as existing between two extremes: censorship and resistance, with the collective occupying the latter mode. Specifically, and akin to the theorizations of the camera as a gun in previous generations, they see their role in "the position of a sniper, lying in ambush behind apparently harmless short films," where their original impetus was to "reach our public right under the censors' nose." In general, Abounaddara films can be identified by their brevity, overabundance of static shots, and an eclectic array of techniques, soundtracks, direct-to-camera testimonials, photomontages, advertisements, and interviews—a mélange of media texts that are repurposed in service of unrelenting opposition. Part of this practice is situational; working in a state of emergency manifests a host of ever-shifting constraints, including unreliable access to an internet connection, constant catastrophic violence and trauma, safe and unsafe sites for filming, among many others. At the same time, Abounaddara notes the "unprecedented sense of freedom" that blurs boundaries between non-fiction and fiction, politics, and aesthetics. The collective argues that they "make aesthetics and political choices that portray the world in which our reference points have been turned upside down by the revolution. It also conveys our pledge to represent our people's enthusiasm by ensuring they are not reduced to stereotyped characters, places or formats."[90]

Part of this assurance against stereotypes lies in the groups' inclination toward individuals and everydayness, as seen in the work of Amiralay, as an affirmative form of resistance against the trauma, destruction, and dying around them. "If you want to resist death and tragedy," they contend, "you have to show life and detail from everyday life . . . because it's the only way to keep faith in the future and in life."[91] This attention to representation also extends to the domain of counterinformation, particularly in the midst of a fragile, inchoate revolutionary situation.

In discussing the 2008 Egyptian revolution centered on Tahrir Square, Abounaddara notes that global television coverage, "by associating a general popular uprising with a particular place," ended up "conditioning people" to the extent that revolution became connected with what was going on in the square; when the people left and traffic returned, the revolution, at least represented via television, was then "over" thus normalizing a moment of great rupture as an event with a coherent beginning, middle, and end—snuffing out sparks of revolutionary fervor.[92] In the context of Syria, which lacks the on-the-ground media access seen in Egypt in 2008, the images that emerge are thus a "vital source of information." Abounaddara argues,

> It is hard to talk calmly about images of the Syrian revolution because they are such a vital source of information, because they have cost so much blood and tears, and because they are the subject of an idolization overflowing with humanitarian reasons. From our point of view, we believe these images express a twofold impotence: that of a defenseless people trying to snatch their freedom from a soldiery of the most barbaric kind, and that of the people filming the images, who are trying to come to terms with a revolutionary saga using devices that are particularly ill-adapted because television has quickly used them to its own advantage.[93]

Television, they contend, "imposes its own codes by appropriating certain images broadcast on the social media" and then "giving them precise orders regarding the filming and choice of subjects."[94] In the film *Media Kill*, for example, a film referenced in the introduction, the anonymous subject of the film recounts a disturbing trend in TV news. "The media play to their markets," he says. "When there is talk of a ceasefire, for example, they tell us, 'send us images of shots being fired. They want to see gunfire, they say it openly."[95] Thus, television actively worked to support a trite conception of the revolution, complete with its "set of clichéd images of suffering and bloodshed, as well as by sanctioning a collection of 'spokespeople' and 'representatives' of dubious legitimacy . . . dumbing down, formatting and manipulating, by taking away everything that was original and authentic about the revolution."[96]

Therefore, Abounaddara adopted a strategy of counterinformation, not only against mainstream news but also against the Assad regime, Daesh, and other fundamentalist extremist groups that use the spectacle of violence tactically in the media to shape narratives to favor their side. They have the correct, slick, visible evidence primed for broadcast and thus set the terms of acceptable debate and legitimate factions. But the enemy in the crosshairs of

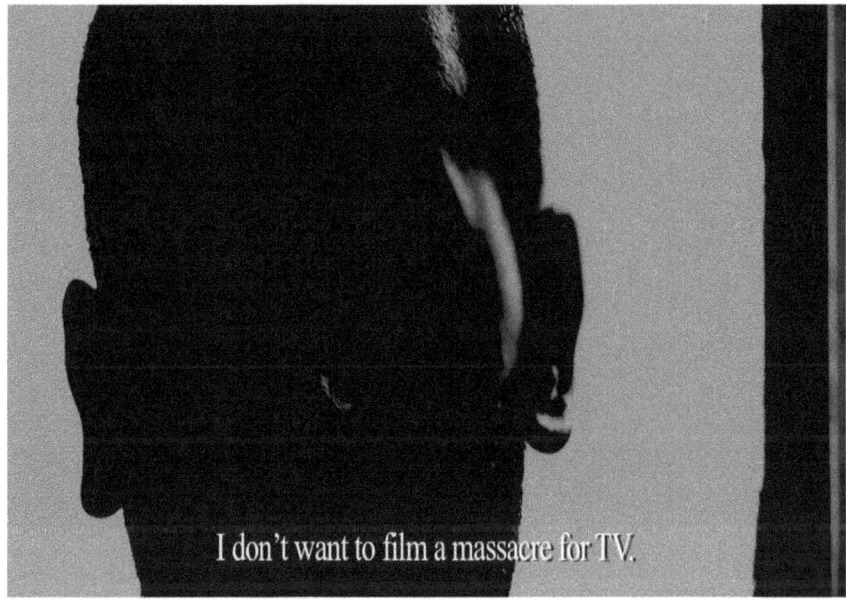

Figure 4.3 Still from *Media Kill*.

Abounaddara's "sniper shots" or "bullet films" is not only the regime. "We're always presented as filmmakers fighting the regime," according to Kiwan, "but we see ourselves as filmmakers empowering our civil society to give it the possibility to produce its own image independent of any political or media agenda."[97] Thus, they seek a productive and creative space outside of current power systems, a task made easier via their anonymity: "To use . . . anonymity, and the mystery [of it] to [their] benefit."[98] The use of anonymity is helpful for the nonsectarian and polyvocal political message that Abounaddara is putting forth. Mainly the group makes its films for Syrians but with an eye toward international viewers as well—though they often lack the full context for deep understanding. This is due to the fact the films are generally released first in Arabic (before being subtitled into French and/or English) and are largely in media res, in the sense that Syrians and native Arabic speakers possess a much deeper context and framing for what is shown.

Their 2017 "Witness" series, for example, features six films, each from a different vantage on the conflict. The films feature a different silhouetted man (to protect identity) against the same backdrop, testifying about their highly specific, personal experiences of the conflict.[99] As a Western viewer, even with knowledge of Arabic, it is hard to make sense of the stories or gain any sense of who the men are. Syrian viewers on the other hand would

Figure 4.4 Still from *The Witness-Jihad*.

recognize regional and class accents, specific historic, geographic, and political references, and other forms of untranslated cultural knowledge. Here, banality serves a dual function: it works to both de-escalate the divisions among Syrians and distance foreign spectators uninterested in actively working to understand. The sniper shots are also targeted at complacent viewers. Here, Abounaddara hopes to confuse, provoke, and activate Western audiences "by playing on the real or imagined differences that characterize our public here and elsewhere."[100] They try and show a "humanity that is the same everywhere," but their eclectic, short films often frustrate "certain left-wing Syrian and European elite" who admonish the group for not representing reality in a proper, easily digestible, morally unambiguous way.[101] As Kiwan asserts, "The idea here is also to confuse people. We want the universal viewer to recognize himself, his place, his country in this Syrian place and voice. We want him to imagine that he could be there."[102]

This recognition is also aided and complicated by many references in Abounaddara's work to larger film traditions and ruptures in the capacity for representation. The film *Syria Today*, for example, aligns the history of cinema and the horror of the Holocaust in one simple shot: a steam train bound down the tracks toward the camera, much like the early Lumiere aculatitè *The Arrival of a Train* or the macabre footage of trains arriving at death camps under the cover of night in Alain Resnais's *Night and Fog*.[103] In other

Figure 4.5 Still from *The Witness-Jihad*.

films, such *Here and Elsewhere*, the group alludes to the militant work of Godard and the Dziga Vertov group as well as the seeming disinterest of the West (elsewhere) at the modern-day genocide happening in Syria (here).[104] Yet, the actual content of the film is a brief interview with a former regime soldier who had defected to revolutionary counterforces while fighting in Homs. The "here" and "elsewhere" within the diegesis of the world of the film refers to the positions available to young people in Syria—with the revolution or against it. While the soldier seems like he is speaking off the cuff, various brief cuts in the film show an unnamed director coaching the soldier. Another film, *The Kid* (2015), borrows its title and soundtrack from the well-known Charlie Chaplin film of the same name, where Chaplin play a tramp who adopts an orphan.[105] The film opens with images of Syrian children neatly dressed in rows while chanting support for Bashar al-Assad. They each hold images of Bashar's face aloft on small, individual placards. The exact opposite sentiments are expressed in the next scene, where a young boy recites rehearsed and rhyming lines about Bashar's murder of children as he shakes his small finger at the camera. In the next scene, we see the same boy, now filmed outside, says while crying, "Bashar has killed us. What did we

Figure 4.6 Still from *Here and Elsewhere*.

Figure 4.7 Still from *The Kid*.

do to him?" In the final scene, the boy appears in a fake Daesh propaganda video. He holds a rifle and declares himself as "a lion cub of the caliphate" and promises death to his enemies. The final title card announces, "To be continued," as the soundtrack from Chaplin's *The Kid* (1921) plays.

Like *Here and Elsewhere*, the film highlights the highly constructed nature of the film as the images of the child's rehearsed antiregime and

Syria and Abounaddara | 197

Figure 4.8 Still from *The Kid*.

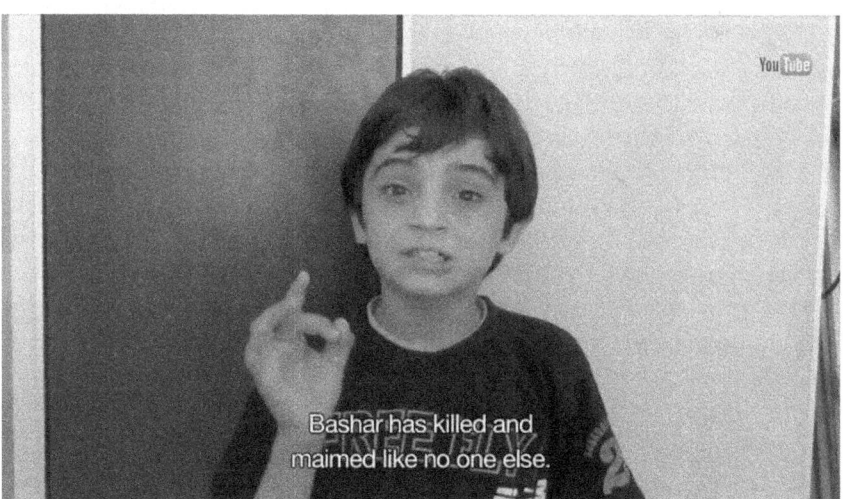

Figure 4.9 Still from *The Kid*.

Daesh speeches are juxtaposed with the highly choreographed propagandistic pro-Assad rallies. Even children are malleable political actors in a state of war. In these and other films, the militant evidence captured, harnessed, and deployed by Abounaddara, sniper shots that make up an emergency cinema composed of militant evidence, function in both an immediate and a long-term way for Syrian and Western audiences. In the immediate term, for both the Syrians making and the Syrians viewing Abounaddara's weekly films, emergency cinema is a collective, anonymous, and largely affirmative practice of resistance. For Western audiences, the emergency nature of the cinema is both a call to engage with the war but also, importantly, to reorientate their vision and conception of "victims" of distant suffering in the digital age. In the *longue durée* sense of the term, emergency cinema is also a practice of digitally archiving and storing, on a weekly basis, images and testimonies of the ongoing war in Syria. This growing digital collection of Abounaddara's work exists as well as what Stuart Hall has called the "living archive."[106] The "living" nature of the archive emerges not just from its dynamic nature but also from the accumulation of short films that evince an affirmative assertion of not just humanity but a humanity in the midst of crisis that is freed from class and religion, unmarked by names, titles, and statuses. But this works two ways. For Syrians, it is a collective practice against the rifts in the country, both concretizing and subjectifying "the other side" for other Syrians, a collectivizing gesture of resistance against the divisions and dictatorship of the regime. At once, it mocks the regime, documents and archives the brutality of war (in a nonspectacular way), and creates an interstice for the collective emergence of a new Syria in the wake of catastrophic destruction. Here, the interstice is open and emerging, purposefully vague. For Westerners, the interstice is more controlled. It is a brief, subjective, and immersive glimpse into a distant conflict that is foreclosed by a lack of knowledge and conditioned by peripatetic Western media narratives reliant on the spectacles of distant suffering. Here, Abounaddara's sniper shots are clearly aimed at journalists, writers, artists, academics, and others who tend to be most interested in these conflicts, or those who might employ the graphic, anonymous images of Syrians in news accounts, documentaries, or media projects. Abounaddara does not ask but rather they demand the right to their images, their cultures, and their subjectivities. They, not others, get to present those to the world and shape their narratives as they see fit.

Toward an Emerging Cinema in Syria

As the war in Syria has worn on and the revolutionary fervor has receded into the weariness of years of armed conflict, the country stands at a crossroads. Through all of the fighting, Bashar al-Assad is still in power. The stakes and situation of image making have shifted, but the importance of wielding militant evidence can be seen in an emerging cinema in Syria that is the longer-term vocation for the filmmakers, activists, and everyday people who have fought for revolution and against decades of state repression and authoritarianism. The terms of the fight have changed, but the mission remains the same: steady and continued opposition to the Assad regime and authoritarian politics—to further strengthen the goals by creating alternatives to state corridors of power in the media, news, and entertainment, which need to be confronted by oppositional images, stories, and evidence. Abounaddara has continued their transmedia advocacy and also ventured into longer form and non-anonymous filmmaking. For example, Maya al-Khoury's *On Revolution*, which premiered at *Documenta 14* in Kassel, Germany, in 2017. The film attempts to make the revolution between 2011 and 2017 visible beyond short bullet films. Al-Khoury directed the film within the framework of the Abounaddara collective, editing footage shot since 2011 into a 140-minute film that followed various narratives and characters over the years of the revolution, fostering a coherent yet complex microhistory that illuminates various stages of the revolution on a human scale.

Other groups, such as Bidayyat for Audiovisual Arts, which was founded in 2013 and is based in Lebanon, have been focused on the education, funding, and distribution of Syrian-made, long-form documentaries as a way to structure and use the creative energy and image-making culture that arose during the war. As the group contends, "It is no longer enough to claim to be objectively documenting reality and conveying it meticulously and professionally to your audience; now, anyone who wishes to make documentary films is obliged to have a viewpoint; to interrogate their relationship with reality in an effort to invoke that reality from their own perspective."[107] For example Ziad Kalthoum's *Taste of Cement* (2018), an essay documentary, focuses on the themes of creation and destruction intertwined with an effective political critique regarding the treatment and rights of Syrian refugee workers in Beirut, Lebanon. Kalthoum was born in Homs, Syria, and began making short documentaries in 2011. The film is comprised of static, dramatically composed long-takes interspersed with war footage, montages of laboring men, and close-ups. The soundtrack is at times quite immersive, particularly in scenes of construction in Beirut and fighting in Syria. *Taste of Cement* documents the construction of an anonymous half-built high-rise on the outskirts of Beirut, a city in the midst of an expansion. Throughout the film, a nameless group of Syrian men, who make up the majority of the construction crew, go about their typical days completing a variety of construction jobs.

Taste of Cement also features disembodied voice-over narration that, coupled with the sound choices, endow the images with the force of critique. For example, early in the film, the camera lingers on a sign that reads "curfew imposed on Syrian workers after 7pm, any violator is punished by law."

The voice-over later notes that racism is spreading toward Syrian refugees in Lebanon. During the day, the men toil away at the construction site, perched high on the skyscraper with the Mediterranean Sea gleaming in the distance. In the evenings, due to both the discriminatory curfew and the low wages, the men live on the construction site in makeshift quarters in the basement of the building. For all intents and purposes, they are imprisoned by the cement. Before the men go to sleep, they gather near one another on damp concrete and in dim light to consume news from Syria on their phones. They scroll through images of Aleppo and Damascus in ruins. In one particularly evocative shot, the camera lingers in an extreme close-up of the eyeball of one the men as he views a video of bombs exploding. The bursts of light flash across his pupils, the mirrored images leave us wondering what he may be thinking and feeling. The film often juxtaposes images of the cement rubble in Syria with the construction cement used in Beirut for the high-rise. In many instances, creation and destruction look similar, but the implicit message of the film is that the workers in this situation are stuck rebuilding a foreign country while their own is being destroyed. The ground for optimism is that one day they can return to Syria to build rather than work in exile. As the opening narration notes, "When war begins, the builders have to leave to another country where the war just ended. Waiting until war has swept through their homeland. Then they return to rebuild it." The film ends with a dedication to all workers in exile.[108]

Other films, such as Saeed al-Batal and Ghiath Ayoub's *Still Recording* (2018), attempts to make sense of the war and revolution through narratives and images culled from an enormous amount of amateur footage. Al Batal and Ayoub edited down over 450 hours of footage supplied by eight cameramen into a taut and powerful 128-minute feature documentary. The film follows the story of Saeed and his friend Milad, formerly nonviolent art students, as they depart their homes in Damascus in 2011 to take part in the armed revolution in Douma (Eastern Ghouta). The film represents various moments in their lives over the next four years as revolutionary fervor and earnestness gives way to weariness and feelings of complete futility. Al Batal and Ayoub smuggled seven hard drives worth of footage out of Syria to edit in the relative safety of Beirut, where Bidayyat's offices are located. As al-Batal argues, "This film is an observation of what happened for us, for all my generation – one that believed in the Revolution ... It is both an attempt to understand the contradictions at play in the exceptional situation of war, and a search to define the word 'artist,' and his or her position in society: what is art in a revolution, in war, in death?"[109] The answers to these questions are also necessary to consider another question. What is art when the initial revolution did not come to fruition? This will be answered in time, once the effects of the emerging cinema in and beyond Syria has grappled with and represented it. Further, this emerging cinema will be buttressed by countless Syrian and global human rights and transmedia advocacy groups as they archive, verify, and deploy militant evidence for effective radicality in their attempt to hold the Assad regime accountable for all manner of crimes against humanity. The revolution is not over, just temporarily stalled, and Abounaddara as well as a new generation of digital active witnesses, film and media collectives, artists, journalists, and revolutionaries will keep it alive.

Notes

1. See https://vimeo.com/36130185.
2. Donatella Della Ratta, *Shooting a Revolution: Visual Media and Warfare in Syria* (London: Pluto, 2018), 131–132.
3. Robin Yassin-Kassab and Leila al-Shami, *Burning Country: Syrians in Revolution and War* (London: Pluto, 2016), 14.
4. Ibid., 137.
5. Jay Weissberg, "*Silvered Water, Syria Self Portrait* Review: A Wrenching Documentary," *Variety*, May 16, 2014, https://variety.com/2014/film/festivals/cannes-film-review-silvered-water-syria-self-portrait-1201183212/.
6. See https://vimeo.com/184030580.
7. Wendy Kozol, *Distant Wars Visible: The Ambivalence of Witnessing* (Minneapolis: University of Minnesota Press, 2014), 206.
8. Ibid., 200.
9. Ibid., 205.
10. Chad Elias, "Emergency Cinema and the Dignified Image: Cell Phone Activism and Filmmaking in Syria," *Film Quarterly* 71, no. 1 (Fall 2017), September 14, 2017, https://filmquarterly.org/2017/09/14/emergency-cinema-and-the-dignified-image-cell-phone-activism-and-filmmaking-in-syria/.
11. Ibid.
12. Moustafa Bayoumi, "The Civil War in Syria Is Invisible—but This Anonymous Film Collective Is Changing That," *Nation*, June 29, 2015, https://www.thenation.com/article/the-civil-war-in-syria-is-invisible-but-this-anonymous-film-collective-is-changing-that/.
13. Susan Sontag, *On Photography* (New York: Macmillan, 1977), 99.
14. Ibid., 111.
15. Elias, "Emergency Cinema and the Dignified Image: Cell Phone Activism and Filmmaking in Syria."
16. Teo Bugbee, "'For Sama' Review: Out of Besieged Aleppo, a Documentary," *New York Times*, July 25, 2019, https://www.nytimes.com/2019/07/25/movies/for-sama-review.html.
17. Ibid.

18. Christy Lange, "Emergency Cinema: How the Anonymous Film Collective Abounaddara Represents Daily Life in Syria," *Frieze*, March 18, 2016, https://frieze.com/article/emergency-cinema.
19. Ibid.
20. Julianne Burton, "Toward a History of Social Documentary in Latin America," in *The Social Documentary in Latin America*, ed. Julianne Burton (Pittsburgh, PA: University of Pittsburgh Press, 1990), 17.
21. Ibid., 18.
22. Ibid., 18–19.
23. Ibid., 17.
24. Ivens and Marker were by no means the only filmmakers to make the pilgrimage to Havana. As Hans Schoots notes, they were part of a "long processions of Europeans and Americans . . . Agnes Varda and Armand Gatti from France, Richard Leacock, D. A. Pennebaker and Albert Maysles from America, Roman Karmen and Mikhail Kalatozov from the Soviet Union, and Cesare Zavattini from Italy." Hans Schoots, *Living Dangerously: A Biography of Joris Ivens* (Amsterdam: Amsterdam University Press, 2000), 266.
25. Burton, "Toward a History of Social Documentary in Latin America," 18.
26. As Waugh argues, "Once there, Ivens got to work without delay. The evening of his arrival, the entire staff of ICAIC, already 300 strong, turned out for the lecture he had been asked to make. The Cubans were aware of Ivens' prodigious reputation as a political filmmaker but hardly knew his work at all: his East German epic, *Song of the Rivers* (1954), a film on the world labor movement, had had some clandestine screenings before the Revolution, and a few Cubans who had recently been to Europe had seen *LA SEINE A RECONTRÉ PARIS* (*PARIS MEETS THE SEINE*, 1957), Ivens lyrical tribute to his adopted home which had won the Palme d'or at Cannes in 1958. Not untypically, the lecture was turned into a dialogue by the Cubans' impatience to get to know their mythical visitor." See Thomas Waugh, "Travel Notebook—A People in Arms: Joris Ivens' Work in Cuba," in *Jump Cut: A Review of Contemporary Media*, no. 22 (May 1980): 25–29.
27. Schoots, *Living Dangerously: A Biography of Joris Ivens*, 269.
28. Ibid.
29. Susan Martin-Márquez, "By Camera and By Gun: Joris Ivens and the Radicalization of Latin American Filmmakers," *Ivens Magazine*, no. 18 (December 2013): 13.
30. Ibid., 14.
31. As Martin-Márquez argues, Ivens's wider strategy, formulated in collaboration with a host of Latin American associates and continuing for some time after his early-1960s visits to Cuba (well beyond the presumed period of Soviet sponsorship), was four-pronged: (1) training of soldier-filmmakers from throughout Latin America who would both participate in and film guerrilla warfare; (2) supporting Latin American "civilians" interested in producing militant films that might be shown in alternative or clandestine circuits, if not through traditional commercial channels; (3) commissioning and/or collecting footage shot by Latin American filmmakers for incorporation into the work of radical European cineastes; and (4) pitching of coproductions of "legitimate" films directed by Ivens. See Martin-Márquez, "By Camera and By Gun," 14–15.
32. Waugh, "Travel Notebook—A People in Arms: Joris Ivens' Work in Cuba."
33. John Mraz, "Santiago Álvarez: From Dramatic Form to Direct Cinema," in *The Social Documentary in Latin America*, ed. Julianne Burton (Pittsburgh, PA: University of Pittsburgh Press, 1990), 131.
34. Fidel Castro, "Word to Intellectuals," in *Fidel Castro Reader*, ed. David Deutschmann (Melbourne, Australia: Ocean, 2008), 225.

35. Michael Chanan, *Cuban Cinema* (Minneapolis: University of Minnesota Press, 2004), 30.
36. Joshua Malitsky, *Post Revolution Non-Fiction Film: Building the Soviet and Cuban Nations* (Bloomington: Indiana University Press, 2013), 25.
37. Michael Chanan. *The Politics of Documentary* (London: British Film Institute, 2007), 199.
38. Travis Wilkerson, "Cuba's Santiago Álvarez, Cinematographer and Revolutionary," *Socialism and Liberation Magazine*. March 1, 2006, https://www.liberationnews.org/06-03-01-cubas-santiago-alvarez-cinemat-html/.
39. Julio Garcia Espinosa, "For an Imperfect Cinema," trans. Julianne Burton, *Jump Cut: A Review of Contemporary Media*, no. 20 (1979), http://www.ejumpcut.org/archive/onlinessays/JC20folder/ImperfectCinema.html. This is an updated translation based the original essay published in *Cine Cubano* issue 66/67 (1969). Burton notes that it "is substantially different from the other English-language version published in the summer 1971 issue of the now defunct British film magazine *Afterimage*, where various sentences and paragraphs were omitted with no acknowledgment of the deletions."
40. Ibid.
41. Ibid.
42. Ibid.
43. Ibid.
44. Della Ratta, *Shooting a Revolution*, 138.
45. Ibid.
46. Chad Elias, "Emergency Cinema and the Dignified Image: Cell Phone Activism and Filmmaking in Syria," *Film Quarterly* 71, no. 1 (2017), September 14, 2017, https://filmquarterly.org/2017/09/14/emergency-cinema-and-the-dignified-image-cell-phone-activism-and-filmmaking-in-syria/.
47. Ibid.
48. Yassin-Kassab and al-Shami, *Burning Country*, 16–17.
49. Ibid., 17.
50. Della Ratta, *Shooting a Revolution*, 19.
51. Yassin-Kassab and al-Shami, *Burning Country*, 39.
52. Ibid., 40.
53. Elias, "Emergency Cinema and the Dignified Image."
54. Della Ratta, *Shooting a Revolution*, 194.
55. Ibid., 160.
56. Josepha I. Wessels, "The Role of Video Recordings in the Collective Memory of the Syrian Uprising" (English Version), in *Konflikten i Syrien: årsager, konsekvenser og handlemuligheder Denmark*, ed. Bjørn Møller and Søren Schmidt (Copenhagen: Djøf, 2016).
57. Josepha I. Wessels, "YouTube and the Role of Digital Video for Transnational Justice in Syria," *Politik* 4 (2016): 14–16.
58. Yassin-Kassab and al-Shami. *Burning Country*, 106.
59. Dia Kayyali and Raja Althaibani, "Vital Human Rights Evidence from Syria Is Disappearing from YouTube," August 2017, https://blog.witness.org/2017/08/vital-human-rights-evidence-syria-disappearing-youtube/.
60. See https://syrianarchive.org/.
61. Ibid.
62. Kayyali and Althaibani, "Vital Human Rights Evidence from Syria Is Disappearing from YouTube."
63. See https://syrianarchive.org/.

64. See https://syrianarchive.org/.
65. See https://syrianarchive.org/en/investigations/Aleppo-Mosque-Bombing.
66. Della Ratta, *Shooting a Revolution*, 13.
67. Laura Feinstein, "This Syrian Filmmaking Collective Shows the Banality of Life in War," *Vice*, June 25, 2015, https://www.vice.com/en_us/article/mvxgap/this-syrian-art-collective-shines-an-intimate-light-on-life-in-their-war-torn-country-456.
68. Melena Ryzik, "Syrian Collective Offers View of Life Behind a Conflict," *New York Times*, October 18, 2015, https://www.nytimes.com/2015/10/19/movies/syrian-film-collective-offers-view-of-life-behind-a-conflict.html?mcubz=0.
69. Ibid.
70. Ibid.
71. Yassin-Kassab and al-Shami, *Burning Country*, 14.
72. Sonja Mejcher-Atassi, "Abounaddara's Take on Images in the Syrian Revolution: A Conversation between Charif Kiwan and Akram Zaatari," *Jadaliyya*, September 2, 2014, http://www.jadaliyya.com/pages/index/19080/abounaddara%E2%80%99s-take-on-images-in-the-syrian-revolut.
73. Bayoumi, "The Civil War in Syria Is Invisible."
74. See https://vimeo.com/43241736.
75. Bayoumi, "The Civil War in Syria Is Invisible."
76. Mejcher-Atassi, "Abounaddara's Take on Images in the Syrian Revolution."
77. Ibid.
78. Ibid.
79. Abounaddara, "A Right to the Image for All" (2012), https://www.fabrikzeitung.ch/a-right-to-the-image-for-all/#/.
80. Ibid.
81. Ibid.
82. Ibid.
83. Ibid.
84. Bayoumi, "The Civil War in Syria Is Invisible."
85. Abounaddara, "Montrons l'horreur en Syrie pour sortir de l'ignominie," *Le Monde*, October 20, 2015, https://www.lemonde.fr/idees/article/2015/10/21/montrons-l-horreur-en-syrie-pour-sortir-de-l-ignominie_4793538_3232.html (translations mine).
86. Ibid.
87. Robyn Creswell, "Voices from a Different Syria" *New York Review of Books*, March 21, 2016, http://www.nybooks.com/daily/2016/03/21/voices-from-different-syria-abounaddara-films/.
88. Mejcher-Atassi, "Abounaddara's Take on Images in the Syrian Revolution."
89. Cécile Boëx, "Emergency Cinema: An Interview with Syrian Collective Abounaddara," *Books and Ideas*, trans. Susannah Dale, October 5, 2012, http://www.booksandideas.net/Emergency-Cinema.html.
90. Ibid.
91. Ibid.
92. Ibid.
93. Ibid.
94. Ibid.
95. See https://vimeo.com/47100634.
96. Boëx, "Emergency Cinema: An Interview with Syrian Collective Abounaddara."
97. Bayoumi, "The Civil War in Syria Is Invisible."
98. Laura Feinstein, "This Syrian Filmmaking Collective Shows the Banality of Life in War."

99. See https://vimeo.com/208817266.
100. Mejcher-Atassi, "Abounaddara's Take on Images in the Syrian Revolution."
101. Ibid.
102. Ibid.
103. See https://vimeo.com/35736955.
104. See https://vimeo.com/194958878.
105. See https://vimeo.com/143357683.
106. Stuart Hall, "Constituting an Archive," *Third Text* (Spring 2001): 89–92.
107. "Our Understanding," Who We Are, Bidayyat, https://bidayyat.org/about.php#.XWbQ2utKgoo.
108. For a broader discussion of documentaries made in the Syrian refugee diaspora, see Ryan Watson, "Refugees Searching for Home in the Syrian Diaspora," *Review of Middle East Studies*, 54, no. 1 (2020): 97–106.
109. See http://www.cinemadureel.org/film/still-recording-2/?lang=en.

Conclusion

Militant Evidence and the Future
of Radical Documentary

VICE NEWS' VIDEO report "Myanmar's Rohingya Genocide" (2020) examined the brutal persecution of the mostly Islamic Rohingya ethnic group in the Rakhine state of Myanmar since 2017. The Rohingya are not officially recognized by the government as one of the 135 ethnic groups in the predominantly Buddhist Myanmar.[1] In a reign of terror and extreme brutality, the Myanmar military has burned villages, raped and killed inhabitants, and brutalized their bodies. These actions have caused a massive wave of more than seven hundred thousand essentially stateless Rohingyans to seek refuge by crossing the Naf River into nearby Bangladesh, which has kept its borders open to the refugees. After arriving in Bangladesh, many of the Rohingya people end up living at the Kutupalong Extension Site in Cox's Bazar, the largest refugee camp in the world. One response to this genocide and forced refugee status has been the formation of the Arakan Rohingya Salvation Army (ARSA), an armed Rohingya liberation group that fights the Myanmar military, on their terms, with guns and munitions. Yet, ordinary people are also fighting in a nonviolent way, using the potential weapons they possess.

Early in the news report, *Vice* correspondent Gianna Toboni visits the camp to speak with some of the Rohingya people who have settled there. She is surrounded by a large group of men and boys who eagerly hand her their cell phones and tablets. Nearly all of them have documented the atrocities committed against the Rohingya people in the Rakhine state. The images are horrifying: charred bodies, decapitated corpses, and burning villages where homes had women and children trapped inside. But, beyond the sickening shock, what force can the images have? When they enter into the realm of the digital network, there is a chance of ungovernability and illegibility. Is there room for a radical documentary practice that does not fetishize the spectacle of atrocity and trauma but uses the forceful affects and effects generated toward activism that has a material effect on the Rohingya people's lives? Where must the images go and who must they be seen by to realize the productive outcomes of this potential force?

As demonstrated throughout the book, a partial answer comes from enmeshing these images in the proper ecologies for resistance, counterarchives, accountability, solidarity, networks of legibility, and visibility. Like in Syria, anonymous groups of citizen journalists, activists, bloggers, and media makers in Myanmar have been collecting militant evidence of the brutal oppression of the Rohingya. They then share it with the world via a WhatsApp group that communicates daily with domestic and international news organizations. The penalty for being caught doing this sort of work is forced disappearance (i.e., death), but those risking the penalty are attempting to document the Myanmar government's ongoing genocide of the Rohingya people by using militant evidence to both stop the killings and preserve proof of their occurrence for when and if the day for justice comes. The militant evidence captured by the Rohingya people is an act of resistance that is helping to form counterarchives and counternarratives of genocide and generate international solidarity.

If these groups are successful in disseminating their captured militant evidence, it could be used for structures of accountability outside of the country in the International Criminal Court (ICC) or other venues. In fact, in January 2020, a seventeen-judge panel of the International Court of Justice (ICJ) unanimously ordered Myanmar to use all measures to prevent genocide, a signal that the international community is well aware of what is going on thanks to the work of digital active witnesses documenting in partnership with other organizations that disseminate and contextualize the militant evidence. The "poor images" captured by these digital active witnesses can become rich with meaning and force when they accumulate to form potent weapons of intervention outside of systems of commodification but within systems of adjudication, engendering an effective radicality. At the same time, agreeing to the profile on *Vice News* and sharing their militant evidence with them, as well as the constant passing of evidence to international news organizations, works to engender affective radicality that builds empathy and solidarity, and is a conduit for action for people outside of Myanmar. As an emerging currency within radical documentary, the use of militant evidence expands and updates frameworks for media activism. These frameworks encompass a new conception of the tactical and strategic deployment of militant evidence as effective and affective forces of radicality for a variety of audiences and platforms and as a catalyst for collective action, adjudication, and/or productive rebellion. This radical use of digital documentary media has been taken up by amateurs, activists, artists, and everyday people on the ground in crises around the globe to document their struggles for rights, representation, and justice. Here, militancy is understood as a non-violent but unrelenting method and practice in a world saturated by images and affective and effective appeals to action or empathy.

In his 2015 book *Exposed: Desire and Disobedience in the Digital Age*, Bernard Harcourt used Gilles Deleuze's 1990 essay, "Postscript on the Societies of Control," to argue that new machines and technologies are expressive of social forms rather than determinative of types of power. He quoted Deleuze's famous line that "there is no need to fear or hope, but only to look for new weapons." Harcourt asked: "Where shall we find them?"[2] As argued throughout *Radical Documentary and Global Crises*, one only needs to look in a pocket for a cell phone with a camera. Documentary studies is currently in its third turn to evidence, a post-9/11 period of global crises and the proliferation of amateur-grade accessible digital technologies that can produce militant evidence to change the visual and media perceptions of these crises as well as the material lives of the people living among them. Documentary media produced by digital active witnesses as militant evidence has engendered an alternative economy of poor images which are the connective tissue of alternative networks, alliances, and connections that forge bonds and create counterpublics and counterarchives while critiquing and challenging the status quo.

The camera has often been analogized as a weapon throughout the history of radical documentary. In the digital age, the camera is not a gun and, in and of itself, it is wholly insufficient. But, the camera can be a type of weapon when the images it produces are deployed and understood within various affective and effective ecologies to provide verification, forms of legibility, and power in accumulation. These images are produced in great quantities by digital active witnesses all over the world, beyond the many places discussed in this book, and the number of digital active witnesses and images produced increases each year. This proliferation of militant evidence offers glimpses of interconnected struggles throughout the world, the basis for global solidarity. Militant evidence emerges from a vast overlapping apparatus of digital active witnesses, on the ground during global crises, who deploy it, in partnership with other groups and organizations, for resistance, counterarchives, counternarratives, extrajudicial structures of accountability, and solidarity. Within the uses of militant evidence, there is an ever-widening, constantly elevating logic of impact that is attuned to acute issues on the ground. Long-term but issue or regionally specific activism gains power by connecting globally and allying with overlapping intersectional struggles and partner organizations. The images and media produced as militant evidence can radically function as witnesses and testimonies, archival traces, effective and affective evidence, and acts of survival.

Chapter 1 explored two human rights organizations that deploy documentary-based transmedia advocacy as their primary means of activism: WITNESS and B'Tselem. Both groups have done groundbreaking and influential human rights work that focuses on the quantifiable and/or material impacts of their advocacy as it manifests in court cases and legal and policy changes. WITNESS and B'Tselem also rely heavily on the creation and amassing of firsthand, amateur footage, witnesses, and testimonies as effective forms of militant evidence; these are often made in partnership with on-the-ground groups and are strategically targeted for maximum impact within specific contexts. Through these transmedia advocacy strategies, WITNESS and B'Tselem utilize militant evidence that is obtained by people on the ground and is then contextualized, narrativized, and/or distributed by partner organizations. The videos produced and disseminated bring forth an effective radicality, and are then aimed at a multitude of government, legal, media, and policy ecologies that place the images and testimonies in settings for adjudication and collaboration to stop human rights abuses and end the occupation of Palestine.

Chapter 2 analyzed Sharon Daniel's *Public Secrets* (2006) and Zohar Kfir's *Points of View* (2014), which uses affective militant evidence produced by women in prison and for B'Tselem, to create radical interactive documentary projects. The interactive documentary form certainly reflects the history and theory of radical documentary practice but offers new possibilities for engagement and intervention. The form of the interactive documentary functions as a semiguided interface for myriad affectively powerful testimonies, bystander videos, and other forms of militant evidence. Interactive documentaries allow viewers/users a multifaceted affective encounter with a range of subjects and evidence, and when this form is used for a radical or activist cause, it can represent and allow for viewer/user critical engagement with systemic problems that are difficult to capture in their scope and complexity in traditional cinematic forms. Daniel and Kfir's interactive documentaries successfully deploy militant evidence as they bring forth an affective radicality, a force that makes visible the many hidden structures of violence and power that inform ways of living around the globe and moves viewers/users into larger ecologies of militant activism; political, legal, and media discourses; and practices of resistance.

In chapter 3, the amateur short documentary films of the Independent Film and Television College (IFTC) were analyzed as affective and effective militant evidence. These films formed counterarchives that, in Iraq, created a microperspectival view of history and memory that documented the war and occupation since 2003 while helping to shape the country's emerging future. These practices served a radical function in the specific time and context of their making and circulation, a notion called the radically banal, which is an assertion of humanity and humanism amid the ruins of war and visual spectacle of modern warfare. In the wake of the Operation Shock and Awe bombings, and then amid crippling US-led occupation, artists and filmmakers reoriented the history that was derailed during Saddam Hussein's reign between 1979 and 2003. Part of this reorientation also came in the context of the massive official film, government, and media archives that were destroyed by coalition forces. The counterarchives produced through amateur short documentary films also challenged the reconstruction of the official state archive. The militant evidence wielded by digital active witnesses in effectively and affectively radical ways in Iraq since 2003 has helped to foster new public domains, spaces of communication and recognition, globally while reshaping the art and media environment and the course, via counterarchives, of Iraq's history. The militant evidence produced by students at the IFTC also set the stage for an expanded media culture and social media–fueled protests as well as the emergence of an independent Iraqi film culture.

Chapter 4 examined the mass of short, militant political documentaries produced anonymously by the Syrian film collective Abounaddara since 2010. The group deploys militant evidence in Syria and throughout the world for a number of reasons. Most importantly, they assert a "right to the image" within a holistic interpretation of international human rights law while also inscribing a notion of universal humanity and personhood into the images of war-scarred landscapes. In addition, they actively resist, through a militant use images, the brutal oppression, media censorship, and dominance of the visual field under the regime of Bashar al-Assad. Abounaddara's bullet films function as sniper shots in ongoing revolution and are an example of "digital imperfect cinema." The films, mostly documentary based but ranging from witness testimonials, montages, newsreel-style satire, mock advertisements, interviews, and remixed and recontextualized historical images, are shared widely throughout the globe on video-sharing sites like Vimeo and form a living archive of Syria in war and revolution. Through their deployment of militant evidence in various global media, art, and human rights ecologies, Abounaddara presents an affectively radical version of Syria to challenge both mainstream representations and depictions of Syrians as powerless victims and the visual power and dominance of the Assad regime.

Throughout *Radical Documentary and Global Crises*, the analysis of all of these global crises was approached from a microhistorical perspective, privileging the images and testimonies produced by the amateurs, artists, activists, and ordinary citizens who bear the brunt of their many cruel effects. The works analyzed in *Radical Documentary and Global Crises*, which instrumentalize images and stories, were examined not only for their form and content but also in and through the ecologies in which they make meaning, through the vectors of access, targeted spectatorship, and distribution that they flow within and between. These ecologies allow for an alternative economy of poor images, produced by digital active witnesses and distributed in partnership with other groups, that are the glue that bind alternative networks, counterpublics, counterarchives, and powerful alliances. Militant evidence is used in a new mode of radical documentary practice in the networked digital age: as a forceful intervention for resistance, abolition, revolution, counterrepresentations, counterarchives, and justice. The use of militant evidence is a collaborative, partnership-based practice that is generated on the ground from afflicted peoples; it is a concrete way for ordinary people to intervene in their worlds.

What is the future of radical documentary? With the ubiquity of cameras and images, activists, amateurs, artists, and everyday people are working to instrumentalize images, emphasizing material reality over theory. The future is in the militant evidence produced by people on the ground documenting the global crises that surround them. The focus and consideration of radical documentary practices, theories, and histories in the coming years should be moved away from the feature-length, festival- and auteur-driven documentary form toward an unwavering commitment to works produced by those directly living through war, occupation, human rights abuses, and mass incarceration. Radical documentary practices in the digital age are a set of mutable practices where militant evidence is instrumentalized from spaces of global crises. These urgent practices also necessitate a larger expansion and rethinking of how a documentary is defined, how and why documentaries are made, what they can do in the world, and how and where they function in the digital age. Documentary media, particularly from a perspective of global crises, must be examined through the vectors of form, content, distribution, access, and spectatorship. Further, the global crises currently ongoing, and the many that will manifest in coming years, require a resolute commitment to collaboration and partnership between digital active witnesses, academics and researchers, artists, coders and technologists, journalists, community groups, lawyers, collectives, activists, and amateurs, together across disciplines, industries, and borders to fight the myriad global crises that increasingly intersect and affect everybody. All the people in these groups who work on or are affected by similar issues must continue to come together and overcome artificial professional distinctions and occupational categories—they do not mean much when everyone is fighting for their lives.

Within an overwhelming image-making environment, the fundamental question is: Can documentary media actually *do* anything to change the material conditions of ordinary people, engender justice, or catalyze radical actions and movements? The answer is yes to all. We *can* act as humans and intervene in the regimes of violence that surround us to assert our values, voices, and agency, producing and deploying militant evidence in spaces of global crises. These images are the unyielding binding agents of struggles throughout the world. The force and power of militant evidence is realized through networks and ecologies of legibility and visibility within the proper frames of reference and contexts. But it is a painfully slow process. Unlike the instant gratification and ease promised by the networked digital age, effectively and affectively deploying militant evidence is a gradual yet affirmative practice of resistance and collective action. Radicality—the root of things—lies not in technology or platforms but in people activating and helping other people fight the oppressive structures that engulf them. Technologies and platforms are just new tools and possible weapons. The accumulated militant evidence examined in *Radical Documentary and Global Crises* is wielded against the many vagaries of global crises in pursuit of a radically different, more just and equitable world.

Notes

1. "Myanmar's Rohingya Genocide," *Vice News*, February 14, 2020, https://youtu.be/AnHizRC6S8U.
2. Bernard Harcourt, *Exposed: Desire and Disobedience in the Digital Age* (Cambridge, MA: Harvard University Press, 2015), 262–263.

Bibliography

Abounaddara. "A Right to the Image for All," https://www.fabrikzeitung.ch/a-right-to-the-image-for-all/#/.
———. "Montrons l'horreur en Syrie pour sortir de l'ignominie." *Le Monde*, October 20, 2015. https://www.lemonde.fr/idees/article/2015/10/21/montrons-l-horreur-en-syrie-pour-sortir-de-l-ignominie_4793538_3232.html.
Abdul-Ahad, Ghaith. "Art under Fire." *Guardian* (UK), November 21, 2004. http://www.guardian.co.uk/artanddesign/2004/nov/22/art-iraq.
Agamben, Giorgio. *Remnants of Auschwitz: The Witness and the Archive*. Translated by Daniel Heller-Roazen. New York: Zone Books, 1999.
Agerholm, Harriet. "Israel Considering Law to Ban Photographing or Filming IDF Soldiers." *Independent* (UK), May 27, 2018. https://www.independent.co.uk/news/world/middle-east/israeli-knesset-ban-photographing filming-idf-soldiers-recording-journalists-robert-ilatov-a8371426.html.
Ahram Online Staff. "Iraq Film Festival Aims to Promote Human Rights." *Ahram Online*, February 28, 2012. http://english.ahram.org.eg/News/35603.aspx.
Aitken, Ian. *European Film Theory and Cinema: A Critical Introduction*. Edinburgh: Edinburgh University Press, 2001.
———. "Introduction." In *The Documentary Film Movement: An Anthology*, edited by Ian Aitken. Edinburgh: Edinburgh University Press, 1998.
———, ed. *The Documentary Film Movement: An Anthology*. Edinburgh: Edinburgh University Press, 1998.
Alexander, William. *Film on the Left: American Documentary Film from 1931 to 1942*. Princeton, NJ: Princeton University Press, 1981.
———. "Frontier Films, 1936–1941: The Aesthetics of Impact." *Cinema Journal* 15, no. 1 (Autumn 1975): 16–28.
Alter, Nora. *Chris Marker*. Urbana: University of Illinois Press, 2006.

Amad, Paula. *Counter-Archive: Film, the Everyday, and Albert Kahn's Archives de la Planète*. New York: Columbia University Press, 2010.
Andrew, Dudley. "*L'âge d'or* and the Eroticism of the Spirit." In *Masterpieces of Modernist Cinema*, edited by Ted Perry, 111–137. Bloomington: Indiana University Press, 2006.
Aronson, Jay D. "Preserving Human Rights Media for Justice, Accountability, and Historical Clarification." *Genocide Studies and Prevention* 11, no. 1 (2017): 82–99.
Ashford, Anne. "Iraq: Filmmaking under Occupation (Interview with Maysoon Pachachi)." *Socialist Review* (July/August 2006). http://socialistreview.org.uk/308/iraq-filmmaking-under-occupation.
Ashuri, Tamar, and Amit Pinchevski. "Witnessing as a Field." In *Media Witnessing: Testimony in the Age of Mass Communication*, edited by Paul Frosh and Amit Pinchevski, 133–158. New York: Palgrave Macmillan, 2009.
Associated Press. "Israeli Supreme Court Rejects Challenge to Open Fire Rules." May 24, 2018. https://apnews.com/da582f11ad4443ddbf44ea6f2fc72c3a.
Azulay, Youval. "B'Tselem Cameras Pay Off for Victims of Settler Attacks." *Haaretz*, June 17, 2008. http://www.haaretz.com/print-edition/news/b-tselem-cameras-pay-off-for-victims-of-settler-attacks-1.247973.
Aufderheide, Patricia. "Public Intimacy: The Development of First-person Documentary." *Afterimage* 25, no. 1 (July–August 1997): 16–18.
Baer, Ulrich. *Spectral Evidence: The Photography of Trauma*. Cambridge, MA: MIT Press, 2002.
Bakker, Kees, ed. *Joris Ivens and the Documentary Context*. Amsterdam: Amsterdam University Press, 1999.
Balsom, Erika, and Hika Peleg, ed. *Documentary Across Disciplines*. Cambridge, MA: MIT Press, 2016.
Barnouw, Erik. *Documentary: A History of the Non-fiction Film*. 2nd ed. New York: Oxford University Press, 1993.
Baron, Jaimie. "Contemporary Documentary Film and 'Archive Fever': History, the Fragment, the Joke." *The Velvet Light Trap* 60 (Fall 2007): 13–24.
Barsam, Richard. *Nonfiction Film: A Critical History*. Bloomington: Indiana University Press, 1992.
Bayoumi, Moustafa. "The Civil War in Syria Is Invisible—But This Anonymous Film Collective Is Changing That." *Nation*, June 29, 2015. https://www.thenation.com/article/the-civil-war-in-syria-is-invisible-but-this-anonymous-film-collective-is-changing-that/.
Bazin, Andre. "On Why We Fight: History, Documentation, and the Newsreel (1946)." In *Bazin at Work: Major Essays & Reviews from the Forties & Fifties*, edited by Bert Cardullo, 187–192. New York: Routledge, 1997.
Beaumont, Peter. "Palestinians Capture Violence of Israeli Occupation on Video." *Guardian* (UK), July 30, 2008. http://www.guardian.co.uk/world/2008/jul/30/israelandthepalestinians.
Benhabib, Seyla. *Dignity in Adversity: Human Rights in Troubled Times*. Cambridge, UK: Polity, 2011.
Benjamin, Walter. *The Arcades Project*. Translated by Howard Eiland and Kevin McLaughlin. Cambridge, MA: Harvard University Press, 1999.
———. *Illuminations*. Translated by Harry Zohn. Edited by Hannah Arendt. New York: Shocken, 1988.

——. *The Work of Art in the Age of Its Technological Reproducibility and Other Writings on Media*, edited by Brigid Doherty, Michael W. Jennings, and Thomas Y. Levin. Cambridge, MA: Belknap/Harvard University Press, 2008.
Berger, Arthur Asa. *Media and Society: A Critical Perspective*. Lanham, MD: Rowan and Littlefield, 2011.
Boëx, Cécile. "Emergency Cinema: An Interview with Syrian Collective Abounaddara." *Books and Ideas*. Translated by Susannah Dale. October 5, 2012. http://www.booksandideas.net/Emergency-Cinema.html.
Bolter, Jay David, and Richard Grusin. *Remediation: Understanding New Media*. Cambridge, MA: MIT Press, 2000.
Boyle, Deidre. "From Portapak to Camcorder: A Brief History of Guerilla Television." *Journal of Film and Video* 44, vols. 1–2 (1992): 67–79.
Brody, Samuel. "The Movies as a Weapon against the Working Class." *Daily Worker*, May 20, 1920.
——. "The Revolutionary Film: Problem of Form." *New Theatre* (February 1934): 21–22.
B'Tselem Staff. "The Army Must Internalize the Gravity of the Ni'lin Shooting Incident." B'Tselem.org, January 27, 2011. http://www.btselem.org/firearms/20110127_nilin_shooting_sentence.
Buchsbaum, Jonathan. *Cinema Engagé: Film in the Popular Front*. Urbana: University of Illinois Press, 1988.
——. *Historical Journal of Film, Radio, and Television* 21, no. 2 (2001): 153–166.
——. "Left Film in France, 1930–35." *Cinema Journal* 25.3 (1986): 22–52.
——. "One, Two . . . Third Cinemas." *Third Text* 25.1 (2011): 13–28.
Buchloh, Benjamin H. D. "Gerhard Richter's 'Atlas': The Anomic Archive." *October* 88 (Spring 1999): 117–145.
Bugbee, Teo. "'For Sama' Review: Out of Besieged Aleppo, a Documentary." *New York Times*, July 25, 2019. https://www.nytimes.com/2019/07/25/movies/for-sama-review.html.
Butler, Judith. *Precarious Life: The Powers of Mourning and Violence*. New York: Verso, 2004.
Burnett, Ron. *Cultures of Vision: Images, Media, and the Imaginary*. Bloomington: Indiana University Press, 1995.
Burton, Julianne. "Toward a History of Social Documentary in Latin America." In *The Social Documentary in Latin America*, edited by Julianne Burton, 3–30. Pittsburgh, PA: University of Pittsburgh Press, 1990.
——. "The Camera as 'Gun': Two Decades of Culture and Resistance in Latin America." *Latin American Perspectives* 5, no. 1 (1978): 49–76.
Caldwell, Gillian, with Peter Gabriel, Sam Gregory, Sara Federlein, and Jenni Wolfson. "Moving Images WITNESS and Human Rights Advocacy." *Innovations* 3, no. 2 (Spring 2008): 35–60.
Campbell, Russell. *Cinema Strikes Back: Radical Filmmaking in the United States 1930–1942*. Ann Arbor: UMI Research Press, 1982.
——. "Introduction: Film and Photo League Radical Cinema in the 30s" *Jump Cut* no. 14 (1977). http://www.ejumpcut.org/archive/onlinessays/JC14folder/FilmPhotoIntro.html.
——. "Radical Documentary in the United States, 1930–1942." In *"Show Us Life": Toward a History and Aesthetics of the Committed Documentary*, edited by Thomas Waugh, 69–88. Metuchen, NJ: Scarecrow, 1984.

Caron, François. *An Economic History of Modern France*. London: Taylor and Francis, 1979.
Castro, Fidel. "Word to Intellectuals." In *Fidel Castro Reader*, edited by David Deutschmann and Deborah Shnookal, 213–240. Melbourne, Australia: Ocean, 2008.
Chapman, James. *Cinemas of the World: Film and Society from 1895 to the Present*. London: Reaktion, 2003.
Chanan, Michael. *Cuban Cinema*. Minneapolis: University of Minnesota Press, 2004.
———. *The Politics of Documentary*. London: British Film Institute, 2007.
Clark, Jessica, and Patricia Aufderheide. "Public Media 2.0: Dynamic, Engaged Publics." Center for Social Media, February 2009. http://cmsimpact.org/sites/default/files/documents/pages/publicmedia2.0.pdf.
Cohen, Hart. "Database Documentary: From *Authorship* to *Authoring* in Remediated/Remixed Documentary." *Culture Unbound* 4 (2012): 327–346.
Costanza-Chock, Sasha. *Out of the Shadows, Into the Streets! Transmedia Organizing and the Immigrant Rights Movement*. Cambridge, MA: MIT Press, 2014.
Creswell, Robyn. "Voices from a Different Syria." *New York Review of Books*, March 21, 2016. http://www.nybooks.com/daily/2016/03/21/voices-from-different-syria-abounaddara-films/.
Crimp, Douglas. "AIDS: Cultural Analysis/ Cultural Activism." *October* 43 (Winter 1987): 3–16.
Critical Art Ensemble. *Digital Resistance: Explorations in Tactical Media*. New York: Autonomedia, 2001.
———. *Electronic Civil Disobedience and Other Unpopular Ideas*. New York: Autonomedia, 1996.
———. *The Electronic Disturbance*. New York: Autonomedia, 1994.
Cuevas, Efrén. "Change of Scale: Home Movies as Microhistory in Documentary Films." In *Amateur Filmmaking: The Home Movie, the Archive, and the Web*, edited by Laura Rascaroli and Gwendolyn Young, with Barry Monahan, 139–152. New York: Bloomsbury, 2014.
Cvetkovich, Ann. "Video, AIDS, and Activism." In *Art, Activism, and Oppositionality: Essays from Afterimage*, edited by Grant Kestor, 182–198. Durham, NC: Duke University Press, 1998.
Czach, Liz. "Home Movies and Amateur Film as National Cinema." In *Amateur Filmmaking: The Home Movie, the Archive, and the Web*, edited by Laura Rascaroli and Gwendolyn Young, with Barry Monahan, 27–38. New York: Bloomsbury, 2014.
Daniel, Sharon. Lecture, "New Media Documentary: Technology and Social Inclusion." YouTube. 2008. https://www.youtube.com/watch?v=JiHBxCDleus.
———. "On Politics and Aesthetics: A Case Study of 'Public Secrets' and 'Blood Sugar.'" *Studies in Documentary Film* 6, no. 2 (2012): 215–227.
———. "Public Secrets: Authors Statement." *Vectors: Journal of Culture and Technology in a Dynamic Vernacular* (2007). http://vectors.usc.edu/projects/index.php?project=57&thread=AuthorsStatement.
———. "The Public Secret: Information and Social Knowledge." *Intelligent Agent* 6, no. 2 (2006). http://www.intelligentagent.com/archive/Vol6_No2_community_domain_daniel.htm.

Davis, Angela Y. *Are Prisons Obsolete?* New York: Seven Stories, 2003.
———. *Freedom Is a Constant Struggle: Ferguson, Palestine, and the Foundations of a Movement.* Chicago: Haymarket Books, 2016.
De Michiel, Helen, and Patricia R. Zimmermann, "Documentary as Open Space." In *The Documentary Film Book*, edited by Brian Winston, 355–365. London: British Film Institute/Palgrave Macmillan, 2013.
De Wachter, Ellen Mara "'I'd Rather Lose Prizes and Win Cases' Interview with Eyal Weizman." *Frieze*, May 2, 2018. https://frieze.com/article/id-rather-lose-prizes-and-win-cases-interview-eyal-weizman-turner-prize-nominated-forensic.
Della Ratta, Donatella. *Shooting a Revolution: Visual Media and Warfare in Syria.* London: Pluto, 2018.
Demos, T. J. *The Migrant Image: The Art and Politics of Documentary During Global Crisis.* Durham, NC: Duke University Press, 2013.
Derrida, Jacques. *Archive Fever.* Translated by Eric Prenowitz. Chicago: University of Chicago Press, 1996.
———. *Demeure: Fiction and Testimony.* Translated by Elizabeth Rottenberg. Stanford, CA: Stanford University Press, 2000.
———. "Poetics and Politics of Witnessing." In *Sovereignties in Question: The Poetics of Paul Celan*, edited by Thomas Dutoit and Outi Pasanen, 65–96. New York: Fordham University Press, 2005.
Douglas, Lawrence. "Film as Witness: Screening Nazi Concentration Camps before the Nuremberg Tribunal." *Yale Law Journal* 105, no. 2 (November 1995): 449–481.
Durkin, Kieran. *The Radical Humanism of Erich Fromm.* New York: Palgrave Macmillan, 2014.
Electronic Frontier Foundation, "Street-Level Surveillance: A Guide to Law Enforcement Technology." 2018. https://www.eff.org/issues/street-level-surveillance.
Electronic Intifada. "Video: Israel Targets Journalists in Gaza." May 24, 2018. https://electronicintifada.net/content/video-israel-targets-journalists-gaza/24431.
Elias, Chad. "Emergency Cinema and the Dignified Image: Cell Phone Activism and Filmmaking in Syria." *Film Quarterly* 7, no. 1 (Fall 2017). https://filmquarterly.org/2017/09/14/emergency-cinema-and-the-dignified-image-cell-phone-activism-and-filmmaking-in-syria/.
Ellis, Jack C., and Betsy A. McLane. *A New History of Documentary Film.* New York: Continuum Books, 2005.
Eshun, Kodwo, and Ros Gray. "The Militant Image: A Ciné-Geography." *Third Text* 25, no. 1 (2011): 1–12.
Eskander, Saad. "The Story of the Cemetery of Books." Keynote Speech at the Internet Librarian International Conference. London, October 10–12, 2004. https://www.infotoday.com/it/deco4/eskander.shtml.
Espinosa, Julio Garcia. "For an Imperfect Cinema." Translated by Julianne Burton. *Jump Cut* no. 20 (1979). http://www.ejumpcut.org/archive/onlinessays/JC20folder/ImperfectCinema.html.
Fassin, Didier. "Humanitarianism as a Politics of Life." *Public Culture* 19, no. 3 (2007): 499–520.
Faruqi, Anwar. "Emad Ali's Film about Iconic Café Screened at Baghdad Festival." *The Daily Star*, May 6, 2011. http://www.dailystar.com.lb/ArticlePrint.aspx?id=137991&mode=print.

Feinstein, Laura. "This Syrian Filmmaking Collective Shows the Banality of Life in War." *Vice*, June 25, 2015. https://www.vice.com/en_us/article/mvxgap/this-syrian-art-collective-shines-an-intimate-light-on-life-in-their-war-torn-country-456.

Felman, Shoshana, and Dori Laub. *Testimony: Crises of Witnessing in Literature, Psychoanalysis, and History*. New York: Routledge, 1992.

Fore, Devin. "Introduction: Soviet Factography." *October* 118 (Fall 2006): 3–10.

Foster, Hal. "An Archival Impulse." *October* 110 (Fall 2004): 3–22.

Foucault, Michel. *The Archaeology of Knowledge*. Translated by Alan Sheridan. New York: Pantheon, 1972.

Gabriel, Peter. "Video Will Bring Us Justice in the Long Run." *Time*, May 16, 2017. http://time.com/4781418/peter-gabriel-video-justice.

Gabriel, Teshome. *Third Cinema in the Third World*. Ann Arbor: University of Michigan Press, 1982.

Gaines, Jane. "Introduction: The Real Returns." In *Collecting Visible Evidence*, edited by Jane Gaines and Michael Renov, 1–18. Minneapolis: University of Minnesota Press, 1999.

———. "Documentary Radicality." *Canadian Journal of Film Studies* 16, no. 1 (Spring 2007): 5–24.

———. "Political Mimesis" In *Collecting Visible Evidence*, edited by Jane Gaines and Michael Renov, 84–102. Minneapolis: University of Minnesota Press, 1999.

———. "The Production of Outrage: The Iraq War and the Radical Documentary Tradition." *Framework* 48, no. 2 (Fall 2007): 36–55.

Geary, Daniel. "C. Wright Mills and the Emergence of the Global New Left." *Journal of American History* 95, no. 3 (December 2008): 710–736.

Getino, Octavio. "The Cinema of Political Fact (1973)." Translated by Jonathan Buchsbaum and Mariano Mestman. *Third Text* 25, no. 1 (2011): 41–53.

Getino, Octavio, and Fernando Solanas. "Towards a Third Cinema." In *Movies and Methods, Volume One*, edited by Bill Nichols, 44–64. Berkeley: University of California Press, 1976.

Gilmore, Ruth Wilson. "Abolition Geography and the Problem of Innocence." In *Futures of Black Radicalism*, edited by Theresa Gaye Johnson and Alex Lubin, 223–240. New York: Verso, 2017.

———. *Golden Gulag: Prisons, Surplus Crisis, and Opposition in Globalizing California*. Berkeley: University of California Press, 2007.

Gomes, P. E. Salles. *Jean Vigo*. Berkeley: University of California Press, 1971.

Gould, Deborah B. *Moving Politics: Emotion and ACT Ups Fight Against AIDS*. Chicago: University of Chicago Press, 2006.

Grant, Paul Douglas. *Cinéma Militant: Political Filmmaking & May 1968*. New York: Wallflower, 2016.

Gregg, Melissa, and Gregory Seigworth, eds. *The Affect Theory Reader*. Durham, NC: Duke University Press, 2010.

Gregory, Sam. "Cameras Everywhere: Ubiquitous Video Documentation of Human Rights, New Forms of Video Advocacy, and Considerations of Safety, Security, Dignity and Consent." *Journal of Human Rights Practice* 2, no. 2 (2010): 1–17.

———. "Transnational Storytelling: Human Rights, WITNESS and Video Advocacy." *American Anthropologist* 108, no. 1 (March 2006): 195–204.

———, and Elizabeth Losh. "Remixing Human Rights: Rethinking Civic Expression, Representation, and Personal Security in Online Video." *First Monday* 17, no. 8 (August 2012). http://firstmonday.org/ojs/index.php/fm/article/view/4104/3279.

———, Gillian Caldwell, Ronit Avni, and Thomas Harding, eds. *Video for Change: A Guide for Advocacy and Activism*. Ann Arbor, MI: Pluto, 2005.

Grierson, John. Unsigned review of *Moana*. *New York Sun*, February 8, 1926. Reprinted in Lewis Jacobs, *The Documentary Tradition*. 2nd ed. New York: W. W. Norton and Company, 1979.

Guyot-Bender, Martine. "Tracking the Global through the Local: Slon/Iskra's Documentaries of Displacement." *SubStance* 43, no. 1 (2014): 138–151.

Hall, Stuart. "Constituting an Archive." *Third Text* (Spring 2001): 89–92.

———. "Life and Times of the New Left." *New Left Review* 61 (Jan/Feb 2010): 177–196.

Harcourt, Bernard. *Exposed: Desire and Disobedience in the Digital Age*. Cambridge, MA: Harvard University Press, 2015.

Hardy, Forsyth, ed. *Grierson on Documentary*. New York: Praeger, 1971.

Hochberg, Gil. *Visual Occupations: Violence and Visibility in a Conflict Zone*. Durham, NC: Duke University Press, 2015.

Human Rights Watch Staff. "Iraq: Intensifying Crackdown on Free Speech, Protests." *Human Rights Watch World Report 2011*, January 22, 2012. http://www.hrw.org/news/2012/01/22/iraq-intensifying-crackdown-free-speech-protests.

Hunt, Lynn. *Inventing Human Rights: A History*. New York: Norton, 2007.

Hurwitz, Leo. "The Revolutionary Film—Next Step." *New Theatre* (May 1934): 14–15.

———, and Ralph Steiner. "A New Approach to Filmmaking." *New Theatre* (September 1945): 22–23.

Ignatieff, Michael, ed. *Human Rights as Politics and Idolatry*. Princeton, NJ: Princeton University Press, 2003.

Isakhan, Benjamin. "Manufacturing Consent in Iraq: Interference in the post-Saddam Media Sector." *International Journal of Contemporary Iraqi Studies* 3, no. 1 (May 2009): 7–25.

———. "The Post-Saddam Iraqi Media: Reporting the Democratic Developments of 2005." *Global Media Journal* 7, no. 13 (Fall 2008): 1–25.

Ivens, Joris. *The Camera and I*. Berlin: Seven Seas, 1969.

———. "Quelques réflexions sur les documentaires d'avant garde." *La Revue des Vivants* 10 (1931): 518–520.

Jameson, Fredric. "Politics of Utopia." *New Left Review* 25 (January/February 2004): 35–54.

Kauffman, L. A. *Direct Action: Protest and the Reinvention of American Radicalism*. London: Verso, 2017.

Kayyali, Dia, and Raja Althaibani. "Vital Human Rights Evidence from Syria Is Disappearing from YouTube." *Witness* (blog), August 2017. https://blog.witness.org/2017/08/vital-human-rights-evidence-syria-disappearing-youtube/.

Keck, Margaret E., and Kathryn Sikkink. *Activists Beyond Borders: Advocacy Networks in International Politics*. Ithaca, NY: Cornell University Press, 1998.

Kellner, Douglas, and Dan Streible, eds. *Emile de Antonio: A Reader*. Minneapolis: University of Minnesota Press, 2000.

Kepley, Vance. "The Workers' International Relief and the Cinema of the Left 1921–1935." *Cinema Journal* 23, no. 1 (Autumn 1983): 7–23.

Kerr, Sarah Stein. "Interactive Documentary 'Points of View' Showcases Citizen Video in Gaza and the West Bank." *Witness* (blog), February 2015. http://blog.witness.org/2015/02/interactive-documentary-points-view-showcases-citizen-video-gaza-west-bank/.

Kleinhans, Chuck. "Forms, Politics, Makers and Contexts: Basic Issues for a Theory of Radical Political Documentary." In *Show Us Life: Toward a History and Aesthetics of the Committed Documentary*, edited by Thomas Waugh, 318–343. Metuchen, NJ: Scarecrow, 1984.

Kozol, Wendy. *Distant Wars Visible: The Ambivalence of Witnessing*. Minneapolis: University of Minnesota Press, 2014.

Kracauer, Siegfried. "Jean Vigo." *Hollywood Quarterly* 2, no. 3 (1947): 261–263.

LaCapra, Dominick. *Writing History, Writing Trauma*. Baltimore: Johns Hopkins University Press, 2001.

Landman, Todd, and Edzia Carvalho. *Measuring Human Rights*. New York: Routledge, 2010.

Lange, Christy. "Emergency Cinema: How the Anonymous Film Collective Abounaddara Represents Daily Life in Syria." *Frieze*, March 18, 2016. https://frieze.com/article/emergency-cinema.

Lawrence, Regina G. *The Politics of Force: Media and the Construction of Police Brutality*. Berkeley: University of California Press, 2000.

Lebow, Alisa. "First Person Political." In *The Documentary Film Book*, edited by Brian Winston, 257–265. London: British Film Institute, 2013.

Lecointe, François. "The Elephants at the End of the World: Chris Marker and Third Cinema." *Third Text* 25, no. 1 (January 2011): 93–104.

Lenin, VI. "Directives of the Film Business (1922)." Marxists Internet Archive. http://www.marxists.org/archive/lenin/works/1922/jan/17.htm.

Lewis, Randolph. *Emile de Antonio: Radical Filmmaker in Cold War America*. Madison: University of Wisconsin Press, 2000.

Levinas, Emmanuel. *Humanism and the Other*. Translated by Nidra Poller. Chicago: University of Illinois Press, 2006.

Lievrouw, Leah. *Alternative and Activist New Media*. Cambridge, UK: Polity, 2011.

Limbrick, Peter. "*14.3 Seconds*: Politics, Art and the Archival Imagination." *Visual Anthropology* 29 (2016): 211–228.

Linington, Jess. "Points of View: Putting Occupied Territories on the (Interactive) Map." *i-Docs.org*, September 9, 2014. http://i-docs.org/points-of-view-putting-occupied-territories-on-the-interactive-map/.

Lippit, Akira. *Atomic Light: Shadow Optics*. Minneapolis: University of Minnesota Press, 2005.

Lupton, Catherine. *Chris Marker: Memories of the Future*. London: Reaktion Books, 2005.

Lynch, Mark, Deen Freelon, and Sean Aday. "Syria's Socially Mediated Civil War." United States Institute of Peace, January 13, 2014. http://www.usip.org/publications/syria-s-socially-mediated-civil-war.

Mackey, Robert. "Israel Tampered with Video Strike That Killed Two Palestinian Boys, Investigators Say." *The Intercept*, December 18. 2019. https://theintercept.com/2018/12/19/israel-airstrike-gaza-two-boys/.

Marcus, Daniel. "Documentary and Video Activism." In *Contemporary Documentary*, edited by Daniel Marcus and Selmin Kara, 187–203. New York: Routledge, 2016.

Martin-Márquez, Susan. "By Camera and By Gun: Joris Ivens and the Radicalization of Latin American Filmmakers." *The Ivens Magazine*, no. 18 (December 2013): 10–22.

Malitsky, Joshua. *Post Revolution Non-Fiction Film: Building the Soviet and Cuban Nations*. Bloomington: Indiana University Press, 2013.

Manovich, Lev. *The Language of New Media*. Cambridge, MA: MIT Press, 2001.

Massumi, Brian. "The Thinking-Feeling of What Happens." *Inflexions* 1.1 (2008): 1–40.

———. *Politics of Affect*. Cambridge, UK: Polity, 2015.

McLagan, Megan. "Making Human Rights Claims Public." *American Anthropologist* 108 (2006): 191–195.

Mejcher-Atassi, Sonja. "Abounadarra's Take on Images in the Syrian Revolution: A Conversation between Charif Kiwan and Akram Zaatari." *Jadaliyya*, September 2, 2014. https://www.jadaliyya.com/Details/30924.

Michelson, Annete. "Film and the Radical Aspiration." In *The Film Culture Reader*, edited by P. Adams Sitney, 404–422. New York: New York University Press, 1970.

———. "Introduction." In *Kino Eye: The Writings of Dziga Vertov*, edited by Annette Michelson. Translated by Kevin O'Brien. Berkeley: University of California Press, 1984.

———, ed. *Kino Eye: The Writings of Dziga Vertov*. Translated by Kevin O'Brien. Berkeley: University of California Press, 1984.

Miles, Adrian. "Interactive Documentary and Affective Ecologies." In *New Documentary Ecologies: Emerging Platforms, Practices and Discourses*, edited by Kate Nash, Craig Hight, and Catherine Summerhayes, 67–82. New York: Palgrave Macmillan, 2014.

Miller, Liz. "The Shore Line and the Practice of Slow Resilience." *Frames Cinema Journal*, 2018. http://framescinemajournal.com/article/the-shore-line-and-the-practice-of-slow-resilience/.

Mills, C. Wright. "Letter to the New Left." *New Left Review*, no. 5 (September/October 1960): 18–23.

Moeller, Susan. *Compassion Fatigue: How the Media Sell Disease, Famine, War and Death*. New York: Routledge, 1999.

Musser, Charles. "War, Documentary and Iraq Dossier: Film Truth in the Age of George W. Bush." *Framework* 48.2 (Fall 2007): 9–35.

Mraz, John. "Santiago Álvarez: From Dramatic Form to Direct Cinema." In *The Social Documentary in Latin America*, edited by Julianne Burton, 131–149. Pittsburgh, PA: University of Pittsburgh Press, 1990.

Nash, Kate. "What Is Interactivity for? The Social Dimension of Web-Documentary Participation." *Continuum: Journal of Media and Cultural Studies* 28, no. 3 (2014): 383–395.

Nash, Kate, Craig Hight, and Catherine Summerhayes, eds. *New Documentary Ecologies: Emerging Platforms, Practices and Discourses*. New York: Palgrave Macmillan, 2014.

New Left Review Editorial Board. "A Brief History of New Left Review: 1960–2010." *New Left Review*. https://newleftreview.org/pages/history.

Nichols, Bill. *Blurred Boundaries: Questions of Meaning in Contemporary Culture.* Bloomington: Indiana University Press, 1994.

———. "Documentary Film and the Modernist Avant-Garde." *Critical Inquiry* (Summer 2001): 581–610.

———. *Introduction to Documentary.* Bloomington: Indiana University Press, 2001.

———. "Newsreel, 1967–1972: Film and Revolution." In *Show Us Life: Toward a History and Aesthetics of the Committed Documentary,* edited by Thomas Waugh, 135–153. Metuchen, NJ: Scarecrow, 1984.

———. *Newsreel: Documentary Filmmaking on the American Left.* New York: Arno, 1980.

———. *Representing Reality: Issues and Concepts in Documentary.* Bloomington: Indiana University Press, 1991.

———. *Speaking Truth with Film: Evidence, Ethics, Politics in Documentary.* Berkeley: University of California Press, 2016.

———, ed. *Movies and Methods.* Berkeley: University of California Press, 1976.

Odorico, Stefano. "Documentary on the Web between Realism and Interaction. A Case Study: *From Zero-People Rebuilding Life after the Emergency* (2009)." *Studies in Documentary Film* 5, nos. 2 and 3 (2011): 235–246.

Peters, John Durham. "Witnessing." *Media, Culture & Society.* 23.6 (2001): 707–723

Petric, Vlada. "Esther Shub: Film as Historical Discourse." In *Show Us Life: Toward a History and Aesthetics of the Committed Documentary,* edited by Thomas Waugh, 21–46. Metuchen, NJ: Scarecrow, 1984.

Puar, Jasbir K. *The Right to Maim: Debility, Capacity, Disability.* Durham, NC: Duke University Press, 2017.

Quilty, Jim. "Bearing Witness to Life in Occupied Baghdad." *Daily Star* (Beirut, Lebanon), June 13, 2009. http://www.dailystar.com.lb/Culture/Arts/Jun/13/Bearing-witness-to-life-in-occupied-Baghdad.ashx#axzz2QwuBn5aI.

Raley, Rita. "The Ordinary Arts of Political Activism." In *Global Activism: Art and Conflict in the 21st Century,* edited by Peter Weibel, 289–297. Cambridge, MA: MIT Press, 2015.

———. *Tactical Media.* Minneapolis: University of Minnesota Press, 2009

Rancière, Jacques. *Dissensus: On Politics and Aesthetics.* Translated by Steven Corcoran. London: Continuum, 2010.

Rangan, Pooja. *Immediations: The Humanitarian Impulse in Documentary.* Durham, NC: Duke University Press, 2017.

Ranvaud, Don. "Fernando Solanas-An Interview." *Framework* 10 (Spring 1979): 35–38.

Renov, Michael. *The Subject of Documentary.* Minneapolis: University of Minnesota Press, 2004.

Richter, Hans. *The Struggle for the Film: Towards a Socially Responsible Cinema.* New York: St. Martin's, 1986.

Rist, Peter. "Agit-prop Cuban Style: Master Montagist Santiago Álvarez." *Off Screen* 11, no. 3 (March 2007). http://offscreen.com/view/agit_prop_cuban_style.

Rose, Mandy. "Not Media about, but Media With." In *iDocs: The Evolving Practices of Interactive Documentary,* edited by Judith Aston, Sandra Gaudenzi, and Mandy Rose, 49–65. New York: Wallflower, 2017.

Rosenthal, Alan. *The Documentary Conscience: A Casebook in Filmmaking.* Berkeley: University of California Press, 1980.

Rosler, Martha. "A Case for Torture Redux." *Jump Cut* 51 (Spring 2009). https://www.ejumpcut.org/archive/jc51.2009/Rosler/text.html.
———. "In, Around, and Afterthoughts (On Documentary Photography)." In *Martha Rosler: 3 Works*, 59–86. Halifax, Canada: Press of the Nova Scotia College of Art and Design, 1981.
Rothberg, Michael. *Traumatic Realism: The Demands of Holocaust Representation*. Minneapolis: University of Minnesota Press, 2000.
Roud, Richard. "Left Bank Cinema." *Sight and Sound* 32, no. 1 (1962–63): 24–27.
Rubenstein, Lenny. "*79 Springtimes*." *Cineaste* 4, no. 3 (Winter 1970): 39.
Ryzik, Melena. "Syrian Collective Offers View of Life Behind a Conflict." *New York Times*, October 18, 2015. https://www.nytimes.com/2015/10/19/movies/syrian-film-collective-offers-view-of-life-behind-a-conflict.html?mcubz=0.
Said, Edward. "Orientalism." *Counterpunch*, August 5, 2003. http://www.counterpunch.org/2003/08/05/orientalism/.
Salucci, Ilario. *A People's History of Iraq: The Iraqi Communist Party, Worker's Movements, and the Left 1924–2004*. Chicago: Haymarket Books, 2005.
Sarkar, Bhaskar, and Janet Walker, ed. *Documentary Testimonies: Global Archives of Suffering*. New York: Routledge, 2010.
Saunders, Dave. *Direct Cinema: Observational Documentary and the Politics of the Sixties*. London: Wallflower, 2007.
Schoots, Hans. *Living Dangerously: A Biography of Joris Ivens*. Amsterdam: Amsterdam University Press, 2000.
Schwartz, Louis-Georges. *Mechanical Witness: Film and Video Evidence in US Courts*. New York: Oxford University Press, 2009.
Sekula, Allan. "Dismantling Modernism, Reinventing Documentary." *Massachusetts Review* 19.4 (Winter 1978): 859–883
Silverman, Kaja. *The Threshold of the Visible World*. New York: Routledge, 1996.
Sliwinski, Sharon. *Human Rights in Camera*. Chicago: University of Chicago Press, 2011.
Sobchack, Vivian. *The Persistence of History: Cinema, Television, and the Modern Event*. New York: Routledge, 1996.
Sontag, Susan. *On Photography*. New York: Macmillan, 1977.
Stam, Robert. "The Two Avant-Gardes: Solanas and Getino's *The Hour of the Furnaces*." In *Documenting the Documentary: Close Readings of Documentary Film and Video*, edited by Barry Keith Grant and Jeannette Sloniowski, 271–286. Detroit, MI: Wayne State University Press, 2014.
Stamberg, Susan. "College Trains Young Iraqi Film Makers." Interview with Maysoon Pachachi. *Weekend Edition Saturday*. National Public Radio, April 8, 2008. http://www.npr.org/templates/story/story.php?storyId=89408895.
Stern, Seymour, "A Working-Class Cinema for America?." *Left* 1, no. 1 (Spring 1931): 71.
Stewart, Kathleen. "Arresting Images." In *Aesthetic Subjects*, edited by Pamela R. Matthews and David McWhirter, 431–448. Minneapolis: University of Minnesota Press.
———. *Ordinary Affects*. Durham, NC: Duke University Press, 2007.
Steyerl, Hito. "In Defense of Poor Images." *e-flux*, November 10, 2009. http://www.e-flux.com/journal/10/61362/in-defense-of-the-poor-image/.
Strebel, Elizabeth Grottle. "French Social Cinema and the Popular Front." *Journal of Contemporary History* 12 (1977): 499–519.

Sturken, Marita. *Tangled Memories: The Vietnam War, The AIDS Epidemic, and the Politics of Remembering*. Berkeley: University of California Press, 1997.
Takahashi, Tess. "The Imaginary Archive: Current Practice." *Camera Obscura 66* 22, no. 3 (2007): 179–184.
Tarzi, Nazli. "The Rebirth of Iraqi Cinema." *openDemocracy*, June 18, 2015. https://www.opendemocracy.net/en/north-africa-west-asia/rebirth-of-iraqi-cinema/.
Taussig, Michael. *Defacement: Public Secrecy and the Labor of the Negative*. Stanford, CA: Stanford University Press, 1999.
Temple, Michael. *Jean Vigo*. Manchester, UK: Manchester University Press, 2005.
Timberg, Craig, and Elizabeth Dwoskin. "Facebook, Twitter and Instagram Sent Feeds That Helped Police Track Minorities in Ferguson and Baltimore, Report Says." *Washington Post*, October 11, 2016. https://www.washingtonpost.com/news/the-switch/wp/2016/10/11/facebook-twitter-and-instagram-sent-feeds-that-helped-police-track-minorities-in-ferguson-and-baltimore-aclu-says.
Tomlinson, John. *Cultural Imperialism*. London: Pinter, 1991.
Torchin, Leshu. *Creating the Witness: Documenting Genocide on Film, Video, and the Internet*. Minneapolis: University of Minnesota Press, 2012.
Turvey, Malcolm. "Iraqis under Occupation: A Survey of Documentaries." *October* 123 (Winter 2008): 234–241.
Ungar, Steven. "Jean Vigo, *L'Atalante*, and the Promise of Social Cinema." *Historical Reflections* 35 (2009): 63–83.
Van Wert, William F. "Chris Marker: The SLON Films." *Film Quarterly* 32, no. 3 (Spring 1979): 8–46.
Vigo, Jean. "Sensitivity of Film." In *The Complete Jean Vigo*, edited by Pierre Lherminier, 37–38. Paris: Lorimer, 1983
———. "Towards a Social Cinema." In *French Film Theory and Criticism, Vol. 2: 1929–1939*, edited by Richard Abel, 60–63. Princeton, NJ: Princeton University Press, 1988.
Virilio, Paul. *War and Cinema: The Logics of Perception*. London: Verso, 1999.
Wahlberg, Malin. *Documentary Time: Film and Phenomenology*. Minneapolis: University of Minnesota Press, 2008.
Wang, Jackie. *Carceral Capitalism*. South Pasadena, CA: Semiotext(e), 2018.
Watson, Ryan. "Affective Radicality: Prisons, Palestine, and Interactive Documentary." *Feminist Media Studies* 17, no. 4 (2017): 600–615.
———. "Art under Occupation: Documentary, Archive, and the Radically Banal." *Afterimage* 36, no. 5 (March/April 2009): 7–12.
———. "In the Wakes of Rodney King: Militant Evidence and Media Activism in the Age of Viral Black Death." *Velvet Light Trap* 84 (Fall 2019): 34–49.
———. "Interview with Sharon Daniel." *Studies in Documentary Film* 13.3 (2009): 283–289.
———. "Refugees Searching for Home in the Syrian Diaspora." *Review of Middle East Studies* 54, no. 1 (2020): 97–106.
Waugh, Thomas. *The Conscience of Cinema: The Works of Joris Ivens 1912–1989*. Amsterdam: Amsterdam University Press, 2016.
———. "Introduction." In *Show Us Life: Toward a History and Aesthetics of the Committed Documentary*, edited by Thomas Waugh, xi–xxvi. Metuchen, NJ: Scarecrow, 1984.

———. "*Loin du Vietnam* (1967), Joris Ivens, and the Left Bank." *Jump Cut: A Review of Contemporary Media* 53 (Summer 2011). http://www.ejumpcut.org/archive/jc53.2011/WaughVietnam/text.html.

———. "Travel Notebook—A People in Arms: Joris Ivens' Work in Cuba." *Jump Cut: A Review of Contemporary Media* 22 (May 1980). http://ejumpcut.org/archive/onlinessays/JC22folder/IvensInCuba.html#7.

Wessels, Josepha I. "The Role of Video Recordings in the Collective Memory of the Syrian Uprising." In *Konflikten i Syrien: årsager, konsekvenser og handlemuligheder Denmark*, edited by Bjørn Møller and Søren Schmidt. Copenhagen: Djøf, 2016. https://www.academia.edu/13016604/The_role_of_video_recordings_in_the_collective_memory_of_the_Syrian_Uprising_English_version_.

———. "YouTube and the Role of Digital Video for Transnational Justice in Syria." *Politik* 4 (2016): 14–16.

Williams, Randall. *The Divided World: Human Rights and Its Violence*. Minneapolis: University of Minnesota Press, 2010.

Wilkerson, Travis. "Cuba's Santiago Álvarez: Cinematographer and Revolutionary." *Socialism and Liberation Magazine*, March 1, 2006. https://www.liberationnews.org/06-03-01-cubas-santiago-alvarez-cinemat-html/.

Winston, Brian. *Claiming the Real II: The Documentary Film Revisited*. London: British Film Institute/Palgrave Macmillan, 2008.

Yassın-Kassab, Robin, and Leila al-Shami. *Burning Country: Syrians in Revolution and War*. London: Pluto, 2016

Yaqub, Nadia. *Palestinian Cinema in the Days of Revolution* Austin: University of Texas Press, 2018.

Zimmermann, Patricia. "Introduction: The Home Movie Movement: Excavations, Artifacts, Minings." In *Mining the Home Movie: Excavations in Histories and Memories*, edited by Karen L. Ishikuza and Patricia R. Zimmermann, 1–28. Berkeley: University of California Press, 2008.

———. "Public Domains: Engaging Iraq Through Experimental Digitalities." *Framework* 48, no. 2 (Fall 2007): 66–83.

———. *States of Emergency: Documentaries, Wars, Democracies*. Minneapolis: University of Minnesota Press, 2000.

Index

Abid, Kasim, 135
Abounaddara collective, 1–3, 167–70, 176–77, 184–85; *Aleppo* (2016), 169; amplification of Syrian voices, 172; anonymity, 186, 193; appeal to dignity, 189–91; emergency cinema, 8, 25, 173, 198; and film history, 194–95; *Of Gods and Dogs* (2014), 185; *Here and Elsewhere*, 195; humanism, 173; hypermediation, 188–89; images as counterinformation, 192–93; imperfect cinema, 173; *The Kid* (2015), 195–97; meaning of name, 185; *Media Kill* (2012), 3; militant evidence, 188; "Montrons l'horreur en Syrie pour sortir de l'ignominie" (2015), 190; *REC* (2012), 1–3, 167; *On Revolution* (dir. Maya al-Khoury, 2017), 199; right to the image, 8, 25, 171–72, 186; "A Right to the Image for All" (2012), 188–89; *Syria Today* (2012), 194; "Witness" series, 193–94
access, 6
accountability, 32–34, 54; and police, 60; shame model and limits of, 58
accumulation, 11
ACT UP. *See* AIDS Coalition to Unleash Power
activism, digital, 23
Adachi, Masao, 104. See also *Red Army/PLFP: Declaration of World War* (dir. with Red Army, 1971)
adjudication, 8, 40, 62
advocacy chains, 63
advocacy video. *See* militant evidence, types of
affect, 93–95, 123–25; and encounter, 125; and mimesis, 20; ordinary, 95. *See also* affective radicality; Melissa Gregg; Kathleen Stewart
affective knowing, 86. *See also* Adrian Miles
affective radicality, 7, 24–25, 85–86, 93, 99–101, 107, 110–11, 121, 124–25
Agamben, Giorgio, 111, 114, 116–17; on archives, 142; homo sacer, 117; *Remnants of Auschwitz: The Witness and the Archive*, 144. *See also* archive; bare life
AIDS Coalition to Unleash Power (ACT UP), 6, 36, 51–53
AJEDI-Ka/PES. *See* Association des Jeunes Pour le Développement Intégré—Kalundu/Projet Enfants Soldats

Alea, Tomas Gutierrez, 175. See also *Memories of Underdevelopment* (1968)
Aleppo (dir. Abounaddara collective, 2016), 169
Alexander, William, 43, 47
Ali, Emad, 132, 154, 159. See also *A Candle for the Shabandar Café* (2017); *Speak Your Mind* (2011)
Álvarez, Santiago, 18, 177–79; *79 Primaveras/79 Springtimes of Ho Chi Minh* (1969), 178–79; *Now* (1975), 178; surrogate public sphere, 177; in Vietnam, 179
Amad, Paula, 25, 133. See also counterarchives
amateur media and independent film, 8
Amiralay, Omar, 187
Amnesty International, 67. See also Citizens Evidence Lab
Angola Three, 89
anonymity, 8, 186
aporia, 114, 117
Arab Spring, 74, 182
Arcades Project, The (Walter Benjamin), 146
archive, 5, 55, 108–109, 142–44, 150–53; and documentary filmmaking, 153; and historical memory, 151; and state, 151; imaginary, 152; turn to, 13–14; visual counterarchive, 152. See also Giorgio Agamben; Jacques Derrida; Michel Foucault
Aronson, Jay, 33
Ashuri, Tamar, 76
Assad, Bashar al-, 25, 181–82, 195–99
Assad, Hafez al-, 1, 186
Association des Jeunes Pour le Développement Intégré—Kalundu/ Projet Enfants Soldats (AJEDI-Ka/ PES), 64–69. See also *A Duty to Protect* (dir. with WITNESS, 2005); *On the Frontlines* (dir. with WITNESS, 2004); WITNESS
Aufderheide, Patricia, 19, 109. See also Jessica Clark; first-person filmmaking; Public Media 2.0

authorship, 109–110
avant-garde: approach to form and content, 5; film, 97–99; and global radical documentary tradition, 14; international, 5; modernist tradition of, 6, 17, 43–44

Baghdad Eye Human Rights Film Festival, 159. See also Iraq
Balthaser, Benjamin, 16
bare life, 116, 189. See also Giorgio Agamben
Bataille des Dix Millions, Le/Battle of the Ten Million (dir. Chris Marker, 1970), 176
Bazin, Andre, 11
Benhabib, Seyla, 34. See also jurisgenerative
Benjamin, Walter, 111, 145–46, 163n37; emergency situation, 187; memory, 146; *The Arcades Project*, 146
Berlin Wall, 12
Bernard, Andrew, 131
Bhalla, Angad Singh, 89. See also *The Deeper They Bury Me* (2015)
Bidayyat for Audiovisual Arts, 199
Bil'in: The Killing of Bassem Abu Rahama (dir. Eyal Weizman and Forensic Architecture, 2010), 92
biopolitics, 55. See also Giorgio Agamben; Jasbir Puar
Black Audio Film Collective (East London), 18–19
Black Journal (National Education Television), 19
Black Lives Matter (BLM), 16–17
Black Panther (dir. Newsreel, 1969), 103
BLM. See Black Lives Matter
Blood of My Brother, The (dir. Andrew Bernard, 2005), 131
Blood Sugar (dir. Sharon Daniel, 2010), 111
body cams, 41
Boyle, Deidre, 18
Brault, Philippe, 88. See also David Deufresne; *Prison Valley* (2010)
Brody, Samuel, 48–49
broken windows, 60

B'Tselem (Israel), 7, 24, 32–38, 42, 51, 53–57, 62–63, 69–73, 76–78, 87, 90–91, 184; "A Camera Changes Reality" (slogan), 56; The Camera Distribution Project, 119, 123; The Camera Project, 54, 119; *Gaza: An Inside Look* (2010), 56; *The Invisible Walls of Occupation*, 56, 90–91; *Living in East Jerusalem* (2011), 56; meaning of name, 81n61. *See also* Zohar Kfir
Burnat, Emad, 72. See also *Five Broken Cameras* (2011); Guy Davidi
Burton, Julianne, 174
Butler, Judith, 4

CAE. *See* Critical Art Ensemble
camera as weapon (trope), 56, 191–93, 198, 209. *See also* Abounaddara collective
Campbell, Russell, 48–49
Candle for the Shabandar Café, A (dir. Emad Ali, 2017), 132, 154–57
Carné, Marcel, 97–98
Casement, Roger, 64
Channel Four, 19
child soldiers, 64–65, 67, 69. *See also* Association des Jeunes Pour le Développement Intégré—Kalundu/Projet Enfants Soldats; *A Duty to Protect* (2005); *On the Frontlines* (2004); WITNESS
cinema-event (cine-acción), 51
cinéma-vérité, 18
citizen journalism, 54
Citizens Evidence Lab, 73. *See also* Amnesty International
Clair, René, 97
Clark, Jessica, 109. *See also* Patricia Aufderheide; Public Media 2.0
Club de l'Ecran, 98. *See also* Joris Ivens
Cocteau, Jean, 97
collective, 23
Columbia Revolt (dir. Newsreel, 1968), 103
commitment, 6, 12, 27n6
communication, 8
communism, 46–47
community. *See* collective
Congo, 63–9. *See also* Association des Jeunes Pour le Développement Intégré—Kalundu/Projet Enfants Soldats; *A Duty to Protect* (2005); *On the Frontlines* (2004); WITNESS
Congo Reform Association (CRA). *See* Congo
consumer-grade digital video (DV) cameras, 19–20
consumer-grade high-definition (HD) cameras, 20
content, 6
Costanza-Chock, Sasha, 33
counterarchives, 8, 25 133, 150–59
counterinformation, 8
Covenant of Economic, Social, and Cultural Rights (ICE-SCR), 189
CRA (Congo Reform Association). *See* Congo
crimes against humanity, 38
Crimp, Douglas, 52. *See also* cultural activism
Critical Art Ensemble (CAE), 22
Cuba Sí! (dir. Chris Marker, 1961), 176
Cuba: Institute of Film Art and Industry (Instituto Cubano del Arte e Industria Cinematograficos, ICAIC), 175–77; film society movement, 173–74; post-Revolution cinema, 6; Revolution, 173–74; "soldiers not artists," 175
cultural activism, 52. *See also* Douglas Crimp
Cvetkovich, Ann, 52

Daesh. *See* Islamic State of Iraq and the Levant (ISIS)
Damen, Rawan, 91. *See also Al Nakba* (2008), 91
Damned Interfering Video Activist Television (DIVA TV), 6, 18, 36, 51–53. *See also* AIDS Coalition to Unleash Power
Daniel, Sharon, 7, 24–25, 85, 110–118; *Blood Sugar* (2010), 111; *Public Secrets* (2006), 7, 24–25, 85, 87, 93, 95–96, 110–18, 124–25
Daradji, Mohamed al-, 159–60. See also *Son of Babylon* (2009)
Davidi, Guy, 72. *See also* Emad Burnat; *Five Broken Cameras* (2010)
Davis, Angela Y., 87–88, 111, 114

de Michiel, Helen, 21, 107. *See also* open space
decolonialism, 102
Deeper They Bury Me, The (dir. Angad Singh Bhalla, 2015), 89
Deleuze, Gilles, 23, 209
Democratic Republic of Congo (DRC). *See* Congo
Demos, T. J., 17
Derrida, Jacques, 142; archive fever, 151
Deufresne, David, 88. *See also* Philippe Brault; *Prison Valley* (2010)
digital active witness, 8, 32–33, 35–36, 56, 58, 62–63, 73–78; and accumulation, 73–74; ethics of, 33, 74; and militant evidence, 32, 76–77
digital technology, rise of, 12
digital turn, 13–14
dissensus, 117. *See also* Jacques Rancière
DIVA TV. *See* Damned Interfering Video Activist Television
documentary: and abundance, 107; and affect, 106; amateur, 137–38; and anti-war activism, 133; and audience engagement, 102, 109–10; as collective project, 21; coinage, 97; efficacy of, 21–22, 51; and ethnography, 13; framing, 48–49; global radical practices, 6; history of, 7; images, 1, 4; interactive form, 24–25, 85–91, 108, 116, 118–121; media, 1, 3–4; militant, 48; participatory, 49, 75; phenomenology of, 157; to prove and to move, 31; radical, 5, 11, 13; and self-representation, 13, 51; for social and political struggle, 50–51; specificity/context, 50–51; theory, 26, 49–50; turn, 13–14
Douglas, Lawrence, 39
DRC (Democratic Republic of Congo). *See* Congo
drones, 90
DuBose, Samuel, 41
Duchamp, Marcel, 97
Duty to Protect, A (dir. WITNESS and AJEDI/Ka-PES, 2005), 64–68
DV cameras. *See* consumer-grade digital video cameras

effective radicality, 24, 32, 34–37, 43–44, 49–50, 53, 63, 77–78, 87, 91
Egypt, Tahrir Square, 192
Eisenstein, Sergei, 97
emergency cinema, 25, 173. *See also* Abounaddara collective; imperfect cinema
empathy, 24
Eshun, Kodwo, 10
Eskander, Saad, 150–51
Espinosa, Julio García, 179–80
everyday, 8, 23
evidence, 5, 15–16, 48–49; accumulation of, 45–46; and affidavits, 39–40; circumstantial, 61–62; as counter-information, 5; direct, 61–62; and discourse, 21; and documentary, 20; facts, 11, 14, 43–53; indexicality, 20, 86; interpretive instability, 16; as intervention, 21; of militancy, 104–105; and Nuremburg trails, 38–39; paradox of visibility, 17; rebuttal, 61; as spectacle, 16–17; statistics, 40; ubiquity of, 3; visibility, 3; weaponization of, 16. *See also* militant evidence; visible evidence
experimentation, 5
eyeWitness to Atrocities (closed-source mobile app), 73

Facebook. *See* social media
factography, 46
facts. *See* evidence
Fahdel, Abbas, 138–141
fake news, 9
Fassin, Didier, 75. *See also* politics of life
Film and Photo League (US), 17, 36, 46–48
film-fact, 45. *See also* Dziga Vertov
filming and mobility, 5
first person political, 135, 137–38, 157. *See also* Alisa Lebow
first-person filmmaking, 19
fist of facts, 45–48. *See also* Dziga Vertov
Five Broken Cameras (dir. Emad Burnat and Guy Davidi, 2011), 72–73
Floyd, George, 16–17
Forensic Architecture, 91, 120, 184. *See also* Bil'in; *The Gaza Platform*; Eyal Weizman

form, 6
Foster, Hal, 153
Foucault, Michel, 151. *See also* archives
143 Seconds (dir. John Greyson, 2009), 140–41
Free Alabama Movement, 88
Frontlines, On the (dir. WITNESS and AJEDI/Ka-PES, 2004), 64, 67–68
Fruchter, Norm, 103. *See also* Robert Kramer; Newsreel

Gabriel, Peter, 37, 57. *See also* WITNESS
Gaines, Jane, 20, 42, 86, 132, 157. *See also* political mimesis; visible evidence
Gaza: An Inside Look (dir. B'Tselem, 2010), 56
Gaza Platform, The (Forensic Architecture and Amnesty International), 92
Gaza War (Operation Cast Lead), 121–23. *See also* Palestine
Georges-Schwartz, Louis, 35. *See also* image events
Getino, Octavio, 36, 49–51, 102. *See also* Fernando Solanas; Third Cinema
Gilmore, Ruth Wilson, 114. *See also* infrastructures of feeling
global archives of suffering, 44
Global War on Terror, 4
globalization, 4
Godard, Jean-Luc, 104. See also *Ici et Ailleurs (Here and Elsewhere)* (1976)
Gods and Dogs, Of (dir. Abounaddara collective, 2014), 185
Gray, Ros, 10
Great March of Return protests, 55
Gregg, Melissa, 93–94, 125. *See also* affect
Gregory, Sam, 37, 58–59, 63, 74. *See also* smart narrowcasting; WITNESS
Greyson, John, 140–141
Groupe Dziga Vertov (Dziga Vertov Group), 104. *See also* Jean-Luc Godard
Grupo Cine-Liberación, 50. *See also* Third Cinema
Guantanamo Bay, 117

Hall, Stuart, 198
Halleck, Dee Dee, 18
Hameed, Sami Abdul, 140

Harcourt, Bernard, 209
HD cameras. *See* consumer-grade high-definition cameras
Healthy Options Project Skopje (HOPS), 59
Here and Elsewhere (dir. Abounaddara), 195
Hill, Marc Lamont, 119
Hip Hop Lessons (dir. Muhammad al-Majdlawi, 2009), 122
HIV/AIDS, 51–52
Hiwar (dir. Kifaya Saleh, 2005), 132, 137, 141–43, 145, 147
Hiwar Center, 141–42, 145. See also *Hiwar* (dir. Kifaya Saleh, 2005); Iraq; Kifaya Saleh
Hochberg, Gil, 90
Holliday, George, 40–41
Holocaust, 38
Homeland: Iraq Year Zero (dir. Abbas Fahdel, 2015), 138–41
homo sacer. *See* Giorgio Agamben
HOPS. *See* Healthy Options Project Skopje
Human Immunodeficiency Virus/Acquired Immunodeficiency Syndrome. *See* HIV/AIDS
human rights: abuses in Congo, 63–69; advocacy, 58; claims, 34; and documentary film, 53; models of representation, 74–75; organizations, 7, 24; survivor-centered model, 61; theory, 26
humanitarian media intervention, 75
Hunger 1932 (film), 48
Hunger Strike (dir. Ashraf Al-Mashharawy, 2014), 91
Hussein, Ahmad Abu, and Yaser Mutaja, IDF killing of, 55
Hussein, Saddam, 25, 133–35, 150
hypermediation, 1, 188–89

IAH. *See* Internationale Arbeiterhilfe
I Will Cross Tomorrow (dir. Bassel Shehadeh, 2012), 187
ICAIC (Cuban Institute of Film Art and Industry/Instituto Cubano del Arte e Industria Cinematograficos). *See* Cuba

ICC. *See* International Criminal Court
ICE-SCR. *See* Covenant of Economic, Social, and Cultural Rights
Ici et Ailleurs (Here and Elsewhere) (dir. Jean-Luc Godard, 1976), 104
ICPR. *See* International Covenant of Civil and Political Rights
IFTC. *See* Independent Film and Television College
IIFC. *See* Iraqi Independent Film Center
image events, 35
impact, 22
imperfect cinema, 173, 179–81. *See also* Abounaddara collective; emergency cinema
Independent Film and Television College (IFTC, Baghdad, Iraq), 8, 25, 132–37, 158–59. *See also* Iraq
Independent Television Service (ITS), 19
indexicality, 20, 86. *See also* evidence
information, quantity, 12
infrastructures of feeling, 114. *See also* Ruth Wilson Gilmore
INLA. *See* Iraq, National Library and Archive
Instagram. *See* social media
interactive documentary. *See* documentary, interactive form
interactivity, 14–15, 108
International Covenant of Civil and Political Rights (ICPR), 189
International Criminal Court (ICC), 64–65, 67–69, 208
International Solidarity Movement, 69
Internationale Arbeiterhilfe (IAH), 47
intersubjectivity, 157
Invisible Walls of Occupation, The (dir. B'Tselem), 56, 90–91. *See also* B'Tselem
Iraq in Fragments (dir. James Longley, 2006), 131–32
Iraq: al-Amiriyah bombing, 139; cinema and film archives, 140–41; Hiwar Center, 141–42, 145; independent film culture, 25; ISIS, 160; kidnapping of journalists, 159; Mobile Cinema Festival, 160; National Library and Archive (INLA), 150; Operation Shock and Awe, 8, 134–35, 158; post-occupation media environment, 160; radical culture, 155; Short Film Festival, 147–49; social media, 160–61; war and occupation, 4, 8, 25, 131–35, 139–40, 158. *See also* Independent Film and Television College
Iraqi Cultural Association, 159
Iraqi Independent Film Center (IIFC), 159–60
Islamic State of Iraq and the Levant (ISIS), 105
ISIS. *See* Islamic State of Iraq and the Levant
Israel, 53–57. *See also* B'Tselem; Palestine, occupation of
Ivens, Joris, 6, 17, 85, 98–99, 100–101; brigade, 175–76; in Cuba, 175; militant cinema, 101–102; *Misere au Borinage* (dir. with Henri Storck, 1934), 98; *People in Arms, A* (1961), 175; *Travel Notebook* (dir. Joris Ivens, 1961), 175

Jackson, Robert, 40
Jameson, Fredric, 111, 114
jurisgenerative, 34–35. *See also* Seyla Benhabib

Kannan, Salam, 69
Kaufman, Boris, 98
Keck, Margaret, 63
Kfir, Zohar, 7, 24–25, 85, 118–124; *Points of View* (2015), 7, 24–25, 56, 85, 87, 93, 95, 118–25; *Testimony* (dir. Zohar Kfir, 2017), 118. *See also* B'Tselem
Kid, The (dir. Abounaddara collective, 2015), 195–97
King, Rodney: beating by LAPD, 5; video tape, 6, 10, 20, 16, 20, 35, 40–42, 57. *See also* visible evidence
kino-eye, 45–46, 146. *See also* Dziga Vertov
kinok, 45–46. *See also* Dziga Vertov
Kiwan, Charif, 170, 186, 188–191, 194
Kleinhans, Chuck, 106
Kozol, Wendy, 75, 169
Kramer, Robert, 103. *See also* Norm Fruchter; Newsreel

Lawyers Committee for Human Rights, 57
Lebow, Alisa, 135, 137–38, 157. *See also* first person political
Left Bank group (France), 18
Let the Show Begin (dir. Dhafir Taleb, 2005), 132, 147–49
Living in East Jerusalem (B'Tselem, 2011), 56
localization, 68
Longley, James, 131–32. *See also Iraq in Fragments* (2006)
Losh, Elizabeth, 74
Lubanga Dyilo, Thomas, 64, 68–69

MacKinnon, Catherine, 111
Making Sand out of Ruins (Unspecified Director, 2010), 122
Maliki, Nuri al , 158
Malitsky, Joshua, 46. *See also* factography
manifesto, 49–50
Manovich, Lev, 14, 108–9
mapping, 120
Marker, Chris, 18, 176. See also *Cuba Si!* (1961); *Le Bataille des Dix Millions/ Battle of the Ten Million* (1970)
Mashharawy, Ashraf al-, 91. See also *Hunger Strike* (2014)
mass incarceration, 4
Massumi, Brian, 94–95, 108. *See also* affect; interactivity
mattering, 169–70
McLagan, Meg, 59, 76
Media Kill (dir. Abounaddara collective, 2012), 3
mediated information, 14
Memories of Underdevelopment (dir. Tomas Gutierrez Alea, 1968), 175
microhistory, 5, 137, 153–54
Miéville, Anne Marie, 104
Miles, Adrian, 86. *See also* affective knowing
militant cinema, 101–102. *See also* Joris Ivens
militant documentary. *See* documentary, militant
militant evidence, 6, 7, 9–11, 21, 23–26, 32–37, 55, 58, 75–77, 133–34;

accumulation and corroboration, 9; and activist intervention, 21; affective form, 9–10; defining, 9; in the digital age, 23–26; effective form, 9–10; human rights-based, 75–77; nonviolence of, 37; and poor images, 10–11; types of, 58; and visible evidence, 10
militant image, 10
militarized gaze, 90
Miller, Liz, 37–38. *See also* slow resilience; WITNESS
Misere au Borinage (dir. Joris Ivens and Henri Storck, 1934), 98
Mobutu, Joseph, 64
montage, 146–47; 163n37
Muslim Brotherhood, 1
Musser, Charles, 131
Mutaja, Yaser, and Ahmad Abu Hussein, IDF killing of, 55
My Country, My Country (dir. Laura Poitras, 2005), 131
Myanmar, 207–9. *See also* Rohingya genocide
"Myanmar's Rohingya Genocide" (dir. VICE, 2020), 207–9

Nakba, Al (dir. Rawan Damen, 2008), 91
National Education Television (NET), 19
Nazi Concentration Camps, The (dir. George Stevens, 1945), 39–40
NET. *See* National Education Television
networks, networked, 1, 4, 15
new documentary movement, 6, 85, 105
New Left, 17–18, 28n31, 103
new media technology, 14–15
Newsreel collective (US), 6, 18, 85, 102–4. See also *Black Panther* (1969); *Columbia Revolt* (1968); *San Francisco State on Strike* (1969)
Nichols, Bill, 21–22, 26n5, 77, 98–99, 103, 107, 156–57. *See also* realism
9/11. *See* September 11, 2001
1968 protests, 18
Now (dir. Santiago Álvarez, 1975), 178
Nuremburg trials, 16, 20, 35, 38–40, 42

Officer Head-butts Palestinian, Youth (dir. Zidan Sharabati, 2012), 123
open-source model, 121
open space, 107. *See also* Helen de Michiel; Patricia Zimmermann
Operation Cast Lead. *See* Gaza War; Palestine
Operation Shock and Awe, 8, 134–35, 158. *See also* Iraq
overmediation, 4–5

Pachachi, Maysoon, 135
Palestine, 4, 7, 53–57, 69–73, 90–94 104, 118–24; Gaza Strip, 54–56, 90–92, 119–23; Gaza War (Operation Cast Lead), 121–23; Israeli occupation of, 4, 7, 53–57, 90–94; Liberation Organization (PLO), 57; militarized gaze, 90; Popular Front for the Liberation of Palestine (PFLP), 104; and US prison industrial complex, 87–88, 90; West Bank, 69, 71–73. *See also* B'Tselem; Israel
Paper Tiger Television, 18
People in Arms, A (dir. Joris Ivens, 1961), 175
perpetrator video. *See* militant evidence, types of
personal video camera, 18
Peters, Durham John, 32
PFLP (Popular Front for the Liberation of Palestine). *See* Palestine
Pinchevski, Amit, 76
PLO. *See* Palestine, Liberation Organization
Point of View (*P.O.V.*, PBS), 19
Points of View (dir. Zohar Kfir, 2015), 7, 24–25, 56, 85, 87, 93, 95, 118–25
Poitras, Laura, 131. *See also My Country, My Country* (2005)
police: as occupying force, 41–42; brutality in US, 4, 48; systemic abuse in New York City, 60; violence toward Black people, 16–17, 41
political mimesis, 20. *See also* Jane Gaines
politics of life, 75. *See also* Didier Fassin
polyvocality, 111
poor images, 10–11, 26, 208; accumulation and deployment, 11; as alternative economy, 26; as facts, 11; and location, 11

Popular Front for the Liberation of Palestine (PFLP). *See* Palestine
power, 23. *See also* Rita Raley
prison: abolition, 114; industrial complex, 87–88; media ban, 112; and Palestine, 87–88; strikes, 88
Prison Valley (dir. David Deufresne and Philippe Brault, 2010), 88–89
privilege, 32
"Profiling the Police: El Grito de Sunset Park" (WITNESS), 60
propaganda, 15–16
propos de Nice, À (dir. Jean Vigo, 1930), 98
Puar, Jasbir, 55. *See also* right to maim
public, 113–14
Public Broadcasting System (PBS), 18–19
public domains, 25, 134, 157–58
Public Media 2.0, 109
Public Secrets (dir. Sharon Daniel, 2006), 7, 24–25, 85, 87, 93, 95–96, 110–18, 124–25
Pudovkin, Vsevolod, 97

Qaeda, al-, 105

radical, 6, 11–13; and banality, 25, 134–35; humanism, 13; as opposed to committed, 12; as oppositional practice, 12–13
radical documentary, 5, 11, 13, 43; and anticolonial struggles, 49; in US, 46–47. *See also* documentary
Rahma, Ashraf Abu, 69–71
Raley, Rita, 22–23. *See also* power; tactical media
Rancière, Jacques, 117, 169
Rangan, Pooja, 75. *See also* humanitarian media intervention
real, realism, 14, 20, 156–157. *See also* Bill Nichols; evidence
REC (dir. Abounaddara collective, 2012), 1–3, 167
Red Army Faction of Japan Revolutionary Communist League (Red Army), 104
Red Army/PLFP: Declaration of World War (dir. Masao Adachi and Red Army, 1971), 104
remediation, 14–15

Remnants of Auschwitz: The Witness and the Archive (Agamben), 144
Renoir, Jean, 97–98
representation, 5, 8
resistance, 8
Revolution, On (dir. Maya al-Khoury, 2017), 199. *See also* Abounaddara collective
Richter, Hans, 43, 97
right to information, 150–51
right to maim, 55. *See also* Jasbir Puar
right to the image, 74–75, 172, 186. *See also* Abounaddara collective
Rohingya genocide, 207–9
Rosler, Martha, 6, 85–86, 105–106. *See also* new documentary movement; *A Simple Case for Torture* (1983)
Rotha, Paul, 15–16

Said, Edward, 13
Salaita, Steven, 119
Saleh, Kifaya, 132
San Francisco State on Strike (dir. Newsreel, 1969), 103
Sarkar, Bhaskar, 22, 44
Sebti, Kasim, 141–45. *See also* Hiwar Center
secrecy, 113–14
Seigworth, Gregory, 93–94, 125. *See also* affect
Sekula, Allan, 105. *See also* new documentary movement
September 11, 2001 (event), 4, 140
79 Primaveras/79 Springtimes of Ho Chi Minh (dir. Santiago Álvarez, 1969), 178–79
sexual assault, 118
sexual violence against women, 65–66
Shamas, Diala, 55. *See also* B'Tselem
Shehadeh, Bassel, 187. *See also* *I Will Cross Tomorrow* (2012)
Shub, Esfir, 14, 17, 97
Sikkink, Kathryn, 63
Silvered Water, Syria Self-Portrait (dir. Ossama Mohammed, 2014), 168
Simple Case for Torture, A (dir. Martha Rosler, 1983), 85–86, 105–6
6x9: A Virtual Experience of Solitary Confinement (dir. Francesca Panetta and Lindsay Poulton, 2016), 89

Sliwinski, Sharon, 63
slow resilience, 37–38
smart narrowcasting, 37, 58–59
social cinema, 14, 96–97
social media, 1, 4, 17, 25
Solanas, Fernando, 36, 49–51, 102
solitary confinement, 89
Son of Babylon (dir. Mohamed al-Daradji, 2009), 160
Sontag, Susan, 171
Sony, 18
Soviet cultural representation, 46
Speak Your Mind (dir. Emad Ali, 2011), 159
spectatorship, 6, 37
Stam, Robert, 50
state of emergency, exception, 12–13
Stern, Seymour, 47–48
Stevens, George, 39. *See also The Nazi Concentration Camps* (1945)
Stewart, Kathleen, 95, 123–24. *See also* affect, ordinary
Steyerl, Hito, 10–11. *See also* poor images, as facts
Still Recording (dir. Saeed al-Batal and Ghiath Ayoub, 2018), 200–201
stop and frisk, 60
Summer Games (dir. Fadi al-Ghorra, 2009), 122
surveillance, 17, 41–42
survivor-centered human rights model. *See* human rights
Syria, 167; Archive, 73, 184; Center for Media and Freedom of Expression, 181; Committees for the Defense of Democratic Freedoms and Human Rights in, 181; conflict in, 1, 4, 25; Daesh and jihadism, 183; ethical responsibilities of filmmakers, 171; and global media/international community, 168–69; image-making, 167–68; overmediation, 183; protests in Daraa, 182; state monopoly on cinema, 186–87; stereotypes of, 170–71, 191–92. *See also* Abounaddara collective
Syria Today (dir. Abounaddara collective, 2012), 194

tactical media, 22–23. *See also* Rita Raley
Taleb, Dhafir, 132, 147–49. *See also Let the Show Begin* (2005)
Taste of Cement (dir. Ziad Kalthoum, 2018), 199–200
Taussig, Michael, 111
technological developments, 85
Tensing, Ray. *See* Samuel DuBose
testimony. *See* witness
Testimony (dir. Zohar Kfir, 2017), 118
Third Cinema (Argentina), 6, 18, 36, 49–51, 85, 102. *See also* Octavio Getino; Fernando Solanas
Third World, 17
Tomlinson, John, 67–68
Torchin, Leshu, 35, 39
Transcultural Psychosocial Organization, 67
transmedia advocacy, 33–37, 77
Travel Notebook (dir. Joris Ivens, 1961), 175
Tunnel Youth (Unspecified Director, 2009), 122–23
Turvey, Malcolm, 131
Twitter. *See* social media

undermediation, 5
Ungar, Steven, 97–98
Union of Congolese Patriots (UPC). *See* Congo
Universal Declaration of Human Rights (UDHR), 34, 117, 159, 189
UPC (Union of Congolese Patriots). *See* Congo
Ushahidi (open-source tool, Kenya), 73

Vertov, Dziga, 5–6, 14, 17, 36, 44–46, 97; "factory of facts," 5; film-fact, 45; fist of facts, 45–48; kino-eye, 45–46, 146; kinok, 45–46; visual bonds, 10–11
VICE, 207–9
video advocacy, 79n7
Vietnam War, 102–3
Vigo, Jean, 6, 14, 17, 85, 96–98. See also *À propos de Nice* (1930)
Vimeo. *See* social media
virtual reality. *See* documentary, interactive form

visibility, 17, 21
visible evidence, 5, 42; and discursive field, 42; human rights-based, 31; limits of, 38–43; and outcomes, 35; and police violence, 41; Rodney King tape and verdict, 10, 20. *See also* evidence; Jane Gaines; Rodney King
Visual Forensics and Metadata Extraction (VFRAME, Syria), 73
Visualizing Palestine (human rights organization), 92

Wahlberg, Malin, 153–55
Walker, Janet, 22, 44
Wallace, Herman, 89
war crimes, 40
War Games (dir. Muhammad al-Aloul, 2009), 122
Weizman, Eyal, 91. *See also* Forensic Architecture
Wessels, Josepha, 183
Why We Fight (propaganda series), 15–16
Williams, George Washington, 63
Williams, Randall, 75
Winston, Brian, 22
witness, 5, 19, 24, 347, 37, 44, 50–51, 62, 75–76, 90–91, 142–44
WITNESS (human rights organization, Brooklyn), 7, 24, 32–40, 51–69, 76–78, 184; Media Lab, 59; *A Duty to Protect* (dir. with AJEDI/Ka-PES, 2005), 64–68; *On the Frontlines* (dir. with AJEDI/Ka-PES, 2004), 64, 67–68; video as evidence, 59; *You Must Know about Me: Rights Not Violence for Sex Workers in Macedonia* (dir. with HOPS, 2009), 59. *See also* Association des Jeunes Pour le Développement Intégré—Kalundu/Projet Enfants Soldats (AJEDI-Ka/PES); child soldiers; Congo; Healthy Options Project Skopje (HOPS)
witness documentation. *See* militant evidence, types of
witnessing witnesses, 39
WIR. *See* Workers International Relief

women in prison, 87, 112, 110–118.
    See also Sharon Daniel; *Public Secrets*
    (2006)
Workers International Relief (WIR), 47

Yakobovich, Oren, 55. *See also*
    B'Tselem
Yaqub, Nadia, 57

*You Must Know about Me: Rights Not
    Violence for Sex Workers in Macedonia*
    (dir. WITNESS and HOPS, 2009), 59
YouTube. *See* social media

Zimmermann, Patricia, 12–13, 21, 107,
    153–54, 157–58. *See also* open space;
    public domains

Ryan Watson is Associate Professor of Film and Media Studies at Misericordia University.

www.ingramcontent.com/pod-product-compliance
Lightning Source LLC
Chambersburg PA
CBHW020835160426
43192CB00007B/656